Teams That Thrive

Five Disciplines Of Collaborative Church Leadership

Ryan T. Hartwig
Warren Bird
Foreword By Dave Ferguson

16pt

Copyright Page from the Original Book

InterVarsity Press
P.O. Box 1400, Downers Grove, IL 60515-1426
ivpress.com
email@ivpress.com

©2015 by Ryan T. Hartwig and Warren Bird

All rights reserved. No part of this book may be reproduced in any form without written permission from InterVarsity Press.

InterVarsity Press® is the book-publishing division of InterVarsity Christian Fellowship/USA®, a movement of students and faculty active on campus at hundreds of universities, colleges and schools of nursing in the United States of America, and a member movement of the International Fellowship of Evangelical Students. For information about local and regional activities, visit intervarsity.org.

Scripture quotations, unless otherwise noted, are from The Holy Bible, English Standard Version, *copyright © 2001 by Crossway Bibles, a division of Good News Publishers. Used by permission. All rights reserved.*

While any stories in this book are true, some names and identifying information may have been changed to protect the privacy of individuals.

Cover design: David Fassett
Interior design: Beth McGill
Images: light blue paper: © billnoll/iStockphoto
    sun burst: © Bierchen/iStockphoto
    group of hands: © Leontura/iStockphoto
    gears: © igorshi/iStockphoto
ISBN 978-0-8308-4119-6 (print)
ISBN 978-0-8308-9757-5 (digital)

Printed in the United States of America ∞

 *As a member of the Green Press Initiative, InterVarsity Press is committed to protecting the environment and to the responsible use of natural resources. To learn more, visit greenpressinitiative.org.*

Library of Congress Cataloging-in-Publication Data
Hartwig, Ryan T., 1978-
  Teams that thrive : five disciplines of collaborative church leadership / Ryan T. Hartwig and Warren Bird.
    pages cm
  Includes bibliographical references and index.
  ISBN 978-0-8308-4119-6 (pbk. : alk. paper)
  1. Christian leadership. 2. Teams in the workplace. I. Title.
BV652.1.H275 2015
253—dc23

                                                                2015000989

P 21 20 19 18 17 16 15 14 13 12 11 10 9 8 7 6 5 4 3 2 1
Y 32 31 30 29 28 27 26 25 24 23 22 21 20 19 18 17 16 15

TABLE OF CONTENTS

Foreword	vii
Preface	x

PART ONE : WHY READ A BOOK ABOUT LEADERSHIP TEAMS?

1: Myths We Believe	3
2: Your Vantage Point	6

PART TWO: WHY DO LEADERSHIP TEAMS MAKE SENSE?

3 : The Bible Speaks	27
4 : Passing Fad or Here to Stay	48

PART THREE : HOW WELL IS YOUR TEAM THRIVING?

5 : Reality Check	67
6 : Our Survey Says	90

PART FOUR : WHAT ARE THE COLLABORATIVE DISCIPLINES OF TEAMS THAT THRIVE?

7 : DISCIPLINE 1: Focus on Purpose, the Invisible Leader of Your Team	109
8: DISCIPLINE 2: Leverage Differences in Team Membership	144
9: DISCIPLINE 3: Rely on Inspiration More Than Control to Lead	185
10: DISCIPLINE 4: Intentionally Structure Your Decision-Making Process	220
11: DISCIPLINE 4: Intentionally Structure Your Decision-Making Process	242
12: DISCIPLINE 5: Build a Culture of Continuous Collaboration	280

PART FIVE: PART FIVE WHAT'S YOUR BEST NEXT STEP?

13 : Six Ways to Avoid Sabotaging Your Team	313
14: Catalyze Your Team's Growth	330
Acknowledgments	343
Appendix	346
Notes	348
Additional Resources	376
About the Authors	377

TABLE OF CONTENTS

Foreword ... vii

Preface ... x

PART ONE: WHY READ A BOOK "ABOUT" LEADERSHIP TEAMS?

1. Why We Believe ... 3
2. Our Vantage Point ... 6

PART TWO: WHY DO LEADERSHIP TEAMS MAKE SENSE?

3. The Bible Speaks ... 17
4. Chasing Fad or Here to Stay ... 46

PART THREE: HOW WELL IS YOUR TEAM THRIVING?

5. Reality Check ... 67
6. Our Survey Says ... 90

PART FOUR: WHAT ARE THE COLLABORATIVE DISCIPLINES OF TEAMS THAT THRIVE?

7. DISCIPLINE 1: Focus on Purpose, the Invisible Leader of Your Team ... 119
8. DISCIPLINE 2: Leverage Differences in Team Membership ... 144
9. DISCIPLINE 3: Keep an Inspiration from Team Charter to Team Life ... 185
10. DISCIPLINE 4: Intentionally Conduct Your Decision-Making Process ... 220
11. DISCIPLINE 5: Intentionally Structure Your Decision-Making Process ... 249
12. DISCIPLINE 6: Build a Culture of Continuous Collaboration ... 280

PART FIVE: WHAT'S YOUR BEST NEXT STEP?

13. Six Ways to Avoid Sabotaging Your Team ... 313
14. Catalyze Your Team's Growth ... 320

Acknowledgments ... 343

Appendix ... 346

Notes ... 348

Additional Resources ... 376

About the Authors ... 379

"The most effective churches in America today have strong leaders who surround themselves with a smart team of leaders. Finally, a practical book on leadership that helps churches develop the right kind of team to lead their church forward. This book is long overdue, greatly needed and high on my recommendation list."

Jim Tomberlin, founder, MultiSite Solutions, author, *Better Together*

"We know that we're supposed to like working in teams, but how many of us actually get excited when we hear the word *teamwork*? It isn't that we hate working with others, it's just that more often than not teams seem to make things harder, not easier. Fortunately, in *Teams That Thrive*, Ryan and Warren promise it doesn't have to be that way. Read this book and start creating teams that work!"

Greg Surratt, founding pastor of Seacoast Church

"Serious leaders are serious about their teams because something extraordinary happens when a team thrives, something much greater than the sum of its parts. *Teams That Thrive* is an unusual blend of spirit and practice. It is fresh, deep and eminently helpful!"

Nancy Ortberg, author of *Lessons in Non-Linear Leadership*

"This practical book is full of tips and tools that church leadership teams can use to become better and to increase in impact. *Teams That*

Thrive will be a great help to my own team as we help church leadership teams get unstuck."

Tony Morgan, founder and chief strategic officer of the Unstuck Group, author of *Take the Lid Off Your Church*

"I can't think of a better, more needed topic than *Teams That Thrive*. The ability to build a culture of collaboration and team leadership is crucial to anyone's effectiveness in ministry. For years, Warren Bird has been a go-to expert for pastors wanting to learn how to do things better, and here he teams well with university professor Ryan Hartwig to pull together top research and great examples."

Dino Rizzo, executive director of the Association of Related Churches, author of *Servolution*

"I wish I had read this book at the beginning of my ministry career! *Teams That Thrive* is an incredible resource to help you and your team rethink how you lead. Packed with outstanding research, helpful tips, practical wisdom and thoughts from expert commentators, this book is the how-to resource you need to move your team (and your church) from simply surviving to thriving."

Jenni Catron, church leader and author of *Clout*

"In this rigorous and readable treatment of church leadership teams, Warren Bird and Ryan Hartwig show how shared leadership and an effective team at the top not only ensure high-functioning church operations, but they also provide the model for a thriving congregation and a healthy community culture. *Teams That Thrive* provides practical solutions and inspiring wisdom to those who would elevate their team leadership capacity in ways that genuinely contribute to effective, purposive and growing church communities."

Ruth Wageman, author of *Senior Leadership Teams*

"I'm a better leader with a healthier leadership team because of the principles outlined in this book. In *Teams That Thrive*, Ryan and Warren have given all of us an accessible roadmap for high-performance leadership teams in any church context."

Chris Lewis, lead pastor of Foothill Church

"*Teams That Thrive* is an incredibly practical guide for church leadership teams. Dr. Bird and Dr. Hartwig understand that pastors don't need another book on leadership theory; they need practical tools to implement collaborative leadership in the context of day-to-day ministry. That's exactly what *Teams That Thrive* delivers."

Geoff Surratt, pastor, coach to church planters, and author of *Ten Stupid Things That Keep Churches from Growing*

"Every time I meet with pastors, the subject of leadership comes up at some point in the conversation. The struggle for all churches is to build new leaders who are unified around a common vision. This is a needed book to help us build better teams and better churches."

Ron Edmondson, pastor of Immanuel Baptist Church

"The daily life of running a church ministry is all about teams. How are they doing? Are they growing? How do we get new folks on teams? *Teams That Thrive* helps us to answer these questions with solid research, stories and examples, and to form and maintain great teams."

David Fletcher, executive pastor at the EvFree Church of Fullerton, California, founder of xpastor.com, author of several books, including *Crisis Leadership*

"What's essential and what's superfluous? What should we tackle head-on and what should we detour around? How do we course correct when we hit trouble? How do we keep momentum when we have it? From a strong mythbuster start to a next-best-step finish, this book is a one-of-a-kind resource for teams. Spoiler alert: help is here."

Kem Meyer, former executive team member and communications director at Granger Community Church, kemmeyer.com

"Rarely does a book debut in the church arena that has a strong combination of understanding, analysis, solutions, research, biblical basis and real life usability. My friends Warren Bird, Ryan Hartwig and their team have produced just that in *Teams That Thrive*. Churches will be stronger because teams will be healthier and more productive, enhancing the kingdom of our Lord. Every leader in your church needs a personal copy of this book."

Samuel R. Chand, leadership consultant, samchand.com, author of *Cracking Your Church's Culture Code*

"*Teams That Thrive* is about the work that leaders do to build high performance teams—and the things that are keeping them from it. If your team embodies the disciplines in this book, you'll be well on your way to a team experience that will not only change your organization but will ultimately change you!"

Josh Whitehead, executive pastor of Faith Promise Church

"I'm a lay leader serving on the leadership team of a church of 225 and this fast-moving book has a lot of practical ideas and relevant application for us."

Ron Keener, former editor, *Church Executive*

To my family, my favorite team. RTH

Foreword

IT WAS AT A LEADERSHIP CONFERENCE that Warren and Ryan approached me and asked if I would write this foreword to *Teams That Thrive: Five Disciplines of Collaborative Church Leadership*. I was flattered when they said, "Dave, your heart and ministry match this book. You not only talk about how to grow teams, you live and model how to develop healthy leadership teams." I was grateful for the compliment, but I also knew the whole truth—I had not always been a part of a thriving leadership team.

When we started Community Christian Church in Naperville, Illinois, we were one of the first in a wave of new churches that started with a leadership team. Until then most new churches were bravely started by a single individual or a couple forging out on their own to do the best they could. My wife, Sue, and I had no interest in doing it on our own. Sue went to work to provide some income and I recruited my brother Jon to partner with me. We started our new church with five full-time staff, ages twenty-one to twenty-five.

This team was composed of people that I grew up with, roomed with in college and loved deeply, but it was not a thriving team. I loved the idea of a strong leadership team, but I didn't know how to make it happen. And within twenty-four months of this team starting a new church the only person remaining on that team was my brother! Not only were we not thriving, we were not surviving.

As I look back on those early years, what I needed most was a resource that could help me and my friends thrive as a leadership team. We desperately needed:

- A tool that would help us assess our strengths and weaknesses and then build on those strengths and compensate for the weaknesses.
- Good examples that we could point to that would help us learn the disciplines of thriving teams.
- A strategy for how we could move forward into the future, not just as a group of friends, but also as a thriving team advancing the mission of Jesus.

What you are holding in your hand is what my team needed most, and that is why I'm so excited that you are reading *Teams That Thrive: Five Disciplines of Collaborative Church Leadership* by Ryan Hartwig and Warren Bird. Ryan is a scholar and a practitioner. Warren is a brilliant researcher and a gifted writer. In *Teams That Thrive* they offer us a rare combination of great research and best practices for leadership teams.

It has now been more than two decades since we started Community Christian Church. Since that time I have had the privilege to work with some amazing leadership teams and consequently to teach and write on this topic. But as I combed through the pages of this book, two thoughts came to mind: "I wish I would have known that twenty years ago" and "Oh, this is really good—this could help my current leadership team thrive!"

So, if you find yourself leading a team or on a leadership team that is passionate about the mission of Jesus and wants to thrive, then devour and discuss the content of Teams That Thrive. This is a book that could have saved me twenty years of hard-learned lessons and that will help your leadership team thrive today!

Dave Ferguson
Lead pastor, Community Christian Church, and visionary for NewThing

Preface

> *If you want to go fast, go alone. If you want to go far, go together.*
> **African Proverb**

When people work together to finish a job, such as building a house, will the job (a) probably get done faster, (b) take longer to finish, or (c) not get done? That simple quiz comes from Richard Hackman, acclaimed Harvard researcher, voiced in the opening pages of his book *Leading Teams*.[1] The expected correct answer is (a), which is no surprise. The author explains that this question came from a standardized fourth-grade test in Ohio. "It illustrates how early we're told that teamwork is good," he says.[2]

Yes, teams do have tremendous potential to create something extraordinary. For that reason, teams are found in every area of life today, including multiple varieties within our churches. Perhaps you've heard and used slogans like these as far back as your earliest school days:

- Teamwork makes the dream work.
- T.E.A.M. = Together Everyone Achieves More!
- *We* is better than *me*.
- There is no *I* in the word *team*.

Unfortunately, reality often doesn't live up to those oft-heard slogans. Maybe you've created or even led teams that simply didn't work, despite all the hoopla about what a well-working team can do.

If so, you're not alone. Enough people have been disillusioned by teams that a number of clever sarcasms have also arisen:
- A committee is a group that keeps minutes and wastes hours.
- A camel is a horse designed by a group.
- If you had to identify in one word the reason why the human race has not achieved and never will achieve its full potential, that word would be *meetings*.
- The major difference between meetings and funerals is that most funerals have a definite purpose. Also, nothing is ever really buried in a meeting.[3]

In fact, the term *teamwork* frequently conjures up images of wandering discussions, unresolved friction, wasted time, pooled ignorance, ineffective decision-making practices and frustrated group members, in spite of good intentions regarding the potential of working together. Harvard researcher Hackman says, "Research consistently shows that teams underperform, despite all the extra resources they have."[4]

We've seen the same sad reality in too many churches. These days it seems that everyone is trying to do ministry through teams, but despite all the resources available on teamwork, many people simply don't know how to improve their teams. Worse, many teams seriously underperform but the team's leaders think the results are just fine, not realizing that their team has huge untapped potential.[5]

> Teams are found in every area of life today, including multiple varieties within our churches.

With frustrating team experiences being all too common, many people have accepted, perhaps without realizing it, a low-bar status quo. Or they've gone further and grown disillusioned with teams. Despite the possible advantages of teams over individual performance, many have concluded that teams are simply not worth the hassle.

THRIVING TEAMS AT YOUR CHURCH?

It doesn't have to be that way. Instead, teams can thrive. Teams can outperform the individual—by far. Teams can accomplish the seemingly impossible. And team life can be quite fulfilling: team members can operate out of humility, develop strong friendships, enjoy their teamwork and interaction, and never want to leave the organization or team.

We've seen great teams in action in churches like yours. The truth is, many church teams are thriving. We surveyed them, watched them and talked with church staff, volunteers and elders that rely on them for direction and guidance. These teams are *truly* leading their churches collaboratively. And so can your team. Your team can grow to be extraordinary. Yes, with coaching, your team can likely accomplish significant goals you never imagined possible!

> With coaching, your team can likely accomplish significant goals you never imagined possible!

We wrote this book to help the teams at your church thrive, especially the senior leadership team. From all our research, we're convinced that the best teams are distinguished in two ways. First, teams that thrive believe that collaborative leadership is practically and biblically the right way to lead. Despite the challenges that teams naturally face (go to any playground to see the inherent challenges of doing anything productive together), these teams are committed to making collaboration work at the executive leadership level. Second, teams that thrive discipline themselves to practice the fundamentals—day in and day out—that make a great team. Teamwork can be hard, for sure, but great teams work hard to become great at it. Because they know it's worthwhile to lead collaboratively, they do what it takes to become extraordinary.

> Teams that thrive (1) believe that collaborative leadership is practically and biblically the right way to lead, and (2) discipline themselves to practice the fundamentals—day in and day out—that make a great team.

That's our dream for you. We hope you'll grow convinced that collaborative leadership is practically beneficial and biblically viable (at minimum), if not biblically mandated. We also hope that you'll learn and commit to the disciplines that if practiced over and over turn teams, even ones that are barely surviving, into teams that thrive.

Take heart: no matter your position on your team, you can make some simple changes to your team's disciplines that will ripple across your congregation and beyond. If you rate your church's leadership team as anything less than exemplary, we'll show you how you can transform your team's potential into a high-performance, thriving, healthy team.

THIS BOOK IS FOR YOU

This book is for leaders across a wide range of churches, both large and small, growing and non-growing, well-established and new.

Struggling teams and thriving teams. Maybe you picked up this book because you could use some help with your team. To lend you a hand, we not only suggest what you might do—no matter your position on the team, whether you are the formal leader or not—to help your team thrive, but also how you can actually do it. In the *Teams That Thrive* framework, we cut through the clutter of ideas and give you research-supported advice on which you can focus your time and efforts. Plus, we offer you a set of tools you can use to facilitate your team's growth.

Or maybe you're part of a pretty solid team and want to be sure your team stays that way. If you are looking for a resource to help your team maintain its health, we hope to help you better understand why your team is winning—so that you can go to even greater levels of effectiveness. Plus, as Andy Stanley, pastor of North Point Church in greater Atlanta, said, "If you don't know why it's working, when it's working, you won't know how to fix it when it breaks."[6] Knowing what your team is doing that is successful enables you to self-correct when performance slips and to translate the success of your team to other teams in your church and in your ecclesial tribe.

Team leaders and team members. If you head a senior leadership team, perhaps as a lead pastor or executive pastor, you'll find advice to help you focus on what matters most to your team's health and effectiveness. We will show you how to truly share leadership with others to everyone's benefit.

But this book isn't just for designated team leaders. It's for everyday team members who want to help take their teams to the next level of health and productivity—with or without the explicit support of the formal team leaders. If that's you, you'll find straightforward tips you can apply right away to increase your influence on the team and steer your team to greater performance. Remember, everyone can lead! We're glad you take your leadership seriously.

Skeptics and enthusiasts. Not everyone is as convinced about the possibilities of teams as we are—fair enough. If you're not fully convinced that shared leadership is biblically viable or practically preferable, we hope you've come with an open mind (the fact that you have this book in your hand suggests that you have). Be sure to notice how we differentiate between work groups and true teams—and you might realize that your issue is not with teams in general, but with groups that never develop the discipline to become high-functioning teams. Regardless, unless you're willing to develop a true sense of team, this book's practices will backfire and perhaps even harm your team. On the other hand, if you're part of the "I love teams" choir, we look forward to preaching to you. You'll find research-grounded, time-tested tips and techniques to turn your teamwork beliefs into reality.

Church planters and revitalizers. If you're a church planter assessing different options for leadership as you launch a new congregation, we seek to help you think through what team leadership requires and offer you a plan for setting your team up for success.

At the same time, this book is for pastors seeking to reenergize the church. Indeed, leadership teams offer more resources—ideas, inputs, time, energy, mental and physical bandwidth—than individuals acting alone to lead large-scale congregational and organizational change.

Church boards and staff observers. If you're a church elder or board member, we believe you'll find insight in these pages to help your eldership or board function at its highest potential. We investigated leadership teams comprising primarily church staff, but the principles we gleaned are aptly applied to other teams and working groups that serve in organizational leadership. In addition, we hope you'll use this book to encourage the members of your church's pastoral leadership team to succeed as a team and therefore increase the leadership capacity of your church.

Likewise, if you're on staff at a church or another ministry organization but not part of the leadership team per se, this book has many applications for you. We believe the findings of our study, as well as the tools we explain that can be used to grow teams, will be relevant and useful for your team, whether it is a worship team, a council that oversees a church's small group leadership or another group of folks working together.

Consultants, professors and trainers. If you work as a consultant or coach to help other teams be successful, or as a professor to train pastors who will one day serve on a church leadership team, we hope to offer you research-based insights and a model for performance that will aid your coaching, consulting or teaching.

HOW THE BOOK UNFOLDS

Part 1 frames the book by showing many of the widespread myths about church teams and by explaining the importance and impact of leadership teams on the churches they lead.

Part 2 answers the question: Why do leadership teams make sense? We realize you may not yet fully buy in to the idea of team leadership, so we offer biblical foundations and models for teams, and we explain the practical benefits of leadership teams.

Part 3 discusses typical problems that plague leadership teams, introduces the five disciplines of teams that thrive and explains our research foundation.

Part 4 describes how to develop a great team in your church. We cover how great teams collaborate to develop their purpose, select a complementary team of players and execute important team processes. We offer very practical advice, all framed around what we call the "Disciplines of Teams That Thrive."

Part 5 helps you determine specifically what to do next. We also describe detours and potholes to avoid and improvements you can begin to make today, whatever your current leadership team situation.

Throughout the book we provide tables and figures with examples from numerous thriving leadership teams, quick diagnostics, questions for individual reflection and group discussion, over two dozen "two-minute tips" and insights by expert commentators (one at the end of most chapters). We encourage you to use this book as a thought-provoker, conversation-starter and guide for taking your team to the next level of health and effectiveness.

WHAT THIS BOOK IS NOT

You will look in vain for the section in this book that shouts tired slogans about teams, such as "Teamwork makes the dream work." Yes, teams are great. But we hope to move beyond those clichés to offer solid advice that helps teams actually work together and reap the benefits that come with it.

This also isn't a book of techniques about "getting along" as a team. It's not specifically about how to improve your team relationships.

It's not about Kumbaya-style camaraderie. To be fair, it's not even about building a cohesive team. It's about building a high-performance team that will most likely also prove to be quite cohesive.

This is not a book of team-building exercises either. There are no trust falls, weeping willows, toilet paper tear-offs or high-ropes-course challenges here, nor are there calls for teams to do them. As we'll explain later, these efforts rarely translate into effective teamwork, so we instead want to simply help you do your team's important work better together.

This is not a book about the church being business-minded or about blindly adopting business principles from the corporate world to use in the church. Rather, we start from the ground-up, studying church leadership teams and identifying patterns in the data that suggest differences in what top teams and underperforming teams do.

Finally, this is not a book that places all the credit for a team's successes or blame for their failures at the team leader's feet. Yes, what the person at the top of the organizational chart does certainly matters, but that individual doesn't get to decide everything about a team's fate. No, every member of a team contributes to a team's wins and losses, whether directly or indirectly. Thus we address this book toward every member of a leadership team. As you read this book, we hope you'll focus on what *you* can do to improve your team more than what someone else can do to improve your team. And if you do think of what other people should do, buy them a copy of the book. Chances are we'll target their issue on some page!

For the record, chapter nine specifically addresses designated leaders of teams. All other chapters are written to general team members. And the principles and insights, though focused on senior leadership teams, are applicable to every type of team at your church, from your worship team to your student ministries leadership team to the group that coaches your small group leaders.

Teams That Thrive is about teams doing the most substantial leadership work for any church—that of making key strategic decisions—together as a team, and thereby shaping the direction and success of the church.

OUR UNIQUE PERSPECTIVE

We believe the perspective we've taken in this book is unique. We've weaved together church-based research on leadership teams, relevant marketplace research, practical examples based on visits we've made to numerous churches and a Christ-focused biblical foundation.

Teams That Thrive draws from several primary sources: our foundation in the Bible's teachings, our recent two-year study described below, our visits with dozens of growing churches across North America, our in-depth knowledge of the best practices of teams in ministry contexts and of senior leadership teams in corporate organizations, and our own involvement in various leadership roles in our own churches.

Strong foundation in Scripture. The role of Scripture is so important that we devote a whole chapter to our own summary of biblical foundations for team leadership. Many other excellent books explore Bible-based patterns of team leadership. These range from widely read books of yesteryear like *The Training of the Twelve* by A.B. Bruce and *The Master Plan of Evangelism* by Robert E. Coleman to a wave of more contemporary titles such as George Barna's *The Power of Team Leadership* or Kenneth Gangel's *Team Leadership in Christian Ministry*.[7]

Our research. Our major research project ran from 2012 to 2013, during which Leadership Network helped us collect questionnaire data from 1,026 senior leadership team members at 253 churches. In addition, we visited many leadership teams and conducted dozens of interviews with members of church senior leadership teams. In chapter six we explain more detail about our research.

Our backgrounds as academics, researchers and observers. This book has been written by a team. As a professor and researcher, Ryan observes, studies and teaches about teams in various contexts, including senior leadership teams in corporate and nonprofit contexts, as well as teams of all types in ministry contexts. In fact, his doctoral work in group and organizational communication included an in-depth study of a church's senior leadership team for nearly two years. With expertise in teams, Ryan brings a rich theoretical base and knowledge of research on senior leadership teams.

Warren has been part of a senior leadership team in four different churches (of varying size) for almost twenty years. In his work overseeing the research department at Leadership Network, he has sat in on numerous senior church team meetings and addressed the issue in hundreds of formal interviews. As an internationally acclaimed researcher on church leadership practices and trends, Warren brings a rich understanding of church dynamics and influences on the modern church.

In addition, we drew on the expertise of Chong Ho Yu, professor of psychology at Azusa Pacific University, for statistical data analysis, as well as Sid Buzzell for theological support. Buzzell is professor of Bible exposition and dean of the School of Theology at Colorado Christian University. We also asked a number of people to give feedback on the research design as well as the material that is in this book. These ranged from students in Ryan's communication classes at Azusa Pacific University to our friends serving on senior leadership teams in various churches. In addition, our own personal church experiences watching or participating in senior leadership teams informed our writing.

In short, we want this book to be a resource you can trust—because of its sound theological grounding, its use of expert statistical analysis, its in-depth knowledge of church leadership movements and practices, its grounding in the science of team and group communication, and its practical, relevant context. We believe this "team" of contributors makes this book a rich and unique resource.

WHAT WE PRAY THIS BOOK WILL DO FOR YOU

Most of us like the idea of teams as the best way to get a job done—with advantages for both creativity and productivity—but research says that too many of us are bad at teamwork. "Most of the time ... team members don't even agree on what the team is supposed to be doing," according to Hackman, the Harvard researcher quoted earlier. He concludes that "the odds are slim that a team will do a good job" without help.[8]

Help is here.

Our prayer is that God would mightily use *Teams That Thrive: Five Disciplines of Collaborative Church Leadership* to assist leadership teams in churches of every size to develop the disciplines necessary to grow more focused, effective, healthy and fruitful.

PART ONE

WHY READ A BOOK ABOUT LEADERSHIP TEAMS?

1

Myths We Believe

How Many of These Do You Think Are True?

The chief object of education is not to learn things; nay, the chief object of education is to unlearn things.

G.K. Chesterton,
All Things Considered

As we've studied, researched and observed senior leadership teams in churches, we've had many "aha!" moments where things we thought we knew about teams turned out to be just the opposite of reality for thriving teams. As we've listened to others, many have voiced similar harmful stereotypes. Here are some of the myths we hear most:

Myth: Great teams are primarily advisers to the top person, who makes the decisions.

Reality: The best teams make decisions as a group.

Myth: Meetings are places not to make decisions but to work through decisions already made.

Reality: The best teams both make decisions and "own" the implementation.

Myth: Teams first build trust, and then they learn to work together.

Reality: Trust is built in the trenches as the team works together, especially on major initiatives and tough, controversial decisions.

Myth: Senior teams are created by drawing a circle around the top positions on your organizational chart.

Reality: The best leadership teams draw from a diversity of roles and positions.

Myth: Bigger teams are better, drawing from eight to twelve people.

Reality: The optimal size is four to five in most cases, and sometimes three.

Myth: Shorter meetings are better than longer meetings.

Reality: Long meetings can be highly productive, if they are carefully structured to accomplish clear objectives and fully engage everyone's strengths.

Myth: Team leaders can't really be accountable to their group if they're the lead pastor.

Reality: The best teams have an amazing level of mutual accountability and genuine camaraderie.

Myth: The senior pastor or person who's been there longest is the best team leader.

Reality: The best teams rotate aspects of providing leadership to the team.

Myth: Most team improvement is haphazard, largely based on each member's growth outside of team meetings.

Reality: The best teams continually work together on improvement as a team.

The last myth helps explain why we wrote the book. We've given you tools for your team not just to improve, but to thrive. Please read on!

2

Your Vantage Point

How Is Your Church Being Led Right Now?

Why collaboration now? Not only because we don't really have a choice—but it's the best choice we've got.

Michael Schrage[1]

Thriving Churches are led by thriving leaders. Not *one* leader but *many* leaders. And not just by a group but by a *team* —there's a big difference between the two.[2]

If it's true that everything rises and falls on leadership, then it's worth examining who—beyond title—is actually leading your church. Who influences others on the team and throughout the staff? Who is being followed? Who establishes vision and direction? Who develops other leaders? Who truly shoulders the main decision-making responsibility?

Every church has some form of senior leadership at its helm. If it's a group rather than an individual, who is in that group, and why? What exactly are they trying to do, and how could they become more effective at it?

This book tackles these questions head-on, ultimately helping you develop a senior leadership team that thrives as it *truly* and *effectively* leads your church.

But first, this chapter provides the context for that discussion. In it, we will
- describe various types of leadership formations
- unpack the importance of a church's senior leadership group
- help you identify who is, or might be, on your senior leadership team
- identify how to maximize your own role in terms of how you'll be reading and applying this book

WHO'S LEADING YOUR CHURCH?

Every Tuesday at 10a.m. the staff and select volunteer leaders gathered in the pastor's office. After he arrived, usually late and without apology, he asked for personal prayer requests, had someone pray and then asked each person "what do you have?" Sometimes it was information that everyone should know, sometimes it was a problem to be solved, and sometimes it was a statement that the person needed to talk about a situation privately with the pastor.

On paper, this group seemed like a caring, involved team. In reality, everyone knew that their information mattered but not their opinion, that the pastor would make all the decisions himself, and that the only people who truly had his ear and could challenge his choices were his administrative assistant and the assistant pastor. All others who disagreed with him were put down verbally or described behind their backs as disloyal. Though the team led the church on paper, in reality the lead pastor held tightly to his role as singular leader.

The more you can clearly identify who provides actual leadership at your church, the better you can explore what it's truly accomplishing—including questions like whether the group is the best size, uses the best meeting strategies or involves the best people for what you actually need.

Identifying your actual leadership "team" might not be as simple as you think. Too often the officially named group is not the actual leadership team. Sometimes no group exists on paper, but one does in reality. On rare occasions, the leadership "group" is largely just one person.

Which of the following terms most closely describes how your church is led? You might pick more than one option:

- *Organic/informal.* Your leadership team is informal, perhaps not even identified as a team. A large number of people have access to the pastor, and all of them feel they are organically influencing the big picture at some level.

- *Fluid.* The leadership team seems to change month-to-month, and sometimes even day-to-day. If people are needed for their expertise or relevance, they're pulled into the decision-making circle. As new issues or circumstances arise, the makeup of the circle changes. Some would go so far as to say there is no fixed leadership "team" beyond the lead pastor.
- *Inner circle.* A designated group is supposed to work with the pastor to lead, but in reality the pastor has a "kitchen cabinet" of just a few people who actually make most leadership decisions.
- *Family based.* If two or more family members are heavily involved in the church's top-tier leadership, a large number of leadership decisions occur at family gatherings, often over meals or in the pastor's home.
- *Better-halved.* Whatever the designated leadership structure, the real person in power is the pastor's spouse. Regardless of how thoroughly a decision is prepared and processed, if it doesn't pass muster over pillow talk at home, the next day it gets voided, reversed or modified.

- *Pastor's staff.* The team is formed by simply drawing a circle around the top one or two tiers of the hierarchical organizational chart.
- *Senior pastor–executive pastor partnership.* The top dogs run the show, connecting with each other regularly but often not inviting significant input from anyone else. Even if they do ask someone's opinion, everyone around knows who the real power brokers are.
- *Ceremonial.* You have the right people with the right titles meeting regularly with a full agenda and making constant decisions—but never about truly big-picture issues. This team is great at perpetuating the status quo, but no one has permission to raise tough or controversial questions. You're called the "leadership team," but you're limited to keeping the train on the tracks rather than charting new territory.
- *Cheerleading only.* Your team focuses only on the good news of what's going well. You thank God for your blessings and affirm the servants God used. Any feedback that seems negative, even if constructively intended, is unwelcome. Any challenge to the status quo is out of place.
- *Advisory only.* Your team discusses true top-level leadership issues but only in an advisory capacity to the pastor. The group

rarely makes the actual decision; instead, the pastor alone weighs the input and makes the final call.

- *First responders.* Your team is mostly responsible to carry out the pastor's plans. You gather to hear the latest idea, which often requires a drop-everything approach to make things happen on short notice. The team contains senior-level people, but they are more implementers than co-dreamers or co-deciders.
- *Fire department.* You meet primarily when someone or something is on fire. When crisis hits, you feverishly meet and extinguish the issue, only to quickly resort back to the status quo of day-to-day individual functioning, to the neglect of strategic envisioning.
- *Leader's support group.* You use the word *team* without truly functioning as one. You look like a team from the outside, but the leader still calls all the shots.
- *A thriving leadership team.* Together your team truly leads your church. You establish and carry out vision, set direction, wrestle with thorny issues and come to conclusions, fight for unity, and model gospel-centered and mission-driven community for your staff and congregation.

SOFTWARE UPGRADE OR NEW OPERATING SYSTEM?

Each option above, except the last one, contains one or more fatal flaws to a high-performance, healthy, thriving team. The goal of this book is to help your team be more intentional, strategic, healthy and effective—an ideal that involves guiding you to move toward more of what a true team is all about.

We want you to understand how to do teamwork well. Good teaming is far more than a pair or loose group learning to work more efficiently. Sure, efficiency is often useful, but great teams aren't necessarily efficient. Rather, they are effective. And great teams are unwilling to sacrifice effectiveness on the altar of efficiency. To become more effective, your team might need not merely a software upgrade but a whole new operating system. For some, that will mean setting up a new team, while for others it will mean doing serious repairs to modify an existing one. Then, even when your team is truly thriving, you'll need tools to know how to keep tweaking it to stay current with issues triggered by growth and change. We appreciate the spirit of one team we interviewed who told us, "One of our values is that of incessant tinkering. That shows up in our programming, our approach to caring for our volunteers, and the way we keep improving our executive team."

> Great teams are unwilling to sacrifice effectiveness on the altar of efficiency.

A true team hitting on all cylinders will exhibit a number of specific qualities that we unpack starting in chapter six. These are measurable and achievable for every church. They can apply whether you're a church of fifty, five hundred, five thousand or even fifty thousand. They apply whether your church is new or long-established, denominational or not, urban or rural, mono-ethnic or multiethnic, traditional or contemporary. Because we offer general principles (such as "keep your team small and diverse"), we're confident you'll be able to apply the principles to your particular ministry context. Likewise, we offer practical and transferrable examples rather than prescribe exact criteria (such as a mandate to compose your team of exactly four people, namely, the youth pastor, worship leader, executive pastor and senior pastor).

NAME AND DEFINE THE TEAM LEADING YOUR CHURCH

Consultant Tony Morgan suggests that a church leadership team is "the team of leaders that usually includes the senior or lead pastor and the group of leaders that oversees the day-to-day operations of the church."[3] These teams go by many different names. Some are generic like lead team, senior leadership team, senior team, executive team (or exec team), directional leadership team, management council or senior staff. Some have a simple handle like "all the directors" or "all the pastors" or "all the elders" while others needs special explanation because they're a unique, carefully designed configuration. Some are subgroups of a board and thus have names related to that group such as the executive team of the elder board or governing board (which typically meets more frequently than the full board). Some are very informal in their name, such as pastor's team or the kitchen cabinet.

To know how to apply this book, it's far more important that you identify who that team is than that the group have a clear name. Sometimes there is no specific name. Consultant and author Bob Frisch writes about similar situations in the business world, saying, "Most companies are run by teams with no names"[4] and "Most of the world's best executives make decisions in ways that don't show up on an organization chart or process flow diagram."[5]

In smaller churches the teams are typically made up of mostly volunteers plus a pastor or other staff such as the pastor's administrative assistant. As a church increases in size, the senior leadership team often draws only from staff members. In even larger churches it's typically certain members of the executive staff. Like team membership, team names vary considerably (see table 2.1). No matter your church's size or station, we want to help you establish, encourage or sustain a leadership team that thrives together. Later, in chapter eight, we'll help you think through and determine who should compose your leadership team.

Table 2.1. Senior Leadership Teams Go by Many Names

Church	Attendance	Team Title
The Church at Argyle, Jacksonville, Florida	400	Senior Staff
Cornerstone West, Los Angeles, California	450	Pastor-Elders
Cross Lanes Baptist Church, Cross Lanes, West Virginia	575	Pastoral Staff
The Journey Church, Newark, Delaware	1,000	Directional Team
Freedom Church, Acworth, Georgia	1,700	Lead Team
Northstar Church, Panama City, Florida	2,500	Directional Leadership Team
Faith Promise Church, Knoxville, Tennessee	5,000	Executive Team

THE RIPPLE EFFECT OF YOUR LEADERSHIP TEAM

Whatever you call it and whoever composes it, many important issues ride on the strength of your church's leadership group. You need an outstanding team because it sets the pace for almost everything in the life of your church. For good or bad, leadership teams shape the culture, direct the mission, establish the vision and model the values of your church.

If that group is haphazard, unfocused, imbalanced or dysfunctional, the ripple effect will show up at every level of your church. By contrast, if your team is thriving, there's a good likelihood that the rest of the church will as well.

> You need an outstanding team because it sets the pace for almost everything in the life of your church.

In researching this book we[6] visited a number of churches to watch teams at work. One Monday morning at Liquid Church in Morristown, New Jersey, we sat in on a team of eight people debriefing the weekend worship services. The sense of unity and camaraderie was obvious immediately. Everyone clearly understood why they were meeting and what they needed to accomplish. Different people were using their gifts, from pastoring to leadership to administration, each with good effect on the group as a whole.

We later sat in on the church's lead team and observed many parallels. The environment was high-trust, honest, fun and truth-seeking. The four team members were all fully engaged. The purpose and desired outcomes for the meeting were clear. The entire group owned the decisions being discussed. Clearly this group looked to God's leading and sensed its responsibility as his representatives in steering this church.

> As goes the senior leadership team, so go most other teams in your church.

These parallels are not unusual: as goes the senior leadership team, so go most other teams in your church. Many have written about this ripple effect, including Pete Scazzero and Warren Bird in *The Emotionally Healthy Church*.[7] When leadership teams fail to reach their potential, their churches follow suit. In short, poorly functioning leadership teams don't bode well for the health and vitality of a church. Instead, churches need vibrant, healthy, effective teams to lead the congregation toward greater Christlikeness.

That's why we've written this book primarily to the core senior leadership team at a church, knowing also that most other teams can look over their shoulders as they read and still benefit.

Once you read and apply *Teams That Thrive*, it's unlikely you'll look at your team in the same way again. You'll more fully leverage the real power and competencies of the many individuals on your team, not just its leader. Your church will get better decisions faster, as well as a higher level of organizational alignment in executing those decisions. Team members, and those who work or volunteer under them, will achieve new levels of effectiveness and fulfillment.

In short, if we've done our job well in this book, you'll know some simple steps you can begin taking today on a journey that will bear much fruit for you personally, for your church's senior team and for your entire congregation.

YOUR VANTAGE POINT

We realize that every reader engages with this book from a distinct place. Some are totally sold on the benefits of teams. You could perhaps write this book. Not only are you convinced that teams are biblically and practically the way to go, but you've also experienced great success in your team efforts.

Figure 2.1. Four spectrums: theology, theory, your experience, your convictions

Others are less than convinced. You truly want the best for your church, but for any number of reasons, you believe leadership by team simply cannot work, and so you cling to solo leadership, believing it is the most efficient way to deal with the dicey issues that arise in your church.

Others of you are somewhere on a continuum that stretches between those two extremes.

To help identify your standpoint as you read this book, mark an X on each of the spectrums in figure 2.1 for theology, theory, your experience and your convictions.

Wherever you are on this spectrum, we hope you'll entertain the positive potential for team leadership in your church and find tools that can help your team truly thrive. And at the end, we hope you'll see why collaborative leadership makes sense and be willing to do what it takes to become extraordinary.

REFLECTION AND DISCUSSION QUESTIONS

1. Who provides the actual leadership to your church?
2. If you have a named senior leadership team, who is on it?
3. What are the key things your leadership team accomplishes?
4. As a team, discuss your responses for figure 2.1. How much agreement do you find among your team members? What are the primary areas of agreement and disagreement?
5. In the areas of disagreement, how does your team's lack of alignment around team philosophy and practice affect your ability to function as a thriving team?

6. Picture Jesus and his twelve apostles as a team. What statements of Jesus indicate his goals and objectives for that team?

EXPERT COMMENTARY: WHAT'S THE SECRET TO GREAT TEAMS?
Jim Tomberlin

Collaboration produces the best decisions, creates more ownership for the outcomes and fosters deeper community.

The day I started working at Willow Creek Community Church, Bill Hybels pulled me aside and said, "As a senior team member, I need you to show up with an opinion. I don't want to hear what you think I want to hear. I want to hear *your* thoughts, *your* opinions, *your* ideas. I need you to bring *your* best thinking and ideas to our team meetings."

Behind every great leader is a team of leaders. Why? None of us is as smart as all of us.

It takes a team to lead. The greater the cause and the more significant the outcome, the more important the team. Why? Everything rises or falls based on leadership, and a plurality of leaders united under a common cause is stronger than a lone-ranger, solo leader.

Collaboration produces better decisions, and better decisions lead to better outcomes. Healthy teams move beyond authoritarian leaders and departmental silos. They become idea factories where the best idea wins and gets improved through collaboration. True collaboration moves beyond the sharing of information or even cooperating to creating something better *together*. Collaborative teams create synergy where the sum is greater than the individual parts. When the best idea wins, the whole church wins.

Great leaders get ownership from their teams. How does that happen? Collaboration. When people feel like they have been heard, have contributed and have helped shape a decision, they own it. They have skin in the game and will work hard to make that decision a reality. If a leader doesn't have ownership from his or her team, he is not leading; the leader is just taking a walk, or, worse, becoming a target.

The most effective churches in America today have strong leaders who surround themselves with a smart team of leaders, and in the process they become a community of leaders. They become a band of brothers and sisters who will take a bullet for the cause and each other. They recognize that they rise or fall together, that they are only as strong as the weakest link on the team. They will pat each other on the back and kick each other in the butt to get the job done. They push each other to be and do their best. They bond

> deeply through the crucible of collaborative leadership. True collaboration not only produces better outcomes; it generates deeper community.

The church team model is not a new innovation. It's as old and effective as the church of Antioch in Acts 13. It was led by a diverse team composed of a Jewish rabbi (Saul of Tarsus), a Jewish marketplace leader (Barnabas), a North African (Niger), a Jewish aristocrat (Manaen) and a cosmopolitan Roman (Lucius). Maybe that explains why the church at Antioch is the best example of a high-impacting, life-giving, sending church recorded in the New Testament.

Local church ministry is best played as a team sport. Effective church leaders surround themselves with a team of leaders. Build your team, invest in them and become a stronger, healthier and more effective church in the process. Go team!

***

Jim Tomberlin is founder and senior strategist at MultiSite Solutions and coauthor of *Church Locality: New Rules for Church Buildings in a Multisite, Church Planting, and Giga-Church World*. Find Jim online at multisite solutions.com.

PART TWO

WHY DO LEADERSHIP TEAMS MAKE SENSE?

PART TWO

WHY DO LEADERSHIP TEAMS MAKE SENSE?

3

The Bible Speaks

Scriptural Foundations for Senior Leadership Teams, with Sid Buzzell

At that time I said to you,... "How can I bear by myself the weight and burden of you and your strife? Choose for your tribes wise, understanding, and experienced men, and I will appoint them as your heads." And you answered me, "The thing that you have spoken is good for us to do." So I took the heads of your tribes, wise and experienced men, and set them as heads over you, commanders of thousands, commanders of hundreds, commanders of fifties, commanders of tens, and officers, throughout your tribes.

Deuteronomy 1:9, 12-15

Now you are the body of Christ and individually members of it.

1 Corinthians 12:27

The more Charles Anderson read his Bible, the more he wanted to fire himself from being the senior pastor of University United Methodist Church in San Antonio, Texas. Founded in 1970, the church had gone through several seasons of remarkable growth before Charles was called there as senior leader in 2006. He loved the people, the community and his denomination, but his study of Scripture kept troubling him that he was not doing what he should be doing. He was the primary preacher, but he needed to be the primary team leader also.

Reflecting on this needed transition, Charles said,

> The more I studied Scripture, the more I became concerned by the whole "senior" pastor and "associate/assistant" pastor language, particularly what it communicated about our sense of being. I began to question whether or not the terminology was more the language of academia instead of ministry. The language of academia is about credentials and flow chart hierarchy, which seemed alien to the kingdom of God's concerns of character, calling and mission. I also was disturbed by the lack of ministry purpose in our common language. After all, my primary ministry as "senior" pastor is not to be the oldest clergy on staff; it's something beyond age or experience or pay grade.

Through a series of Bible reflections with his boards, and with his bishop's blessing, Charles has taken on a new title: directing pastor, which includes his preaching role. "The term means I can work with other leaders to be the chief visioner and chief leadership development officer," he explained. "Together we focus on hearing and articulating the vision and values of the church, we personify the identity and unity of a diverse multisite community, and we identify and mentor leaders for the entire system."[1]

This approach works better for both Charles and the church, but he's still looking to Scripture to find even better ways to lead in the way it models and teaches.

Similarly, when three friends joined together to plant The Parks Church in McKinney, Texas, they looked to the Scriptures to determine how to provide leadership to their new congregation. As they read their Bibles, they saw plurality of leadership through and through.

Having experienced unhealthy single-person leadership and having seen so many other church planters burn out or struggle through church planting, they endeavored to do leadership in a way that would force them to pursue knowing God and abiding in Christ above all else. "If your ambition and desire to see the church grow is driving you, things like team will get in the way of your true ambition," said Sam Deford, who planted the church along with Kyle Redel and Aaron Snell. But, he concludes, "if your desire is to know God, you will know his humility, and then it becomes so easy to submit as part of a team."

Just like these four leaders, people who take the Bible seriously are governed by the question, "What does God's Word say about the topic I am investigating?" While you won't find the exact term *leadership team* in your Bible, you will find myriad examples of leadership teams. You'll also find many biblical teachings that strongly support the idea of a leadership team, whatever your church polity.

Though our aim is not to fully explore what the Scriptures say about leadership in general, and team leadership in particular, we do want to offer a high-level tour of biblical texts that point to team leadership.[2] Toward that end, this chapter

- suggests that the Trinity demonstrates a certain "team" quality about God
- shows how the body of Christ metaphor undergirds the idea of teams in the church
- applies New Testament principles for church leadership to leadership teams
- affirms that collaborative leadership can work in your particular ecclesial context

THE TRINITY MODELS TEAMWORK

From one cover of the Bible to the other, the Creator of the universe works as a team. The first glimpse of this dynamic appears in the

Bible's opening chapter. It speaks of God creating by means of his Word and Spirit (Gen 1:2-3; see also Jn 1:1-3; 1 Cor 8:6). Then Genesis 1:26 makes a similar point with its use of the plural: "Let *us* make man in *our* image, after *our* likeness" (emphasis added). God, Word and Spirit are brought together.

By New Testament times, the picture becomes clearer. Father, Son and Spirit work together at the annunciation to Mary (Lk 1:26-38), at Jesus' baptism (Mt 3:11, 16) and in Jesus' teachings (such as Jn 14), especially his final commission (Mt 28:19-20). Likewise, the rest of the New Testament contains repeated reference to the idea of one God as a divine Trinity of Father, Son and Holy Spirit.

This model of divine collaboration causes seminary professor Robert Crosby to conclude, "The foremost metaphor or model for teams in the Bible is the Trinity."[3] Presbyterian pastor Stan Ott voices a similar thought, expanding on how that divine collaboration works:

> For the ultimate picture of a ministry team, we need look no further than the Trinity: the Father, Son, and the Holy Spirit. The members of the Trinity share a common vision for ministry. They enjoy fellowship in wonderfully loving relationships. And each member of the Trinity has a unique "task" or role in the process known as salvation history [or God's work in revealing salvation]. They are the essential

fusion of relationships and work—*the missional fellowship.*[4]

Christianity is unique among major religions in presenting one God who eternally exists and functions as a divine team. certainly undergirds the idea of God's people likewise working in unity through teams.

> Christianity is unique among major religions in presenting one God who eternally exists and functions as a divine team.

THE BODY OF CHRIST WORKS AS A TEAM

Not only does God work as a team, but he calls his church to function collaboratively as well. One of the most prevalent images of the church in the New Testament is that of the body of Christ. "Now you are the body of Christ and individually members of it" (1 Cor 12:27), the apostle Paul teaches. He also explains, "To each is given the manifestation of the Spirit for the common good" (1 Cor 12:7), encouraging the church's members to unite their efforts so they could benefit each other and best engage in the church's mission.

In this passage, Paul brings out two emphases: there are *varieties* of "gifts," "services" and "functions," but the *same* "Spirit," "Lord" and "God" gives and empowers them in each person. Paul is emphasizing the essential roles of diversity and unity that are necessary for the body of Christ to work well. With the essential strength of diversity comes the inherent danger of disunity. To address that danger, Paul underscored that the church is *one* body, not multiple: "For just as the body is one and has many members, and all the members of the body, though many, are one body, so it is with Christ" (1 Cor 12:12).

To help his readers understand how the church can coordinate all this variety of function into one cohesive unit, he landed on this marvelous parallel: the church combines its variety of functions in the same church much like a human body coordinates its variety of functions. A human body, like the church, has varieties of parts, each with an essential function, but all are members of the same body. In the church as a body, diversity and unity combine seamlessly.

To make the metaphor stand the test of real people in a real church, Paul needed to address two problems that arise when we combine the strengths of diversity and unity. He addressed the problem of low-status members feeling they have little to contribute (1 Cor 12:15-20). In addition, he spoke to the problem of dominant members minimizing others' contributions (1 Cor 12:21-26).

A functioning body, whether literally or metaphorically, needs to respect, honor and nurture all its members. And it needs to give what it can and receive what it must from each other member.

> In the church as a body, diversity and unity combine seamlessly.

If we searched long and hard for a modern term to describe how Paul envisioned the members of the church relating to each other, none comes to mind that is more accurate than the word *team*. Is it possible that functioning as a team fleshes out Paul's vision of the church's members operating as a body? If not, what other option could work better? If the members of the church are taught the importance of working as a body, how much more should the leaders whose model they are told to imitate?

Indeed, it is the diversity of thought, perspective and skill integrated in a unified fashion that enables teams to outperform individuals. A team without diversity is no better than a single individual. But a team without unity will fracture from fighting and disparate visions. Instead, true teams value, respect, encourage and combine the contributions of diverse members to create a united effort. The body of Christ provides an exemplary model for teamwork.

> A team without diversity is no better than a single individual.

THE NEW TESTAMENT DESCRIBES MANY LEADERSHIP TEAMS

Jesus Christ, who is the head of the body of Christ, gave various leaders to the church (Eph 4:11-16). While the New Testament contains many mandates that require leadership, such as "Go therefore and make disciples" (Mt 28:19-20) and "preach the word" (2 Tim 4:2), the Bible is often less specific on precisely how to do so.

We find much biblical support for the idea of team-based leadership, even though Scripture does not expressly use this term. Our basis is that leadership teams are not ends in themselves; they are means to ends. They are not mandates. They are methods consistent with the New Testament teaching and modeling. So instead of searching for a Bible passage that says, "Thou shalt lead your church with teams," we explore the question, "Are there biblical models or principles to support the idea that church leaders can be more effective and efficient stewards of their leadership responsibilities if they function as a team?"

To answer that question, we asked Sid Buzzell[5] to survey the various New Testament passages that refer to leaders and their functions to discern what they say related to leading a church as a team. The New Testament uses eight different Greek words: the first three refer to people who serve in the office of leader, and the last five refer to leaders, but more to leadership function than to leadership office.

1. *Episkopos* (πίσοκπος) occurs five times and is translated *overseer* in the ESV (the ESV is used in the following translations as well). One example is 1 Timothy 3:1: "The saying is trustworthy: If anyone aspires to the office of *overseer*, he desires a noble task" (emphasis added).

2. *Presbyteros* (πρεσβύτερος) occurs sixty-six times and is translated as *elder* or *elders* sixty times. In twenty-seven instances the term refers to Israel's elders; five references are to church elders. One example is Titus 1:5: "This is why I left you in Crete, so that you might put what remained into order, and appoint *elders* in every town as I directed you" (emphasis added).

3. *Diakonos* (διάκονος) occurs twenty-nine times and is translated *servant, minister* or *deacon*. It's used eleven times to describe servants, apart from any leadership function, four times in the Gospels to state that the path to greatness was to serve or be a servant, and seven times as minister. For instance, Paul referred to himself or his team members as ministers. Examples

include 2 Corinthians 6:4: "as *servants* of God we commend ourselves in every way," and 1 Timothy 3:8: "*Deacons* likewise must be dignified, not double-tongued, not addicted to much wine, not greedy for dishonest gain" (emphasis added in both verses).

4. *Poimena* (ποιμένα) is translated *shepherd*. It's used eighteen times and refers to literal shepherds, such as when Jesus referred to Israel as "sheep without a shepherd" (Mt 9:36; Mk 6:34). Jesus and Peter refer to Jesus as the "Great Shepherd." The word was used only once in reference to a church office: "And he gave the apostles, the prophets, the evangelists, the shepherds and teachers" (Eph 4:11).

5. *Poimain* ō(ποιμαίνω) is a verb meaning *to shepherd* and is related to the noun *shepherd*. It occurs eleven times and is used twice to refer to Jesus as a shepherd. The Ephesian elders were told to "care for" the church (Acts 20:28). Peter instructed the fellow elders he was addressing to "shepherd the flock of God that is among you" (1 Pet 5:2).

6. *Proistamenos* (προϊστ□μενος) is a participle that's used eight times. In Romans 12:8 it is listed as a spiritual gift and translated

lead. In other passages it is translated *rule*, *manage* or *devote*. "We ask you, brothers, to respect those who labor among you and *are over you* in the Lord and admonish you, and to esteem them very highly in love because of their work" (1 Thess 5:12-13; emphasis added).

7. *Hē goumenos* (ἡγούμενος) is used twenty-eight times, two times of Jesus as ruler and four times translated *leader(s)*. For example: "Obey your *leaders* and submit to them, for they are keeping watch over your souls, as those who will have to give an account" (Heb 13:17; emphasis added). The word is also used in other references not related to leading.

8. *Apostolos* (ἀπόστολος), used eighty times, initially referred to the original Twelve who were appointed by Jesus (Lk 6 and Acts 1). In addition, Paul and Barnabas are referred to as apostles (Acts 14:14), and perhaps others are as well.

> The practice of multiple leadership—or teams—existed from the church's birth.

These eight words in their various contexts offer many insights about team leadership in the New Testament. Most compelling to us is the idea that the practice of multiple leadership—or teams—existed from the church's birth. At each stage of the early church's structural development, when a new form of leadership shows up, it looks like a team. he departed. As one writer says, "Jesus gave the Church plurality of Jesus set the first precedent for church leadership when he "called his disciples and chose from them twelve, whom he named apostles" (Lk 6:13). Jesus then prepared them to lead his fledgling movement after leadership."[6]

In the book of Acts, the apostles were the obvious leaders. As the church grew, the ministry needs overwhelmed the apostles and they could no longer perform all the leadership functions. Some of the people complained about this oversight, so the apostles said, "pick out from among you seven men of good repute, full of the Spirit and of wisdom, whom we will appoint to this duty" (Acts 6:3).

Thus a second layer of official ministers was added so the apostles could specialize in what they were called to do, as indicated in Acts 6:4: "But we will devote ourselves to prayer and to the ministry of the word." Added responsibility required added leadership. Although this may or may not have constituted the origin of the deacon office, appointing a second group to assist in the ministry was undoubtedly the prototype for it.

A third development in the church's leadership structure is noted when the church at Antioch sent a gift to the Jerusalem church. Those who officially received the gift were called elders (Acts 11:30). The apostles were still active. The seven who were appointed in Acts 6 (and who were later referred to as an official group called "the seven" in Acts 21:8) were also still functioning. Now Luke refers to another official group of leaders called elders.

The status of Jerusalem's elders was demonstrated at the Jerusalem Council. The leadership team that made the crucial decision at this council was composed of the apostles *and* the elders. In addition, the letter announcing their decision was signed by "The brothers, both the apostles and elders" (Acts 15:23).

The office of elder became a recognized position in other churches besides Jerusalem. Paul and Barnabas returned to the churches they planted and appointed elders in each church (Acts 14:23). Even these new churches needed people to whom the congregation could look for direction and ministry. Small as most of these churches likely were, Luke points out that elders (in the plural) were appointed.

PATTERNS OF CHURCH LEADERSHIP

One consistent pattern across all these roles and references is the use of plural: not one apostle, but a team of apostles; not one deacon or elder, but elders and deacons, always referred to in the plural. Some churches had multiple elders, while others had multiple elders and multiple deacons. Typical is Philippians 1:1 where more than one leadership office is named, but all leadership groups are referred to in the plural: "*Paul and Timothy, servants* of Christ Jesus, to all the saints in Christ Jesus who are at Philippi, with the *overseers* and *deacons*" (emphasis added). Indeed, this pattern is so strong that one commentator concluded, "In all these passages, there is not one passage which describes a church being governed by one pastor."[7]

Another pattern is that New Testament churches added leaders to meet ministry needs, sometimes resulting in multiple leadership groups. The qualifications for both elder and deacon suggest that leaders needed to work well both with church members and with other leaders. Leaders were required to function in a variety of roles that sometimes overlapped. For example, most of the leadership qualifications listed in 1 Timothy 3 and Titus 1 deal with how leaders would relate to others as they conducted their leadership responsibilities, such as the requirements for leaders to be sober-minded, self-controlled, respectable, not violent but gentle, and not quarrelsome. The list describes people who could not only minister to the congregation, but who would also function well in a multifaceted leadership setting.

Further, clear leader–follower relationships also existed. Followers are told to respect their leaders who are "over" them. The Thessalonian believers were encouraged to "respect those who labor among you" and "to esteem them very highly in love because of their work" (1 Thess 5:12-13). Leaders were expected to perform their leadership duties with diligence and skill.

And certainly, leaders are to lead. Hebrews 13:17 reminds us that leaders will have to "give an account" for how they lead. As such, leaders are responsible for the people under their care.

TEAMS CAN WORK WITHIN ANY CHURCH POLITY

Historically, three approaches have developed for how to apply the Bible's teaching and modeling to church leadership and governance today. In the twenty-first century, church structures are more complex than churches in the New Testament, whether megachurches, multisite satellite campuses or even traditional single-site churches; however, each of these formats draws biblical support for their leadership system:

- Episcopal: each local church is under the control of a hierarchy of leaders.
- Presbyterian: each local church is led by elected elders from within the congregation as well as by higher authorities.

- Congregational: each local church is autonomous with a democratic structure, with limited relationship between local churches and higher authorities.

Because teams never exist in isolation, it is important to understand the way that a church's governance structure shapes the leadership team. Leadership teams' roles and functions at their churches are shaped by cultural values and practices, practical exigencies of their surrounding community and the ecclesial tribe to whom the church belongs and with whom leaders align. However a church achieves collaborative leadership within these various ecclesial forms, team leadership excludes forms of "unitary leadership, monarchical rule, or one-man leadership."[8]

> Functioning as leaders in a collaborative manner is certainly part of God's design for local church leadership.

No matter what governance structure a church adopts, functioning as leaders in a collaborative manner is certainly part of God's design for local church leadership. Just because the terminology of leadership teams has come into vogue in the beginning of the twenty-first century doesn't mean they're a new innovation. As this brief review indicates, leadership teams have been around since the church's founding.

At the same time, however, there's a modern resurgence of interest in practicing shared leadership. Why?

While we can argue that if collaborative leadership is part of God's design, then there must be good reasons for it, we suspect that organizations of all types are turning to team leadership because of the pragmatic benefits it offers. Chapter four picks up there.

REFLECTION AND DISCUSSION QUESTIONS

1. In what ways does your current leadership structure align with biblical principles for church leadership? In what ways does it not?
2. In your leadership team, how do diversity and unity combine seamlessly?
3. How could a senior leadership team work best in your church's governance structure?
4. Are the constraints that challenge your ability to work as a team more theologically based or practically based?
5. Read and reflect on Ephesians 4:11-16 as a team. How does this passage instruct on why and how to do leadership as a team?

EXPERT COMMENTARY: GOSPEL-CENTERED LEADERSHIP TEAMS

Matt Carter

The gospel gives us both the structure and the culture of how leadership teams should look. In the gospel, the Father sends the Son, who is empowered by and sends the Holy Spirit. The Godhead himself models the original leadership team.

Not only is the structure of a leadership team modeled by the Godhead in the gospel, but also the culture of a perfect and healthy leadership team is modeled. The Father's heart is set on loving and glorifying the Son. In turn the Son submits himself completely to the Father's will, and the Holy Spirit directs all of creation to glorify the Father and Son. This culture of mutual love and submission is key to any leadership team's success and flourishing. Specifically, we see this mutual submission played out in three primary ways for gospel-centered leadership teams (GCLTs).

First, GCLTs wash feet. Taking their cues from the original leadership team, the Trinity, team members humbly serve. As we see in Philippians 2:6-8, Jesus, "though he was in the form of God, did not count equality with God a thing to be grasped, but emptied himself, by taking the form of a servant, being born in the likeness of men. And being found in human form, he humbled himself by becoming obedient to the point of death, even death on a cross." And in John 13, Jesus assumed the posture of a slave, washing the feet of his disciples, even the one who would betray him. Jesus took the initiative. A GCLT isn't a platform for power and control, but for humility, sacrifice and humble submission.

Second, GCLTs boast in weakness. This isn't about who has the dirtiest sins. It's about making much of Jesus. The gospel is the ultimate pride killer. It reveals who we are apart from Christ and wrecks us. But then it tells who we are in Christ and transforms us. GCLTs realize no individual, or team for that matter, is equal to the task, but Jesus is. So, following the instruction of 1 Corinthians 2:3-5, members of GCLTs come "in weakness and in fear and much trembling" so "that [others'] faith might not rest in the wisdom of [the leadership team as a whole or any one member of it] but in the power of God." Woe to the leadership team with all the answers and no weaknesses.

Third, GCLTs willingly defer to and serve others for the sake of *the* mission, rather than controlling others for the sake of *their* mission. Members of leadership teams do this individually and as a team. It's not about them and their success, but God and his glory.

Gospel-centered leadership teams know and live out their conviction that Jesus' "power is made perfect in weakness," that his "grace is sufficient," and position themselves "so that the power of Christ may rest upon [them]" (2 Cor 12:9).

***

Matt Carter is pastor of preaching and vision at the Austin Stone Community Church in Austin, Texas, and author of *The Real Win* (with Colt McCoy). Connect with him on Twitter (@_Matt_Carter).

4

Passing Fad or Here to Stay

Ten Practical Reasons for Senior Leadership Teams

Teamwork is not a virtue. It is a choice—and a strategic one. That means leaders who choose to operate as a real team willingly accept the work and the sacrifices that are necessary for any group that wants to reap the benefits of true teamwork.

Patrick Lencioni, The Advantage

Two years into their journey as a new church, Reality LA in Hollywood, California, moved toward the idea of a senior leadership team. With the help of the elders and other pastors from the Reality family of churches, lead pastor Tim Chaddick realized that as the congregation's solo leader he wasn't adequately using the gifts and strengths of his staff. "I knew some of the other pastors were more gifted in some areas than I was; I needed to let them lead," Tim reflected.

That jumpstarted a gradual shift toward doing leadership as a team. Today, the four members of their executive team—the pastor of preaching and vision, executive pastor, pastor for community groups and pastor for equipping theology—truly share leadership responsibilities, even rotating the designation of "first among equals"[1] among the team, based on who holds the most expertise in any given area.

They've bought solidly into shared leadership, but why? From our review of biblical principles for ecclesial leadership unpacked in chapter three, we know that team leadership is biblically viable, but what are the practical benefits it offers?

What happened at Reality LA is increasingly commonplace in today's church. As a Leadership Network report analyzes the current situation, "In North American church leadership, the structure is changing from a single leader calling all the shots to flattened-hierarchy leadership teams that share crucial strategic and directional responsibilities."[2] Influenced by the for-profit corporation's move to leadership teams in the 1990s and 2000s, many churches today utilize senior leadership teams to provide optimal leadership to their churches. Pastors, similar to corporate executives, have found "that the demands of leadership necessitate the creation, building, and management of executive teams ... [to assist them in] running the whole enterprise."[3]

Though leadership teams come in just about as many shapes and sizes as do churches, one fact remains: many churches have found leadership teams to be a wise choice for organizational leadership. To help us better understand the value of leadership by a team, this chapter explores why leadership teams have proliferated in the church and examines the practical arguments for leadership by team. To do so, this chapter

- explains the practical benefits of senior leadership teams for church leadership
- offers a diagnostic to help church leaders distinguish whether their leadership group is more of a working group or team

THE BENEFITS AND POWER OF SHARED LEADERSHIP

Not only do the Scriptures point toward the values of plural leadership, as chapter three outlined, but copious research shows the benefit of a team approach to complex tasks. Providing effective executive leadership to a church is no different. Well-functioning leadership teams enjoy numerous advantages. Let's look at ten practical benefits of team leadership.

1. Greater productivity. As the Bible emphatically illustrates in 1 Corinthians 12–14 and the "strengths-based" movement highlights, not everyone is gifted in the same way.[4] When each team member fully operates out of various gifts, talents and strengths toward a common goal, instead of constantly trying to mitigate personal weaknesses, leadership teams are able to outpace the combination of individual contributions.

> Copious research shows the benefit of a team approach to complex tasks.

2. Less stress and pressure on the lead pastor. Leadership teams take pressure off the organizational senior leader, spreading out the responsibility for organizational leadership to several persons. Solomon expressed the power of collaboration well: "Two are better than one, because they have a good reward for their toil. For if they fall, one will lift up his fellow. But woe to him who is alone when he falls and has not another to lift him up!" (Eccles 4:9-10).

In addition, teams somewhat level the proverbial playing field so that participants with lower status can more freely offer their ideas, knowledge and concerns. The extent that the playing field is leveled depends, however, on the level to which responsibility is shared and power distributed among the team. In other words, it is determined by how the team deals with the notion of "first among equals"—how much first and how much equal.

3. Greater leadership development. By inviting additional staff into the most crucial conversations about mission, values and strategy, and then inviting the team to make key decisions, team members are spurred to develop their own leadership capacity. In fact, inviting a group of emerging leaders into the church's most significant decision-making tasks is a fantastic way to develop leaders.

> Inviting a group of emerging leaders into the church's most significant decision-making tasks is a fantastic way to develop leaders.

4. More creativity and innovation. It's a well-trod myth that bursts of creativity are developed in the private closet.[5] In reality, innovative solutions to pressing problems are more typically developed through collaboration with others. Leadership teams, therefore, enable individuals to build upon one another's ideas to create solutions that go beyond one person's limited vision of possibilities.

5. Better decision making. The issues discussed at the senior level of any organization are often complex, necessitating a breadth of perspectives to address the challenges. Well-staffed and well-structured leadership teams potentially have more information (because of the knowledge brought by each member) and should be able to process it better that individuals, and they bring together people with multiple perspectives and insights into how to respond to those issues.

6. *More safety and accountability.* Because leadership teams provide strength in numbers, increase opportunities for cross-training and promote mutual accountability, they offer stability to organizations in times of distress or change, and they provide checks and balances to each member's individual performance. Based on his extensive study of power and status in the early church, social historian and pastor Joseph Hellerman argues, "A community of leaders has the ability to maximize a pastor's strengths, while simultaneously intercepting and derailing potential abuses of spiritual authority before irreparable damage is done."[6] News accounts of pastoral sin and other types of abuse are all too rampant and offer a timely, important reminder of the need for accountability with the responsibilities and privileges of leadership.

Similarly, leadership teams provide a setting where multiple people can lead, teach, preach, strategize, counsel and administrate, which prevents potentially harmful specialization among team members. Though a reasonable level of specialty is warranted, too much of a good thing can put a church in dangerous territory in the case that only one person can effectively teach, manage the books, run programs and so on. Teams create a setting for collaboration and cross-training, an important guard against church collapse when a senior leader can no longer continue in leadership. Along those lines, "in a [leadership] team setting, leadership is shared by a community of people, which counters the tendency for pastors to form congregations in their own images."[7]

> "A [leadership] team setting ... counters the tendency for pastors to form congregations in their own images."
> Adam S. McHugh, *Introverts in the Church*

7. Less loneliness. Leadership doesn't have to be lonely. Leadership teams combat isolationism in several ways: placing senior leaders in mutually accountable relationships, sharing the burdens of personnel issues, resource conflicts and difficult decisions that rise to the top of any organization, and developing camaraderie and trust among co-laborers. One of the primary causes of pastoral burnout and turnover is lack of community. Too many pastors are seen, or see themselves, as a "sacred person over the church who can never really become a part of the congregation."[8] Leadership teams combat such isolation, pushing pastors to experience community, which they can then also use to model community to the church.

8. Greater joy and satisfaction among team members. Teams offer a space where members can voice their feelings, disagreements, opinions and ideas, and also be social as they work. Both of these practices promote the finding of greater enjoyment of the task. They also invite the joy that comes from being in real relationships. The greatest joys of life are found in community; teams create a space for extraordinary achievement in the midst of connection.

9. *Greater trust among the congregation.* The benefits of healthy leadership teams extend beyond the team itself. Many staff and congregants who are wary of the pitfalls of one-person leadership find great comfort in knowing that several godly people are involved in shaping the direction of the church, determining what to do in difficult personnel situations and, in some cases, developing what is taught to the church. For instance, though several staff members at one church we visited were sometimes confused and even distraught by decisions that had been made by the executive team, they found great confidence in knowing that one staff member they really trusted (other than the senior pastor) was part of making those decisions.

> Teams create a space for extraordinary achievement in the midst of connection.

10. *Provide better organizational leadership.* Putting it all together, organizations

benefit from true teamwork at the top of the organization, as it produces the following:
- *better decisions* based on greater perspective and information
- *greater accountability* for senior leaders
- *enhanced productivity* that reduces bottlenecks at the executive level
- *spread out weight of responsibility* among several organizational leaders
- *opportunities for leadership development* for more staff members or high-capacity lay leaders
- *greater community and satisfaction* among team members

The best organizations and the teams that they comprise understand these benefits. It's no wonder modern management practice, inside and outside the church, has embraced team leadership. In fact, when we asked the exceptional teams in our research sample (details coming in chap. 6) why they used a leadership team, they told us they did so to take pressure off the lead pastor, to increase representation for decision making, to increase coordination across departments or campuses and, ultimately, to provide better leadership to the church than the lead pastor alone could provide. However, we know that leadership teams work—and experience all these benefits—because God designed the church to be led collaboratively.

When churches do so, they experience the blessing that comes with leading in a manner consistent with God's Word.

MOVING FROM SOLO LEADERSHIP AND WORKING GROUPS TO A TRUE TEAM

The above benefits are available only to those teams who are willing to do the hard work to be a team. In fact, many groups call themselves a team but in reality are not—relying on a single leader while feigning teamwork.

> Many groups call themselves a team but in reality are not—relying on a single leader while feigning teamwork.

Single-leader approaches can take several forms. One of the most prominent is the benevolent dictatorship where the lead pastor runs the show but is generally kind and generous with staff. No one questions the pastor's authority; indeed, they benefit from it. This approach does work in a limited capacity, as it benefits from the wisdom of experience, makes decision making efficient and centralizes control and authority.[9] However, when that single leader, who is human, makes a mistake—big or small—the church can suffer dramatically. None of the benefits listed earlier in the chapter can be realized.

The working group approach is not much different. In an effort to appease those who call for group leadership at the top of an organization, some pastors put a group in place to "lead" the church. But as the exercise below fleshes out, a pure working group is often just a fancy way for saying the "leader's support group" and a thinly-veiled attempt to look like a team without truly functioning as one. The leader still calls all the shots.

We suspect that the majority of church "leadership teams" function instead as working groups. But, just as calling a tree a car doesn't make it one, renaming a collection of people a team doesn't make it a team.

Unfortunately, those working groups won't experience the benefits listed above at their fullest level, as they are reserved for true teams.

In their classic text *The Wisdom of Teams*, consultants Jon Katzenbach and Doug Smith delineate differences between working groups and teams.[10] Take a moment and use the following figure to take stock of your senior leadership team by marking an X on the continuum between each of the two statements showing the extent to which your team is a working group versus a true team (see fig. 4.1).

Take Stock: Do You Have More Working Group or Team?
Place an X on the Continuum

Working Group	Team
One strong, clearly focused leader	Shared leadership roles
Individual accountability	Both individual and mutual accountability
Group's purpose is same as the broader organizational mission	Specific team purpose that the team itself delivers
Individual work products	Collective work products
Runs efficient meetings	Encourages open-ended discussions and active problem-solving meetings
Measures its effectiveness indirectly by its influence on others	Measures performance directly by assessing collective work products
Discusses, decides and delegates	Discusses, decides and does real work together

Figure 4.1. Senior leadership: working group or team?

Now that you've assessed your leadership group, we should offer a bit of clarification. Many thriving teams find value in exhibiting the attributes of both teams and working groups. For instance, running efficient meetings and engaging open-ended discussions are not mutually exclusive. In fact, chapters eleven (on decision making) and twelve (on meetings) explain how you can have your cake and eat it too. At the same time, strong, focused leaders don't necessarily preclude shared leadership roles; instead, those strong leaders can lead in a way that invites others to offer their best to the task (the topic of chap. 9).

If you believe your leadership group should operate as a team, bestselling leadership writer Patrick Lencioni advises that you should ask yourself and your team members five key questions:

- Can we keep our egos in check?
- Are we capable of admitting to mistakes, weaknesses, or insufficient knowledge?
- Can we speak up openly when we disagree?
- Will we confront behavioral problems directly?
- Can we put the success of the team or organization over our own?[11]

He goes on to suggest that "if the answer to one or more of these questions is 'probably not,' then a group of executives should think twice about declaring themselves a team."[12] In that case, the sobering reality is that you'd be better off not trying to become a team and instead setting your sights on being the best work group you can be.

TAKING THE PLUNGE

By now we hope you, like the leaders of Reality LA and The Parks Church, are saying, "I get the benefits, and we're willing to take a shot at becoming more of a true team." But we hope you are also asking, How exactly can we improve to the point of becoming an *exceptional* team?

Read on. We will show you a path.

REFLECTION AND DISCUSSION QUESTIONS

1. After reading this chapter, what sticks out to you as the most compelling reason to figure out how to make your leadership team thrive?
2. What challenge is your church facing that would encourage you to more fully adopt a senior leadership team?
3. Of the ten benefits of team leadership explained in this chapter, which one, if your team could achieve it, would most transform your team's leadership of your church? What could you do this week to take advantage of that benefit?
4. What gets in the way of your team being a true team rather than merely a work group?
5. What can you do this week to help your leadership group function more like a true team?
6. Where in the Bible do you see "the power of shared leadership"?

EXPERT COMMENTARY: GOOD GOVERNANCE REQUIRES

PLURALITY OF LEADERSHIP GOOD GOVERNANCE REQUIRES PLURALITY OF LEADERSHIP

David Fletcher

Recently, I was hosting one of our XPastor certification classes. My guest for that day's webinar was a banker. He was to share with thirty-five students the bank's perspective on the process of getting a church building loan.

The class was going along quite well. Students were involved and asking lots of questions. It was a hot topic. We were talking about money and the best ways to borrow it. Then the banker gave a bell-ringer qualification, "In our process of understanding, if a church is healthy enough for a building loan, we look for good governance. This includes plurality of leadership."

I had to pause the class after hearing this amazing statement. We then explored what he meant—and quite simply it was that churches need teams of strong and gifted leaders. If the bankers are looking for plurality of church leadership, then there must be solid fiduciary sense to it! For years I have been urging churches to have talented people on executive teams. Now the bankers of the world were encouraging it—even demanding it.

The roots of the banker's problem are unfortunate but true. Take a powerful communicator in the lead role, and then surround him with "yes people." Who will have the courage to say, "We can't afford it"? What if the leader's desires become stronger than his ethics? Who will say, "It's not right to take money from a designated fund," or "It's against the law to pay an employee as a contractor," or, even stronger, "It's essentially stealing when we don't report that money as income." From misconduct to malfeasance to bankruptcy, the banks have seen it all.

Solid executive teams trust each other. There is enough trust for crazy ideas to be floated and wild options to be explored. The trust also extends to times when hard decisions must be made. Trust is based on expertise. We trust our lead pastors to deliver God's Word. We trust executive pastors to lead the organization of the church. We trust other key team members to give input and advice according to their skill sets and gift mix. In my current role, we describe the lead pastor as the directional leader. As the executive pastor, I'm the organizational leader, and other team members advise me.

I expect to hear leadership and management gurus state that "financial accountability is a great reason for a church to have an executive team." But when the bankers start demanding churches to have executive teams and plurality of leadership, it means they have learned lessons from the "school of hard knocks." I'm listening.

***

David Fletcher is executive pastor at the EvFree Church in Fullerton, California, founder of XPastor and author of several books including *Crisis Leadership*. Connect with him online at xpastor.org.

PART THREE
HOW WELL IS YOUR TEAM THRIVING?

5

Reality Check

Eight Common Reasons Teams Fail

Success comes from taking the path of maximum advantage instead of the path of least resistance.

George Bernard Shaw, Nobel Prize–winning playwright

One of our church visits involved one-on-one interviews with more than a dozen key players in a certain church. Some were on the church's executive team, and some were not. If you reviewed the interview transcripts, you would have trouble believing the people were describing the same church.

The pastor's passions revolved around his preaching, both at the church and in his continual outside speaking. That's clearly his strength—but it was pretty much all he was interested in. Knowing that reality, the lead pastor authorized several key volunteers and senior staff members to lead, oversee and develop everything else. Unfortunately, their assignments weren't clear or well communicated. Instead of working together, they each built a little silo and generally succeeded in making their small kingdom work well. Predictably, they were frustrated with any players outside their world, so they largely avoided each other.

Sensing that things still weren't working right, the lead pastor's solution was to bring in new players and try new organizational structures. At the time of the interview, he was convinced that now he had the winning formula. But his action only made things messier. No one was addressing the deeper and more systemic problems, so his newest configuration likewise fell apart within a year, with the high turnover rates continuing for staff and volunteers.

That senior leadership team needed to pull out some mirrors and take a hard look at why they were failing—and how to instead build a culture in which they thrived.

So far, we've tried to help you identify your senior leadership team, reflect on its importance and potential, and explore the biblical viability and practical benefits of team leadership. Now, we want to help you take stock of your current team so you know what to do to strengthen it.

In this chapter, we hope to help you
- take an honest assessment of your team
- identify some of the most common reasons that teams fail to thrive
- learn to think differently about the impact of your team's communication practices

Not only do we want to provide you with a framework against which you can measure your team, but we also want to assist you in seeing, understanding and explaining the reasons why your team is thriving or not. As any good athletic coach will tell you, it's important not only to know *how* your team is doing but also *why*.

ASSESSING YOUR TEAM'S LEADERSHIP

Teams that thrive truly and effectively lead their churches. How's your team doing? Take a few moments and answer two questions.

First, *Does your team **truly** lead your church?* Rate your team on whether it superficially or truly leads your church. To help you, figure 5.1 identifies several practices that may indicate the seriousness of your team's leadership. Of course, your team will only truly lead your church if you are convinced that collaborative leadership is essential to the health of your church. Mark an X on the continuum between each of the two statements showing the extent to which your team superficially or truly leads your church.

To What Extent Does Your Team Truly Lead Your Church? Place an X on the Continuum	
Superficially Leads	**Truly Leads**
There's a leadership team on paper, but the pastor really makes all the decisions.	The leadership team truly leads the church.
The leadership team manages minutiae.	The leadership team makes key strategic decisions.
Membership on the leadership team is a privilege, carrying with it great prestige.	Membership on the leadership team carries the weight of great responsibility.
The team meets only when the lead pastor is in town.	The team makes regular meetings a serious priority.
Staff and congregants talk about the leadership team as individual leaders, but not as a cohesive unit.	The leadership team is perceived as a unified team with collective outputs.

Figure 5.1. Practices that indicate effective team leadership

Second, *Does your team **effectively** lead your church?* In the same fashion, rate the extent your team is effective in leading your church (see fig. 5.2).[1]

Only leadership teams that truly and effectively lead their congregations will be teams that thrive. Next we explore typical reasons teams don't perform as well as they could.

COMMON REASONS LEADERSHIP TEAMS FAIL

Most leadership teams that we see struggle do so because of one or more breakdowns in the team's focus, structure, process and personalities involved. Figure 5.2 includes the most common reasons for team failure that we have heard and seen in churches. It also covers how this book seeks to help you overcome these common problems.

1. Everything is a priority, so nothing is. Pastors often tell us that their teams are forever scrambling—there's the next sermon series to plan, a new opportunity to be involved in the community, a fire to put out, another meeting to attend or a discipleship program to launch. With such full plates, they often struggle to take the time and dedicate the energy needed to develop a great team. One possible reason is that their team is trying to do too much or the team doesn't possess the necessary horsepower to do its important work well.

How Effective Is Your Team's Leadership?
Place an X on the Continuum

Ineffectively Leads	Effectively Leads
The leadership team manages the status quo.	The leadership team stays in front of the staff and congregation, determining and championing the church's vision.
The church is stagnant.	The church is growing.
The team sputters without clear direction and purpose.	The team knows and achieves its unique purpose.
Other staff members can't articulate the specific contribution the leadership team makes.	Everyone knows the role of the leadership team and relies on it to accomplish it.
Most work is done individually; team meetings are just for sharing information with one another.	Meetings are full of collaborative work.
One person holds on to all team leadership functions.	Leadership functions are shared among several members of the team.
The team's development is stagnant.	The team is getting better at working together, day by day, month by month.
Artificial harmony prevails.	Conflict is cultivated in the interest of making the best decisions.
The team is trained to think like the leader and to do what the leader would do.	Diverse perspectives are welcomed, encouraged and acted on.
Team members do just enough to get by.	Team members are internally motivated to produce at a high level.
Team members haven't changed in years.	Team members are growing personally and professionally through their work on the team.

Figure 5.2. Practices that indicate effective team leadership

In this way, teams often suffer from the same problems as individuals—trying to take on too much, thereby overwhelming the team and preventing others from making meaningful contributions. If this describes your team, we encourage you to limit the work done by the senior leadership team and its members, and take stock of whether you have the right team members in place. We explain how you might do so in chapter seven (on team purpose) and chapter eight (on team membership).

2. Lack of team leadership skill and understanding. Many church leaders have not been specifically trained in how to run and grow teams and organizations. Too often the best seminary education breezes through the leadership and management skill training that are crucial to effective pastoral ministry and leadership of staff. In particular, our research found that only 18 percent of team leaders have received special training in how to lead teams.

Moreover, we found that thriving teams were more likely found in churches established more recently, whereas underperforming teams were, on average, housed in churches that have been around for twice as long as the churches that housed the top teams. Similarly, the average age of lead pastors in thriving teams was forty-five compared to fifty-three in underperforming teams. Certainly this data doesn't suggest that teams with older pastors and in long-established churches cannot thrive. However, it does suggest that offering special attention to developing teams in older churches and with older senior pastors would be wise. Indeed, our data confirmed that coaching or consulting made a difference for teams in older churches.

Regardless of the reason, many church teams need greater understanding of what makes teams thrive and the skills that can enable them to do so. We hope to help you cut to the chase with our research-based suggestions in part four (chaps. 7-12). There we show you how to cultivate a compelling team purpose; implement crucial team processes related to decision making, communication and meetings; and select and develop the right people for team membership and leadership. In chapter fourteen, we lay out a road map for the next steps you can take to help your team thrive.

3. No inspiration or model for becoming a great team. As the well-trod saying goes, the enemy of the best is the good enough. Is that how you feel about your team? Do you feel it's "good enough"?

When we talk to pastors about their leadership team, we often hear pastors admit that improving it simply isn't a priority. With many other issues loudly calling for attention, a good-enough leadership team is left alone, subjected to continual mediocre performance. It's not terrible, but it's still not great.

If this is you, we want to remind you that as goes the senior leadership team, so go most other teams in the church, as well as the congregation. Great leadership teams lead great churches, and mediocre leadership teams lead mediocre churches. Perhaps while reading this book you'll somehow hear pleas from your staff and team members to provide greater leadership that will prompt you to make improving your leadership team a top priority.

> Great leadership teams lead great churches, and mediocre leadership teams lead mediocre churches.

To lead a thriving church, you need a thriving leadership team. And to develop a thriving leadership team, you may have to boldly challenge the status quo of how things have been done by default or by design in order to find new ways to work together as a team.

4. ***Undisciplined efforts.*** Sometimes undisciplined efforts trace back to small-mindedness. Leaders think of the church as much smaller than its potential, so they do sloppy, poor or no planning, seeing no lost potential when they regularly fly by the seat of their pants. Other times, the lack of discipline allows too many distractions. Teams can't find a clear focus and get distracted by all sorts of unimportant issues. For instance, we know of one church where the senior pastor was so focused on developing a media ministry to sell his products that he recorded staff meetings to sell the recordings. Senior leadership team

meetings were largely a show, contrived, all about every word sounding impressive and insightful on record, but the benefit as a genuine staff meeting was a sham. He used people more than he helped to develop them. Even more simply, teams that don't have a regular or undistracted time to regularly meet are unable to make the meaningful progress that justifies the team's existence and causes it to gel together.

Developing a great team takes a lot of work; it doesn't just happen. Disciplined efforts by people wanting to become true teams rather than just a work group (see chap. 6) is the only way to develop a high-performance, thriving team. Chapters six through twelve lay out the five disciplines of thriving teams. In addition, a lack of discipline is often a core part of an organization's culture, a topic we take up in chapter thirteen.

5. Absence of godly character among the team. Pastors are humans, and leadership teams are full of sinful people. Of course no one is perfect, but when leadership team members don't demonstrate Christlike character, such as laid out by Paul in his letters to Timothy and Titus, and when they are not held accountable for it, bad things happen. For instance, in those letters, Paul suggests that church leaders be temperate, sober, patient, self-controlled and gentle, and *not* violent, pugnacious, contentious or quickly angered (1 Tim 3; Tit 1). And Peter exhorted church leaders to "clothe yourselves, all of you, with humility toward one another, for 'God opposes the proud but gives grace to the humble'" (1 Pet 5:5).

Imagine how well a team would function if every member acted in accordance with those instructions. Unfortunately, unruly or misbehaving members can destroy a team if no one challenges their unhealthy behavior and people accept it as "that's just the way it is."

For instance, a lack of humility plays out quite perniciously on teams. Pride among leadership team members causes them to feel they're the exception to the rules. Though they know healthy patterns, their pride convinces them that they don't need to personally practice them.

Frankly, your team will never perform at a high level if your team members, including the senior leaders, fail to demonstrate the character essential for effective church leadership. Alexander Strauch, author of *Biblical Eldership*, puts it succinctly:

> Much of the weakness and waywardness of our churches today is due directly to our failure to require that church shepherds meet God's standards for office. If we want our local churches to be spiritually fit, then we must require our shepherds to be spiritually fit.[2]

To help you cultivate the right membership for your team, we explain how to select members of your leadership team and discuss challenging membership transitions in chapter eight (on membership). Chapter nine discusses the unique role of the team leader, and is full of practical tips for lead pastors and executive pastors who coordinate the work of leadership teams.

6. Confusion over the team's purpose. Rather than tackle important matters, some teams meander about doing only moderately important work. Chapter two offered a bunch of team descriptions—such as "cheerleading only" or "advisory only." Many of those word pictures imply a purpose that's confused or conflicted. Chapter seven explains the über-significance of team purpose as well as how your team can come to agreement on your team's unique purpose and then pursue it with zeal and focus.

7. Overreliance on the lead pastor. Great churches are often led by great pastors. However, without care, a great strength can become a terrible weakness. When "team" members (quotation marks are used purposely—we wouldn't call such groups teams) think too highly of their lead pastors and look *too much* to them for direction and leadership, team efforts are hampered and the team cannot reach its full potential.

Likewise, when lead pastors equate their church's success almost exclusively to their own individual contributions—seeing themselves as first on the team with no one anywhere close as second—they often neutralize efforts toward teamwork. A classic scriptural example is

Diotrephes, whom John singled out in his letter: "I have written something to the church, but Diotrephes, who likes to put himself first, does not acknowledge our authority. So if I come, I will bring up what he is doing, talking wicked nonsense against us" (3 Jn 1:9-10). Such a desire to be first, or an attribution by others that someone is always first, will wreak havoc on a leadership team.

The problems are easy to spot with the person who wants to be first: they often push others down to push themselves up and become puffed up by their efforts to be successful. However, the issues with putting someone else first, even if they don't ask for it, are more difficult to perceive. Often done out of a desire to "honor" the senior pastor,[3] staff members talk about how they "personally serve the senior pastor" and implore other staff to do the same, giving greater deference, title (such as "pastor" or "bishop") and prestige to the senior pastor than others, guarding the leader from direct contact with the congregation, celebrating the senior leader's accomplishments or investments at a much greater level than others or lamenting how much the church would struggle without the senior leader. When staff show partiality (Jas 2:1) by doing these things on their own, acting out of good intentions rather than compulsion by the senior pastor, they can create an unhealthy atmosphere that problematically elevates the worth of one above others. Teams don't thrive in such circumstances.

If your team is hampered by a staff-inflicted or pastor-demanded overreliance on the lead pastor, we urge you to dive into chapter three (on biblical foundations for leadership teams) as well as chapter nine (on team leadership).

8. *Dysfunctional team communication practices.* "Who is doing communication well?" asked Kason Branch, a leadership team member at Concord Church in Dallas, Texas, during a recent roundtable we convened in researching this book. The discussion focused on the challenges facing senior leadership teams. Of the ten pastors in the room, no one jumped up and said, "We communicate well." Instead, the group explained the challenges they face in ensuring that their church staff has the right information at the right time and is on the same page.

Indeed, communication is a key problem on most church staffs. It's a big issue in churches small and large, old and new, growing and declining. It is also a great problem for many senior leadership teams. In fact, our research showed that the *greatest* predictor of leadership team performance was the amount of stress the team members experienced related to dysfunctional communication practices. The more dysfunctional the communication, the lower the team's performance. The less dysfunctional the communication, the greater the team's performance. That's what this book is primarily about: eliminating dysfunction in your team's communication practices and replacing it with communicative disciplines that characterize teams that thrive. Indeed, chapters six through twelve explain how you can change your team by changing your team's communication.

COMMUNICATION: MORE THAN INFORMATION EXCHANGE

One of the reasons teams struggle so much with the practice of communication is because members don't understand what communication actually is. When communication is seen simplistically—as the transfer of information from one place to another—teams don't give it the attention needed to communicate effectively. Instead, teams try to mitigate their "communication" problems by spending more time and effort exchanging information with one another, even though research shows that focusing on doing so yields few results for teams beyond members being on the same page. Contrary to conventional wisdom, studies show that increased information exchange does not relate to better leadership team performance.[4] Our own research indicates likewise: the leadership teams that "communicated more" to exchange information did not perform as well as other teams that communicated to collaboratively make key, strategic decisions and coordinate important leadership activities.

The higher-performing teams adopt a fuller view of communication. They see communication as human interaction, responsible for far more than transmitting information to one another. Communication creates and shares meaning,[5] and it constructs social realities, structures and institutions—such as churches, teams and boards—that are then coordinated and actively managed.[6] As one professor affirms, "When we communicate, we create, maintain, and change shared ways of life."[7] Viewed this way, communication is the very thing that births, structures and shapes teams, including senior leadership teams. It is the very thing that develops and molds churches and all of their organizational dynamics.

The good news: if you see things differently, you will do things differently.[8] The quantity or quality of *information exchange* within a team doesn't make much of a difference on our teams. So if your leadership team is healthy, it's not simply focused on getting the right information to the right people. Instead, it is focused on the impact of its interaction on creating the team's reality. In fact, when we asked team members what made their team great, the responses almost always pointed to When we asked team members their communication practices. what made their team great, the responses almost Pastors mentioned notions such as, always pointed to their "there's safety to talk about anything," communication practices. "we work together every day" and "we met for two days and knocked a bunch of stuff out."

The good news: if you see things differently, you will do things differently.[8] The quantity or quality of *information exchange* within a team doesn't make much of a difference on our teams. So if your leadership team is healthy, it's not simply focused on getting the right information to the right people. Instead, it is focused on the impact of its interaction on creating the team's reality. In fact, when we asked team members what made their team great, the responses almost always pointed to their communication practices. Pastors mentioned notions such as, "there's safety to talk about anything," "we work together every day" and "we met for two days and knocked a bunch of stuff out."

> When we asked team members what made their team great, the responses almost always pointed to their communication practices.

The better news: if your team needs improvement, simply changing the ways you interact is a great place to start. Your interaction does far more than getting information to the right places at the right times or getting everyone on the same page.

- When you make key decisions, you create and shape your church's culture.
- When you pray (or don't pray), you're shaping everyone's understanding of and relationship with God.
- When you develop, shift or label positions, you're shaping the identities of the members of your staff and congregation.
- When you deal (or don't deal) with conflict, you're making your team healthy or unhealthy—and setting an example of how to do (or avoid) conflict resolution.
- When you cast vision and determine future ministry direction, you're establishing (not just communicating) vision for your ministries.
- When you evaluate the performance of programs and people, you're identifying and solving problems.
- When you make personnel decisions, you're determining who should be involved in key decisions that will further affect the church.
- When you meet, you're establishing the team's purpose, regardless of what is written in your staff manual or even your bylaws.

COMMUNICATION TO CREATE NEW REALITY

When your team interacts, you're shaping your team, staff, congregation and church. Seen this way, communication is not *a* thing that teams should pay attention to; it is *the* thing that accounts for the health and effectiveness of a team. Fundamentally, the primary work of a team is communication that creates new reality. Interaction. Talk. And if our work is to be, as Tim Keller suggests, "rearranging the raw material of God's creation in such a way that it helps the world in general, and people in particular, to thrive and flourish,"[9] then we must focus on what is being created through our interaction and how we can best interact to create thriving teams and flourishing churches.

To focus on creating new reality is to focus on communication. And that's what this book is all about: communicating in a way that causes your team to become exceptional. The question then becomes, How should we best communicate? The remainder of the book seeks to answer that question.

REFLECTION AND DISCUSSION QUESTIONS

1. On the three elements of team effectiveness—task accomplishment, member health and development, and growing in working as a team—how is your team doing (see note 1 for chap. 5)?
2. Which of the eight common reasons that teams fail explains your team's failure to thrive? What could your team do today to mitigate the ill effects of those behaviors?
3. What of your team's communication practices would you consider dysfunctional? Based on what you read here, how might you take action on that dysfunctionality this week?
4. What could your team do in your next meeting to limit information-sharing and invest time to collaboratively make key, strategic decisions and coordinate important leadership activities? Think small first.
5. Think of as many Proverbs, as well as other Scriptures, as you can that speak to the eight common reasons teams fail.

EXPERT COMMENTARY: THREE REASONS SOME PASTORS DON'T MAKE GOOD TEAM LEADERS

Geoff Surratt

While I agree with Ryan and Warren that teams fail to thrive when there is an overreliance on the lead pastor, I think there is an another reason this is a common pitfall: many successful lead pastors make poor team leaders. They are gifted to preach, cast vision and think strategically, but they are poorly equipped to lead teams.

This is a common phenomenon in sports: the MVP seldom makes a good coach. Michael Jordan, one of the greatest players in NBA history, made a terrible coach. His natural talent on the basketball court didn't translate to the bench. The lead pastor may be an all-star in the pulpit but an also-ran at the conference table.

There are at least three reasons why lead pastors don't always make good team leaders:

Schedule overload. Lead pastors have to preach on Sunday, interact with the elders, counsel, marry, bury, keep an eye on the budget and care for the staff, all while modeling a healthy ministry/family balance to the congregation. Add to that the stereotypical limited attention span of many lead pastors, and it is easy to understand why they are often distracted during team meetings.

All vision all the time. Many lead pastors live in the world of vision. They love to dream about new directions and new initiatives; their

> preferred mode is focusing on a better tomorrow. While vision is important, the real task of most teams is the nitty-gritty details of getting from here to there. Teams need focus that many lead pastors can't bring.
>
> *Elephant in the room.* When the lead pastor is also the team leader, his ideas are the best, his opinion is the most important and his decisions are final. Sometimes it is because he is an egomaniacal tyrant, but most often it is the natural tendency to defer to the leader. The lead pastor can't see the impact his presence makes because he never experiences how the team operates without him.

The principal leader in any organization faces these same challenges when leading a team. Effective US presidents learn to utilize a chief of staff to mitigate the negative aspects of strong leadership and build strong teams. Ed Catmull, the president of Pixar Studios, writes that Steve Jobs, who owned the company, had such an overwhelming personality that they asked him not to attend brainstorming meetings at the studio.[10]

When I worked with my brother Greg, who is the lead pastor at Seacoast Church based in South Carolina, he recognized these challenges whenever he served as a team leader. His input and perspective were indispensable, but his influence could unintentionally undermine the purpose of the team. To ensure the teams were as effective as possible, Greg delegated team leadership to other staff members who were gifted in that area. He continued to guide the overall vision and purpose of the church, but he left the execution to others.

***

Geoff Surratt is pastor of church planting at Southeast Christian Church in Parker, Colorado, and author of *Ten Stupid Things That Keep Churches from Growing*. He blogs regularly at geoffsurratt.com.

6

Our Survey Says

The Collaborative Disciplines of Teams That Thrive

Nothing new that is really interesting comes without collaboration.

James Watson, Co-discoverer of DNA

We know some teams are thriving. We know some teams truly are high-performance machines, models of the healthy body of Christ, and places where team members find personal, spiritual and professional fulfillment. We also know that many other teams are ineffective. We wanted to find many of those teams that thrive and discover what makes them so successful.

What's the best way to learn what separates teams that thrive from teams that barely survive? This book is unique because it offers guidance based on empirical research more than anecdotal evidence, and research that comes directly from church leadership teams rather than corporate teams.

This approach offers a level above consultants or pastors who draw from a much smaller context. Though experienced pastors and consultants have taught us much by explaining what works for them or for other churches they know, their findings are often difficult to transfer to other churches. What works for one church or leader, or even for a few, might not work for other leaders in different contexts facing different challenges. This is where a broad research base across many church leadership teams can help.

At the same time, many business books on corporate leadership teams can help you assess and develop your church's leadership team. But the marketplace-to-church parallel is not direct.

Since God is a God of order, good organizational practice often applies to churches as well, but often the for-profit values on which corporate practices and advice-giving are based differ from the gospel-focused values of a church. To combat those challenges, this book offers a broad research base taken directly from hundreds of church leadership teams from churches across the United States and around the world.

Therefore, in this chapter, we'll
- present the *five disciplines of teams that thrive* as a pathway to bring out the best in your team
- detail the research process behind our model
- highlight the major findings from our research study

THE FIVE DISCIPLINES OF TEAMS THAT THRIVE

Studying more than 250 church leadership teams over two years, we discovered several distinctive features of thriving leadership teams. We investigated how the best teams interact, and we share our findings with you through five disciplines your team can develop to communicate effectively and grow into a thriving unit (see fig. 6.1). We summarize them here, and then each receives a full chapter of further development in what follows.

Discipline 1: Focus on purpose, the invisible leader of your team. Great teams pursue a shared purpose that prioritizes making decisions together rather than advising one member who then makes key decisions. Mediocre teams spend most of their time advising the lead pastor, sharing information and coordinating operations, but they rarely go beyond that point. Exceptional leadership teams work together to do the most important strategic work in the church—making critical decisions—regularly and continually.

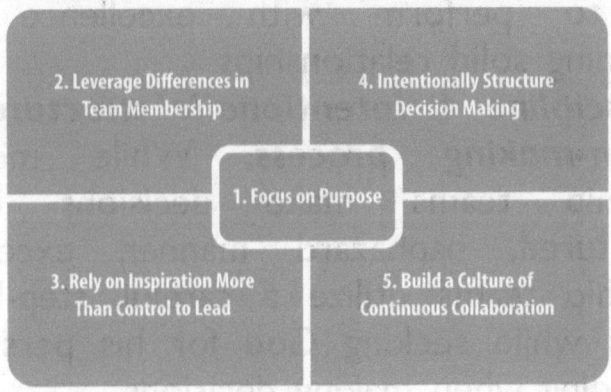

Figure 6.1. The five disciplines of teams that thrive

Discipline 2: Leverage differences in team membership. Great teams pursue diversity in personality, background and perspective rather than democracy or uniformity. Mediocre teams have too many people with the same gifts, styles and backgrounds, or seek to include too many persons. Exceptional leadership teams are small, diverse and consist of members with complementary skills who concentrate their work on the leadership team.

Discipline 3: Rely on inspiration more than control to lead. Outstanding teams prioritize leadership through relationship-based inspiration rather than role-based giving of directives. Leaders of mediocre teams prioritize control and directive leadership and neglect the development of positive working relationships. Leaders of exceptional teams focus on transformational leadership and the building of trust that together inspire and free the leadership team to perform with excellence while maintaining solid relationships.

Discipline 4: Intentionally structure your decision-making process. While mediocre leadership teams make decisions in an unstructured, haphazard manner, exceptional leadership teams utilize a careful, step-by-step process while seeking God for his perspective and leading when making decisions.

Discipline 5: Build a culture of continuous collaboration. Exceptional teams meet with intentionality, utilize collaboratively developed agendas and work together continuously to make the most of meetings. In contrast, mediocre teams tend to limit their collaboration to scheduled team meetings, and even when they meet, they fail to recognize the benefits of effective meetings.

HOW WE RESEARCHED CHURCHES

We developed this model based on a major research project, which ran from 2012 to 2013. During that time, Leadership Network helped us collect questionnaire data from 1,026 senior leadership team members at 253 churches. We invited churches from all over the world to assess their team using the well-respected Team Diagnostic Survey[1] developed by acclaimed Harvard researchers and corporate consultants, and normally offered only to corporate senior leadership teams through a private consulting arrangement. As they completed the Team Diagnostic Survey, we were also able to collect a significant set of data through a questionnaire that we designed.[2] A total of 253 churches participated at some level in the assessment, and 145 church leadership teams completed all aspects of the survey, as 75 percent of the members of those leadership team completed both assessments.

The Team Diagnostic Survey (TDS) offered a reliable measure of team performance. By combining a team's scores on five conditions for team success (listed below), we developed a TDS Sum Score, which we used as the key dependent variable in our research. Throughout this book, we refer to top-performing and underperforming teams. Those designations come directly from a team's score on elements of the Team Diagnostic Survey. Specifically, the scoring converts individual team member responses from a variety of questions into team "scores" for five key conditions that existing research has shown to predict team effectiveness. Those five conditions are

1. a real work team, rather than a team in name only
2. a compelling direction for the team's work
3. an enabling team structure
4. a supportive organizational context

5. available, expert coaching in teamwork

By adding the team scores for each of those five conditions, we were able to give each team a total survey score and use that as the outcome variable for several elements of our data analysis. When we discuss team performance, we are referring to the team's score on those five factors. The higher the score, the greater the performance.

We used that variable, along with church average growth rates for the previous three years, to identify top-performing churches. When we profile top-performing churches in this book (variously calling them top teams, thriving teams, great teams or exceptional teams), we are referring to teams in growing churches with Team Diagnostic Survey scores at the top 10 percent. Finally, we used the same rationale to identify a group of teams whose scores were the top 25 percent, as well as a group with the lowest 25 percent of scores. When we compare top-performing teams to underperforming teams, we utilized those groups.

The second survey, named the Team Communication Questionnaire, probed specific compositional, contextual and communication variables of the teams. It was designed to determine which of these factors correlated with team performance. In this survey, we asked about nearly everything that existing research (mostly on corporate teams) has shown to impact team performance, from team membership to leadership behaviors, to team stressors, to team purpose, to decision-making practices, to meeting practices, to relationships, to power enactment and so on.

After collapsing the individual-level data to group-level data for both surveys, we engaged rigorous data analysis with the able assistance of professional statisticians, identifying top-performing and underperforming teams and investigating which factors predicted variance in team performance and meaningful differences among top-and underperforming teams. This data provides the framework for the model we present in the book. As committed researchers, everything that we report is based on a statistically significant finding or is derived from the profile of the top-rated teams.

WHAT WE LEARNED

The following explains our process and what we found.

First, using a statistical technique known as a random forest analysis, we found five variables that were the most important. In this analysis, we identified significant positive relationships between higher team performance and the following:
- the time a team spent making critical decisions

- the degree to which a team sought God for his perspective
- a team's utilization of careful decision-making processes
- the percentage of time that team members adopted a churchwide perspective (rather than a position-based perspective) during meetings

In addition, we discovered a strong negative relationship between team performance and team members' stress concerning the team's dysfunctional communication processes.

Then we grouped similar variables together and compared top teams and underperforming teams using decision tree analysis and analysis of variance (also known as ANOVAs), with many important findings:

1. In terms of *purpose*, top teams articulated their purpose more about critical decision making and less about exchanging information or advising the lead pastor. Not only did they articulate their team's purpose differently, but top teams also spent more time coordinating leadership activities and making decisions and less time exchanging information with each other. Top teams were more likely to create leadership teams to take pressure off the lead pastor, to provide better decision making and activity coordination and to generally provide better

leadership than one person could alone (see chap. 7).

2. In reference to team *composition,* top teams were smaller than underperforming teams, and more likely found in younger churches. Additionally, members of top teams gave a greater percentage of time to their work on the leadership team than members of underperforming teams, though that work was only one part—not the entire job description—of each team member's role (see chap. 8).

3. In regard to *leadership,* we found that leaders on top teams exhibited more transformational, big-picture, motivational, visionary, relational and biblical leadership qualities but not autocratic, hands-off or laissez-faire qualities; and they were, on average, eight years younger than their counterparts. In addition, team members on top teams reported they were more likely to be able to disagree with the lead pastor and maintain a relationship, and less likely to feel stress in their relationship with the lead pastor than members on underperforming teams (see chap. 9).

4. In regard to *decision making,* top teams made more decisions, particularly in terms of finances and strategy; more often

dialogued on important matters, used problem-solving techniques and sought God for his leading; and more often took on a churchwide perspective when making decisions than underperforming teams. In addition, they listened less to what the senior pastor desired, deferred decisions to the lead pastor less often, and spent less time discussing programs and ministry direction than their counterparts on the underperforming teams. Finally, underperforming teams experienced greater stress because there was not enough time to deliberate and make decisions than top teams (see chaps. 10-11).

5. With regard to team *meetings,* top teams more often worked together continuously or one to two times a day and met more than one hour per week. In addition, they were more likely to distribute agendas that clearly delineated the meeting's tasks (and to do so more than one day in advance), and they were less likely than underperforming teams to have the senior pastor develop the agenda. Interestingly, there were no significant differences related to the number of meetings per week (see chap. 12).

6. In reference to team *relationships,* top teams more often rated high-quality relationships among team members and reported that they could disagree with team members as well as the lead pastor and maintain their relationships, and that they felt less stress regarding personal concerns with team members, compared to underperforming teams. Also, top teams were more likely to engage in some team building and to spend time getting to know team members. Consulting was found to be especially helpful for churches with a longer tenure (see chap. 9).

Finally, we reviewed an average profile of the teams that scored in the top 10 percent of the sample, looking for important normative characteristics. To aid you in comparing your team to the best teams, we share some of what we learned from this profile in the chapters that follow.

After we collected and analyzed that data, we visited many leadership teams around the country and conducted dozens of interviews with members of church senior leadership teams, especially the top performing ones. In addition, we conducted multiple focus groups with senior and executive pastors to learn about their teams' experiences, challenges and practices.

We draw on this rich set of data to develop the recommendations designed to make your senior leadership team great.

CUTTING TO THE CHASE

Our data set is rich, and it led to many important findings. Throughout this book we've tried to make sense of all that data and offer you a model that provides direction, focus and implementation strategies. To that end, we've organized the five disciplines of teams that thrive into three primary elements: team purpose, team players and team processes. We believe that if you can properly set up or fix these elements, you can improve your team.

To help you strengthen your team, each chapter in the next section not only focuses on what you should do but also offers a framework you can use to actually do it. We want to show you not only *what* to do but *how* to do it. So we also include several *two-minute tips* in each chapter. They are simple, quick activities you can do with your team to assess or improve your team's performance (and don't worry, none of them are awkward team-building games). Are you ready to create a new reality for your team?

REFLECTION AND DISCUSSION QUESTIONS

1. Which of the *five disciplines of teams that thrive* does your team already practice well?
2. Which of the *five disciplines of teams that thrive* is most foreign to your team?
3. What most surprised you when reading the "What We Learned" section above?
4. Read Acts 2 and 6, looking for examples that support or critique the six sets of research findings listed in this chapter.

> **EXPERT COMMENTARY: GOOD RESEARCH LEADS TO BETTER CHOICES**
> *Ed Stetzer*
>
> One of my "aha!" moments about the importance of good research occurred as I was facing a room full of reporters in a Religion Newswriters Association session at the *Washington Post* building in D.C. As I describe the event in a widely cited article in *Christianity Today* ("Curing Christians' Stats Abuse"), the reporters had invited me to explain the difference between good religious research and bad. News reports are always batting around some new bit of bad research.
>
> Here was a room of skillful writers, most well-schooled in the field of religion, and yet

many of the "statistics" they asked me to explain were inaccurate or misused. The lesson to me: sometimes a snippet from good research gets pulled out of context, then mangled, garbled and spewed all over. And once a choice morsel of misinformation gets out, it multiplies faster than dandelions in the spring.

Bad and misinterpreted data is a real problem among evangelical church leaders as well. As my friend Christian Smith, a highly respected professor of sociology at the University of Notre Dame, wrote in *Books & Culture* magazine ("Evangelicals Behaving Badly with Statistics," January/February 2007), American evangelicals "are among the worst abusers of simple descriptive statistics." LifeWay Research did a survey of Protestant pastors and found that 66 percent agreed that "Christians frequently misuse statistics to fit their own agenda."

I offer all that build up to affirm the importance of a book like this based in solid research from multiple sources. I predict that many will skim or skip over this chapter's description of the research, thinking that it won't do much to help them take their team to new levels of effectiveness. Maybe not in the short term. But what this book's research basis *can* do is to give you confidence that the advice in this book has a sound

> foundation—adding a vital component to the biblical basis for teams outlined in chapter three.

In short, good research leads to better choices about how to move forward. Facts are our friends when used wisely. Ryan and Warren's research drew responses from 1,026 members of 253 church teams across North America, a picture of team life that's even more robust in scope than the leading book on corporate senior leadership teams,[3] which drew from 120 teams. Plus, Ryan and Warren have gone beyond the reporting of survey frequencies to interpreting the responses with reputable statistical models.

Discerning research used with integrity can help us diagnose our condition and find ways that advance the cause of Christ—even through better team leadership in our churches.

***

Ed Stetzer, PhD, is executive director of LifeWay Research and author of several books including *Viral Churches: Helping Church Planters Become Movement Makers*, coauthored with Warren Bird. Follow Ed online at edstetzer.com.

PART FOUR

WHAT ARE THE COLLABORATIVE DISCIPLINES OF TEAMS THAT THRIVE?

7

DISCIPLINE 1: Focus on Purpose, the Invisible Leader of Your Team

It's any sort of common purpose being arrived at through a tough middle that brings people together.

Donald Miller, *A Million Miles in a Thousand Years*

A TALE OF TWO TEAMS

Faith Promise is a church with more than 5,000 people across six campuses in Eastern Tennessee. We observed their senior leadership team during one of their regular weekly leadership team meetings.

In two hours the team not only covered a bunch of small issues, but they spent the lion's share of their time in two significant discussions. First, they worked on establishing a Wildly Important Goal that would frame the staff's initiatives and establish their accountability for the coming year.[1] Second, they determined whether to move forward on a campus redevelopment project that would cost up to three million dollars. Team members argued with and challenged one another, but ultimately decided, as a team, how to move forward with both of these crucial initiatives.

The team made key decisions together. They did not simply offer their opinions to the authorized decision maker. Nor did they simply serve as a sounding board for the lead pastor. They certainly did not abdicate their team role of making key decisions for the church.

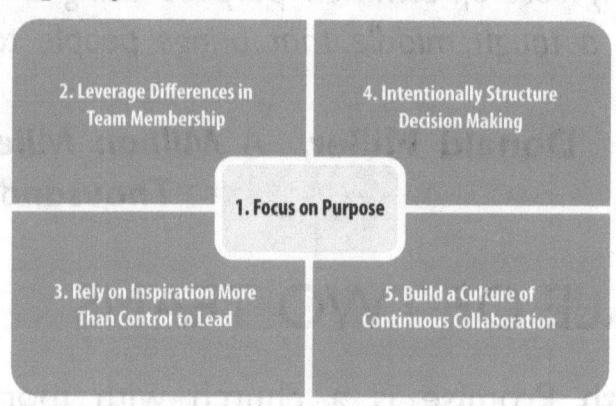

Figure 7.1. Teams that thrive focus on purpose

Oak Street Church (not its real name, but an actual church we visited) is a church very similar to Faith Promise. With approximately 3,000 in attendance each week across three campuses, the church has experienced tremendous growth since it was planted about fifteen years ago.

However, Oak Street's senior leadership team meetings look dramatically different. First, their meetings are bogged down by discussions of operational details such as why the microphones didn't work during Sunday's third service or drawn-out discussions about which announcements are important enough to make the weekend video announcements. Second, the lead pastor exercises executive decision authority frequently, from decisions about who will be the next worship pastor at one of the campuses to how to structure a staff calendaring meeting.

The rest of the team members know he's the ultimate decision-maker, so they defer all decisions to him and spend the lion's share of their meetings advising him on all sorts of issues that need direction and strategy. Or they discuss low-level issues such as those mentioned above.

The differences in meeting practices between these teams go deeper than personality and tradition. They are a reflection of the teams' purposes (see fig. 7.1). The Faith Promise leadership team's purpose was succinctly articulated by lead pastor Chris Stephens as well as his team members, such as the pastor who explained the team's purpose in one short phrase: "We set the course—the direction—of the church."

Oak Street's leadership team purpose is quite different: "overseeing the 'big picture' in many different areas and providing vision and direction for the different teams that the team members lead, both staff members and volunteers." Faith Promise's team sets direction and makes decisions for the entire church. Oak Street's team is limited to providing vision and direction for their individual teams and simply *overseeing* the big picture. In large part, providing leadership to the church is done by the lead pastor.

Is one of these approaches better than the other? Is one more effective than another? Does one lead to a healthier church?

In this chapter, we
- discuss problems related to purpose that senior leadership teams frequently face according to our research
- explain how to get team purpose right by focusing on what we define as the $_5$Cs of purpose
- discuss the benefits of a $_5$C purpose
- explore the most important purposes for church leadership teams
- offer a framework you can use to craft your team's unique purpose

DOES YOUR TEAM SUFFER FROM THESE PURPOSE PROBLEMS?

Every team is guided by some purpose—or set of purposes. Sometimes they're stated and sometimes they're not. Everything the team is and does, from membership, to meetings, to communication, to relationships, to topics of conversation, is informed by that purpose, for good or bad.

When it comes to teams, nothing is more important than purpose.

You (and everyone else) might readily agree that purpose is crucial, but our research uncovered something surprising: unfortunately, many teams don't know or can't articulate their team's purpose. Worse, even if they can, they're too often pursuing a purpose that fails to compel the team toward high performance.

> Unfortunately, many teams don't know or can't articulate their team's purpose. In fact, members of more than 75 percent of the teams in our sample indicated significant disagreement about their team's purpose.

Lack of clarity. When we asked team members to share the purpose of their team, we found incredible disagreement among members of the same team. In fact, members of more than 75 percent of the teams in our sample indicated significant disagreement about their team's purpose. In other words, members of only one quarter of the teams in our sample were able to articulate a similar statement of purpose for their teams. Instead, the vast majority of team members offered different purpose statements for their leadership teams, as the lists below illustrate (and later in this chapter we'll offer more positive examples). Team members vary dramatically about their team's purpose. Consider these five churches. Each line represents what a different team member voiced.

Church 1 team purpose statements

• To equip and facilitate church members for mission and ministry
• Glorifying God by leading people to a relationship with Christ
• Leading the church to fulfill its vision and purpose
• Ministering/leading each age group
• To make Christ known to all
• To teach, lead and instruct our congregation and community
• To provide vision, resources and implementation to our congregation
• To grow the church and find ways to do it
• Unity, to teach the congregation that we are one in Christ

Church 2 team purpose statements

• To guide the church through various functions
• To continue to build the kingdom
• To bring people in, teach the Word and then send them out to serve

- To be leaders of the faith being the prime examples of God's love
- To connect, grow and glow

Church 3 team purpose statements

- To coordinate direction
- To connect people to Christ
- To share God's love and empower others to do likewise

Church 4 team purpose statements

- To have input on and implement ideas for church issues
- To help fulfill the vision of the church under the pastor's leadership
- To be accountable for the finances and be a steward of how we prayerfully go about finding means and ways of using the money wisely for God's glory
- To reach, love, grow, go
- To lead our church to fulfill vision
- Spiritual/emotional and practical support for the members of the congregation
- To follow God's lead
- To work for Christ
- To reach, love, grow and go
- To do the work that Christ Jesus has commanded us to do

Church 5 team purpose statements

- To ensure the effectiveness of the various ministries of the church
- To grow the kingdom numerically while strengthening members
- To bring glory to God almighty
- To make it to heaven and take as many people with us as possible
- To oversee the day-to-day operations of the church

More discouraging, when our assessment survey gave members of leadership teams various items to rate, the idea of clarity of their team's purpose rated terribly—second to the bottom. Yet they ranked the consequentiality of their team's purposes the highest of any performance indicator. Translation: pastors believe that what they are doing—even though it may be largely esoteric and amorphous—is really important. It is consequential. But too many team members don't have a clear sense of what, specifically, they are doing.

> Too many team members don't have a clear sense of what, specifically, they are doing.

This is crucial because a team without a clear sense of purpose will wander around in its meetings. They won't know what is most important for them to tackle, and they will likely spend far too much time, like Oak Street's team did, on operational minutiae that detracts from tackling meaty issues that will propel the church's vision forward. If team members don't know where they're going, they likely won't be able to find better ways to get there.

Lack of challenge. The second major problem we noticed regarding team purpose—one that was even more pronounced in our data—was the lack of challenge the team's purpose provided. The very lowest-rated performance indicator across our entire research assessment was the challenge of the team's purpose. As above, team members argued their team's work was important but not appropriately challenging. When teams don't appropriately challenge members, team members don't commit their best efforts to the team's work. Instead, they channel their best toward the parts of their jobs that demand utmost attention, skill and effort. As the statements in the lists above indicate, when asked to state the distinct purpose of their leadership team, most team members were general and vague.

Two-Minute Tip:

Pay attention to how often members of your team become distracted by their phones, iPads or laptops during a meeting. When they do, that's a likely sign that the work being accomplished is so

> *simple that team members can divide their attention (it's not challenging), feels like a waste of time (it's not consequential) or is so confusing that they'll wait until the fog clears to reengage (it's not clear). You might want to rearticulate the team's purpose or steer toward work that actually accomplishes the team's specific purpose. Or simply ask frankly, "What could we do to make these meetings a better use of your time and talents?"*

GETTING PURPOSE RIGHT

Rick Warren's bestselling book *The Purpose-Driven Life* repeatedly asks, echoing its subtitle, "What on earth are you here for?"[2] He challenges individuals to determine their unique calling that best utilizes their strengths and impacts the world around them.

Teams need to ask the same question: What on earth are we here for? What is it that we must do? What is it that only we, as a senior leadership team, can do for this church?

Ryan has found that great teams coalesce around a $_5$C purpose. The idea comes from an alliteration he developed from both church and marketplace research. Carl Larson and Frank LaFasto, luminary researchers and authors of the classic book *When Teams Work Best*, found that great teams held a clear and elevating purpose.[3] Likewise, Harvard researcher Richard Hackman identified that the best teams pursue a compelling direction that is clear, challenging and consequential.[4] And in faith-based contexts the best teams don't ask their members to check their callings at the door; rather, they enable them to pursue calling as part of the team's work. Pulling these concepts together yields these five Cs:

- *Clear.* Does the team's purpose paint a *clear picture of value?*
- *Compelling.* Do team members view the purpose as consequential? Does it address something that *truly matters, drawing people into it?*
- *Challenging.* To accomplish the purpose, is each member of the team required to contribute in a *meaningful and interdependent way?*
- *Calling-oriented.* Does accomplishing the purpose help members *accomplish God's calling on their lives and pursue their goals?*
- *Consistently held.* Do the members of a group *truly know the group's purpose and pursue it with fervor?*

The purpose of your leadership team must be crystal clear, as everything else hinges on purpose. With that in mind, you might want to adopt clarity evangelist Will Mancini's five characteristics of viral vision statements, also stated as "five Cs," as you articulate your team's purpose. A purpose statement is *clear* if a teenager could understand it, *concise* if it can be stated in one breath, *compelling* if people want to keep on talking about it, *catalytic* if it drives action of all members of the team, not just the team leader, and *contextual* if it specifically fits the particular church's vision and personality.[5]

If you forget everything else, remember that all teams form around purpose, and they bond by pursuing that purpose. In fact, true teams are differentiated from mere work groups based on (1) the extent to which the collective purpose is shared among the group, (2) the level of commitment members have toward that purpose and (3) the clarity of and commitment to performance goals that drive toward the purpose. By contrast, members of work groups don't share any overarching purpose and vary in their commitment to the group's tasks and goals.

"A common, meaningful purpose sets the tone and aspiration"[6] for any real team. Does your team have one? Without a $_5$C purpose, a team will never reach its potential or be able to set meaningful performance goals, which transform the broad purpose into specific and measurable performance challenges, focus the team on pursuing results, facilitate decision making and constructive conflict, and drive the development of an approach to get the work done.

> All teams form around purpose, and they bond by pursuing that purpose.

> **Two-Minute Tip:**
>
> *In your next team meeting, hand out a 3x5 card to each member and ask each one to write your team's purpose on it. Then ask everyone to rate the team purpose—from 1 to 5 (5 being the highest)—on each of the 5Cs. Share what each person wrote as the purpose statement and their ratings on the 5Cs. You'll quickly learn where your team's sense of purpose is both strongest and weakest.*

SIX BENEFITS OF A 5C PURPOSE

A $_5$C purpose offers extensive benefits for your team, as the following points illustrate. A $_5$C purpose:

1. Narrows your team's scope. It's easy for senior leadership teams to equate their purpose with "leading the church." The problem with that, however, is that nothing is excluded from that purpose. If everything is supposedly the team's purpose, then in actuality nothing is. Teams that don't narrow their focus end up trying to do too much, which typically results in actually accomplishing very little. These teams spend seemingly countless hours meeting, leaving little time left for accomplishing key elements of their work outside of team meetings, such as meeting with staff or volunteers, building teams, executing strategies and the like.

2. *Creates space for staff or volunteers to contribute at a high level.* When a leadership team takes on all leadership functions, they don't leave any of those functions to others, ultimately disempowering others at the church. A leadership team with a too-broad purpose takes on too much, tends to overmanage and prevents others from feeling that they're making an important contribution to the church's mission. At one church with a leadership team that took on too much, staff pastors who were not on that senior team indicated that they couldn't see their own fingerprints on their ministry. Combined with working long, hard hours to serve a burgeoning church, more than one of these pastors expressed thoughts of leaving to go to another church where they would have the opportunity to more meaningfully contribute.

When a leadership team limits its role of leadership, it takes seriously Paul's instruction in Ephesians 4:12 for pastors and teachers to "equip the saints for the work of ministry" rather than do all ministry themselves. When it doesn't, it prevents others from doing crucial ministry work. In chapter eight on membership, we discuss how key leadership functions can be spread among a few different pastoral staff and volunteer groups.

> If everything is supposedly the team's purpose, then in actuality nothing is.

3. Compels people to contribute their best to the team. Too often, the work of teams does not call for people's best efforts. Too often team members tolerate the group work, all the while wishing they could get on with their most important work outside of meetings. In fact, we joke that it was sitting in meetings of teams without a $_5$C purpose that led management guru Peter Drucker to quip: "One either meets or one works. One cannot do both at the same time."[7]

However, for teams marked by a strong $_5$C purpose, meetings are crucial because they provide a venue for argument, conflict and meaningful discussion. When people know that their team's work requires their best efforts while contributing to accomplishing their own personal calling, they'll stay focused, resist the urge to halfheartedly engage in discussions and offer their best to the team's consequential work.

4. Inspires and energizes the team. A common purpose serves as a sort of invisible leader, providing "inspiration for participants to use their strengths willingly in leader or follower roles."[8] To garner needed energy, many teams unfortunately rely too heavily on a strong, charismatic leader to provide inspiration, when they could instead establish a $_5$C purpose. In fact, a strong leader becomes less necessary when a team is committed to a $_5$C purpose, because the purpose itself provides necessary motivation.

5. Distinguishes the leadership team's unique contribution at the church. One of the key distinctions between teams and work groups is the perceived identity of the team as a team versus a collection of individuals. In many of our interviews with church staff members, staff were unable to talk about the role of the leadership team as a team; instead, they discussed only the individual roles of the members of the team. Great teams are recognized by others as a team. A $_5$C purpose, when shared with others, articulates the value to the church of the leadership team, establishing the team as an important part of the church's governance and leadership structure. For churches that have experienced conflict over decision-making authority (what church hasn't?), a $_5$C purpose aids in clarifying the role of the leadership team against other groups, individuals and governing bodies.

Two-Minute Tip:

On a white board, create a flow chart that shows how the work done by your leadership team connects to the work of other staff and volunteers, in the following five areas: vision and direction, strategy, finances, programs, and staff selection and development.[9] Then, discuss what is owned

> *by the leadership team and by others and if that ownership mix is ideal. Use that discussion to identify needed changes.*

6. Cultivates trust and relationships among team members. Teams bond around purpose. In fact, a common purpose "cultivates a strong shared bond that connects participants to each other in pursuit of their purpose."[10] In other words, a team gels as it gets to work in pursuing a $_5$C purpose. To accomplish a really challenging purpose, team members quickly realize they must trust one another and build relationships. And, as they work together to successfully navigate conflict, make decisions and produce quality work, they do so.[11] Trust is built in the trenches as teams pursue their team's unique purpose.

> Trust is built in the trenches as teams pursue their team's unique purpose.

As a sort of invisible leader, a team's common purpose inspires team members, cultivates trust among them, bonds them together in its pursuit and compels them to perform at a high level.

WHAT DO THRIVING LEADERSHIP TEAMS DO?

Senior leadership teams typically spend the lion's share of their time doing one or more of four primary tasks: exchanging information, advising the senior leader on decision making, coordinating leadership activities and making crucial, enterprise-wide decisions.[12] Previous research makes clear that the latter two tasks—coordinating leadership activities and making key decisions—require teamwork that is exemplified by communication, interdependence, commitment and trust. On the other hand, exchanging information and advising a senior leader are easily done by executives without ever functioning as a team.

In our study, we found that thriving leadership teams existed to regularly, collaboratively and continually do the most important work in the church. That is, their purpose centered around making critical decisions, those decisions that shape the church's vision, strategy and culture.

Leadership teams that thrive **make decisions.** Not only did the top-rated teams in our study consistently affirm that the most important purpose for their senior leadership team was making critical decisions, but they spent more of their time in meetings doing just that rather than anything else. At the same time, they articulated "exchanging information" and "advising lead pastor" as the least important purposes of senior leadership teams, spending less time doing those functions.

However, as illustrated in figure 7.2, underperforming teams spent a great amount of their time advising the lead pastor, sharing information and coordinating operations, but they rarely went beyond that point to make important decisions.

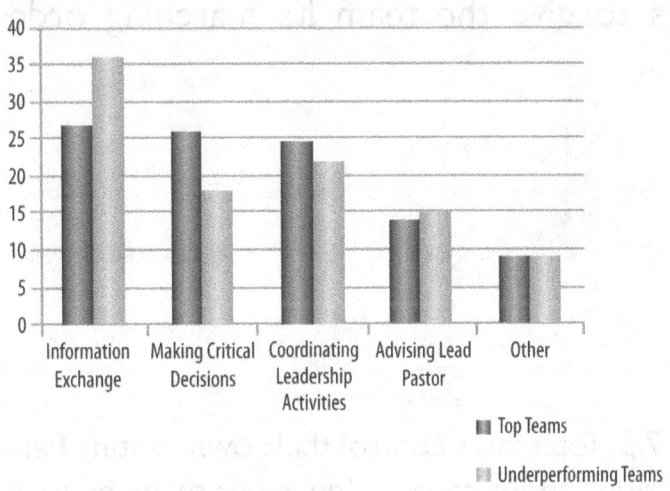

Figure 7.2. Top teams do more decision making and leadership coordinating. Percentage of meeting time devoted to each type of task.

Leadership teams that thrive make key decisions as a team. Furthermore, top-performing senior leadership teams told us that the *team* made decisions 64 percent of time, while underperforming teams made decisions 43 percent of the time. Lead pastors in top teams made decisions 25 percent of time, but in underperforming teams, they made them 37 percent of the time. Finally, others outside of the team, such as board members or other staff members, made decisions 13 percent of time for top teams, where as they made 24 percent of the decisions for underperforming teams. This data, illustrated in figure 7.3, points to the fact that thriving leadership teams collaboratively make decisions rather than advising or waiting for others to give the team its marching orders.

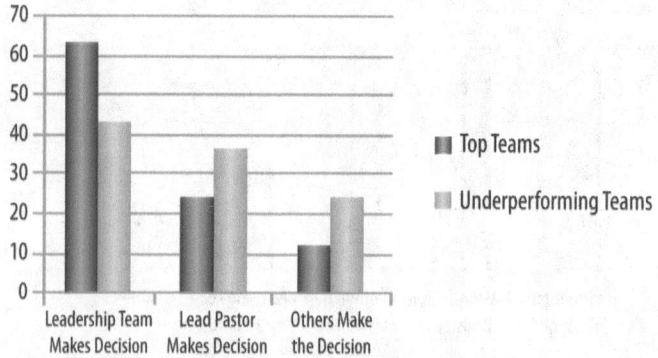

Figure 7.3. Top teams control their own destiny. Percentage of decisions about churchwide issues made by each entity in the past six months.

At the end of the day, teams that do not make decisions don't control their own destiny. Consequently, team members in underperforming teams are often less invested than their counterparts in teams that make a lion's share of the key decisions.

Leadership teams that thrive make decisions about the most important issues.

In our research we found that top teams frequently made significant decisions on certain topics at a statistically significant difference than underperforming teams. These topics are
- finances (budgets, allocating funds)
- policy and procedures (processes)
- ministry direction (service themes, discipleship programs, etc.)
- staff issues (hiring, firing, etc.)
- strategic planning (setting goals, processes)

However, we found similar amounts of decision making regarding programming (activities and events) among top and underperforming teams.

More interestingly, though, the biggest gaps between the top and underperforming teams showed up in decisions made around finances and strategic planning, perhaps because these constitute the *crucial* issues.

For instance, at Faith Promise Church, as mentioned above, the leadership team's time and energy was focused around strategic planning issues and financial issues as they identified key organizational metrics for the coming year and planned their campus expansion plan, including implications for funding.

The key here is determining which decisions the leadership team must be responsible for. A useful tool for determining which decisions need to live where in the organization is a RACI decision right chart. A RACI (RAY-see) chart[13]

can be developed for every type of decision in an organization, as follows:
- *Responsible.* The team or individual responsible for decision making and overall execution. In an organization that values collaboration, teams, like the leadership team, are responsible for many decisions.
- *Accountable.* The team or individual accountable for the decision outcome, for guaranteeing the decision is made with the participation of designated stakeholders (Rs), and for gaining alignment during the decision-making process. Typically, this role is best assigned to an individual in a supervisory role, such as a lead or executive pastor.
- *Consulted.* The persons who are consulted by the responsible party to provide input to the process, but who are not directly involved in the decision-making activity.
- *Informed.* Persons who need to be notified about the decision after the decision has been made, but not directly involved in the decision-making activities.

Determining what decisions the leadership team as a whole is responsible for, as well as those that certain members of the leadership team or others in the church are responsible for, is a great starting point for continuing a RACI chart for the important decisions made at all staff and volunteer levels.

For instance, the leadership team at Country Bible Church near Omaha, Nebraska, is responsible to establish the guiding principles for all ministries at the church rather than make decisions about particular ministry programs. By limiting the team's role to establishing and setting principles for ministry, they encourage the rest of the staff to go out and make decisions in accordance with those principles. For instance, they mandate that all programs at the church are easy to join, easy to understand and consistently offered. Any new program, or any adjustments to current programs, must fit within those boundaries, but the team precludes itself from actually designing ministry programs.

Similarly, Reality LA's leadership team uses the analogy of the railing on the deck of a cruise ship to determine its role. A lot of activity happens on the deck of a cruise ship, but the railings provide safe boundaries for that activity. They believe the leadership team's role is to clarify where the railings are, while allowing other members of the staff to determine what happens within those boundaries. When issues arise that press up against those previously established boundaries, the team determines whether and how those boundaries might need to shift.

Leadership teams that thrive structure their meetings to make decisions. The best teams don't leave accomplishing their purpose to chance. Instead, they structure their time—militantly if they have to—to minimize spending time in less important activities, such as advising the lead pastor and exchanging information so that they can maximize their time making decisions and coordinating important leadership activities.

> ### Two-Minute Tip:
>
> *Review your most recent meeting agenda. Identify 10 percent of the agenda that doesn't have to be accomplished by the senior leadership team. In your next meeting, discuss where that task can go—to an individual, to another staff team, etc. Then, reclaim that 10 percent of time saved to discuss something important that needs senior leadership attention but has been crowded out by other matters.*

In summary, when it comes to team purpose, the best leadership teams
1. bring together their most outstanding leaders to discern and make decisions about the church's vision, strategy and culture
2. give themselves the church's most thorny, substantial work of the church—making key decisions about finances and strategic planning—and force the team to do it together
3. structure their meetings to maximize time and effort on key decision-making tasks while giving other work away to designated

individuals or teams (chaps. 10-11 discuss exactly how to do this)

You might object, "That sounds good in theory, but there sure is a lot of basic information sharing that must occur at the senior leadership level, such that everyone is on the same page and we're able to present a unified front to the rest of the staff and congregation." We agree: information exchange needs to happen, but the best teams minimize time spent doing that. Chapter eleven discusses how to structure meetings to effectively manage and therefore limit "communications" functions such as exchanging information and advising the lead pastor among the senior leadership team, and instead prioritize coordination and decision-making activities.

IDENTIFYING YOUR TEAM'S UNIQUE PURPOSE

Now that you understand why a purpose is so important, what a great team purpose looks like and how to deal with the most common challenges to becoming laser-focused, we offer a framework you can use to establish a $_5$C purpose.

To establish and pursue a $_5$C team purpose, work through the following, answering the italicized questions below as you go along.

1. Brainstorm the crucial tasks that must be handled by your church's executive level staff

(not necessarily the senior team). Write on a white board. You might identify things like
- establishing vision
- executing the vision
- determining or modifying strategy
- building organizational capability (financial or human resources)
- monitoring or managing performance

What does "leadership" look like for our church? What is involved in leadership?

2. Next, draw several large, equal-size circles spread out over a large, clear section of the board (make each one as big as possible, but not touching each other, so you can later write inside them). Draw one circle for each member of the lead team, one for the lead team as a whole, one for your church's board or eldership (if it is distinct from the leadership team) and one for other staff. You should now have three circles more than the total number of people on your team.

What specific teams, groups and individuals are responsible for leadership functions at our church?

3. Now, as a group, determine where each of those tasks is best handled—by the team, by an individual, by the board or by another group of staff or individual. Write the task in the corresponding circle that indicates who owns the task. Those tasks that go to the team should be those that require or greatly benefit from multiple perspectives, interdependence and

collaborative activity. In other words, these tasks are those that must be handled by the senior leadership team and become the foundation of your team's unique purpose.

What are the core outcomes for our team? What is it that our team, and only our team, can accomplish as we work together as a team?

4. Engage in robust dialogue to narrow and establish the team's purpose, different from the organization's purpose, and write it down. For many senior leadership teams, the team purpose is something far too broad like "fulfilling the mission and vision of the church." But a good team purpose is distinct from that of the organization it serves, even for the leadership team. (We offer a few examples later in this chapter.)

How can we frame our team's purpose, making sure it is distinct from the purpose of our larger organization?

5. Check to ensure the purpose is clear, compelling, challenging, calling-oriented and consistently held. If it is, good. If not, continue to hone it until everyone agrees that it meets the $_5$C standards.

Are we all in agreement that we've framed a winning team purpose?

6. Then, identify everything your team has been doing that doesn't fit the purpose. As John Maxwell said, leaders "learn to say 'no' to the good so you can say 'yes' to the best."[14] For senior leadership teams, that might mean saying

"no" to administrative minutiae or coordinating activities. Give all of it away to other teams or individuals, creating new teams if necessary.

What are we doing that is outside of our team purpose? How else can it get done?

7. Increase assessment of your team's outcomes, so that team members know whether they have performed effectively or not.

How do we know if we've accomplished our goals or not?

8. If your team has accomplished its outcomes, celebrate success. Then, raise the bar for team performance by establishing the next challenge for the team to pursue. This way, team members are continually challenged and continue to advance the organization's mission. Don't rest on your laurels.

How can we continue to improve our work as a team and increase our impact?

When it comes to team purpose, there's no one-size-fits-all approach. Teams in smaller churches will likely own greater portions of necessary leadership tasks, whereas larger church teams will take on more targeted initiatives. As a church grows, more staff are available to lead, thereby relieving the senior leadership team of certain leadership tasks. To help you see what a $_5$C purpose might look like, we offer a few basic models in table 7.1.

Table 7.1. Sample Leadership Team Purpose Statements

Type of Church	Leadership Team Purpose Statement
New church plant	Identify and remove barriers to an effective church plant.
Smaller church	Determine the church's shared vision and drive its execution through strategic decision making and ministry alignment.
Medium-sized church	Provide spiritual and strategic leadership to our church by discerning vision and shaping ministry direction.
Larger church	Collaboratively shape vision, determine macro-level strategy and establish guiding principles that energize the staff to do the work of the ministry.

Notice how each statement, in some way: specifically identifies the core elements of the team's work, restricts "leadership" work to a few key activities, designates both process and outcomes of the team's work, and frames the work in a way that it can only be done by a team rather than an individual.

PURPOSE: THE INVISIBLE LEADER OF YOUR LEADERSHIP TEAM

Your team's success hinges on its purpose. Make sure it's clear to your team. Everything else we discuss depends on your team's purpose. Purpose is the invisible leader of exceptional teams. You'll select the members for your team based on its purpose. You'll require a certain kind of leadership based on your team's purpose. You'll call and structure your meetings based on purpose. You'll employ various tactics for making decisions and interact in certain ways and not in other ways because of your purpose. Is it clear what's leading your team? Do you have a $_5$C purpose?

So, before you go any further, ask yourself, What is the longing—the deeply felt longing—that will drive this team even if it does not already have all the tools to achieve it? What will wake up the members of the team every day and make them want to go where they are dreaming of going? For, as leadership author and consultant Vineet Nayar said, "When you, as a leader, can articulate that longing and inculcate purpose, you will be well on your way to fostering collaboration among the people in your organization."[15]

Our research suggests that the best teams focus on making crucial decisions on the most important issues as a team. That's why they exist—to establish direction for the church. We encourage you to emulate them—focus your team's purpose on deciding and coordinating rather than advising the lead pastor or exchanging information.

> If you want your team to work well together, start with a focus on your purpose.

Our research suggests that the best teams focus on making crucial decisions on the most important issues as a team. That's why they exist—to establish direction for the church. We encourage you to emulate them—focus your team's purpose on deciding and coordinating rather than advising the lead pastor or exchanging information.

> If you want your team to work well together, start with a focus on your purpose.

Bottom line: if you want your team to work well together, start with a focus on your purpose.

REFLECTION AND DISCUSSION QUESTIONS

1. What is your team's articulated purpose? That is, what do *you* say is your team's purpose?
2. If guests were to come to one of your meetings and watch you in action, what might *they* say your team's purpose is?
3. If applicable, why is there a gap between your articulated and lived-out purpose?
4. What can you do to shrink the gap between your articulated and lived-out purpose?

5. Think about your most recent meetings. What percentage of your time is spent:
   - Advising the lead pastor?
   - Exchanging information among one another?
   - Coordinating leadership activities?
   - Making important decisions?
   - Doing something else?

   How could you improve that mix?
6. In what areas does your team make decisions? What areas are off-limits to the team? Should it be that way?
7. How many insights can you draw from the book of Proverbs that speak to team purpose? Start with "Without counsel plans fail, but with many advisers they succeed" (Prov 15:22).

EXPERT COMMENTARY: CLARITY ISN'T EVERYTHING BUT IT CHANGES EVERYTHING

EXPERT COMMENTARY: CLARITY ISN'T EVERYTHING BUT IT CHANGES EVERYTHING
Will Mancini

The work of creating clarity itself is an underpracticed discipline by most leaders. But when a leader is determined to seek and find a greater definition and articulation of what matters most, a bit of magic is released and everyone benefits.

Ryan and Warren do an excellent job equipping us for the fruitful work of clarifying team purpose. My response is to highlight from my experience the greatest obstacle to a clear $_5$C team purpose. It's this: operating with a *general sense* of what your team purpose is. This good, albeit vague, idea is a big problem because having only a general sense of your team's purpose inoculates you from the real thing. It prevents you from achieving the game-changing, breakthrough clarity your team may be longing for.

Think about it: most everyone can latch on to a general sense of a team's purpose. That's an easy starting point. In fact, all of the team purpose statements listed in this chapter convey a general sense. You don't have to think that hard or work that much to have a general sense.

But to be a top performing team, a general sense is not enough. A $_5$C purpose requires meaningful specificity that is defined, felt and applied. Until you are tired of living with *generica,* you won't take the time to create the clarity that can make such a powerful difference.

So if that's our greatest challenge, why should you take the time to process this chapter with your team and carefully define your team's purpose? Again, Ryan and Warren outline many benefits, but allow me to amplify.

What do I mean with my assertion that "Clarity isn't everything, but it changes everything"? My dad was an F-5 instructor pilot in the Air Force. As a young boy he taught me that if a plane is off just one degree on its compass, it will be one mile off target for every sixty miles it flies. (This happens pretty fast at high speeds.) In other words, one small directional mistake now will snowball into a much bigger problem later.

Another way to think about it is that creating clarity is logically prior work. You don't have to do it all the time (it isn't everything), but whether or not you have it dramatically affects all you do (it changes everything).

That's why I love the clear purpose at the center of the disciplines of teams that thrive diagram (see fig. 7.1). It's the axle that drives everything else. It's the center around which everything revolves.

Why should you work on your team's purpose today? It will make
- decision making more accessible
- dialogue more powerful
- meetings more meaningful
- synergy more possible
- focus more sustainable
- enthusiasm more transferable
- progress more attainable

Who doesn't want more clarity? You are busy and you have a thousand things to do today. But one ounce of clarity is worth a hundred pounds of activity.

***

Will Mancini is founder and team leader of Auxano and author of *Church Unique: How Missional Leaders Cast Vision and Create Movement.* Connect with Will at willmancini.com.

8
DISCIPLINE 2: Leverage Differences in Team Membership

The saying is trustworthy: If anyone aspires to the office of overseer, he desires a noble task. Therefore an overseer must be above reproach, the husband of one wife, sober-minded, self-controlled, respectable, hospitable, able to teach, not a drunkard, not violent but gentle, not quarrelsome, not a lover of money.

Apostle Paul (1 Timothy 3:1-3)

Get the right people on the bus, the wrong people off the bus, and the right people in the right seats.

Jim Collins, Good to Great

In 1999, Tim Lucas started a Bible class in an established Baptist church in New Jersey. Dave Brooks, a seasoned oil and gas CFO, attended it because his young adult daughter had found rich community and strong biblical teaching, and he wanted to learn more about it. The study grew into a Sunday evening contemporary worship service, and in 2007 Liquid Church was officially born.

The church grew quickly, and the leadership responsibilities outpaced the capacity of Tim and his volunteer leadership. "I've always been drawn to the idea of a leadership team," Tim reflected recently. "So I began looking for leaders with different strengths, abilities and potentials than mine."

First, he asked one of their key volunteers, local Christian school administrator Mike Leahy, to join the team. He was a people magnet with a keen ability to build teams.

Around that same time, Dave experienced an unexpected career transition, and he told his wife, "You know, if there was an opportunity with Liquid, I think I'd consider it." The next week, Tim called Dave: "We have to figure out a way to get you to come to work for Liquid. You have management skills and an attention to detail that far exceed my own."

Dave recalls that "over the next six weeks, God did several things to confirm that this was the right next step for us." Dave joined the staff to provide administrative support to the fast-growing young church.

Two years later, convinced that a multisite strategy was a cornerstone of their future growth plan, they sought out experienced multisite pioneer Rich Birch and hired him from a large church in Canada. The church's leadership team was now quite the mix of gifts, perspectives and experiences. Tim brought a strong vision and preaching skill set; Dave provided a robust administrate leadership skill set; and Rich knew the ins and outs of church growth, technology and strategy. Two professionally "grew up" in the church, and two served in successful careers before coming on to the church staff.

Together, these guys make a formidable senior leadership team. Their diverse backgrounds, top-of-the-class aptitudes and deep commitment to Liquid Church fuel a church that is pushing back the gates of hell in suburban New Jersey. And they model how teams that thrive can leverage the differences of various team members (see fig. 8.1).

As the Liquid Church executive team will affirm, perhaps nothing we recommend in this book is more important than getting the right people on your team. And perhaps nothing is more difficult. We don't take it lightly that we're asking you to make some potentially painful "people" decisions here, and that the actions you take will affect the lives of people you love and God loves. We hope our guiding principles will help you as you seek God to make these crucial decisions.

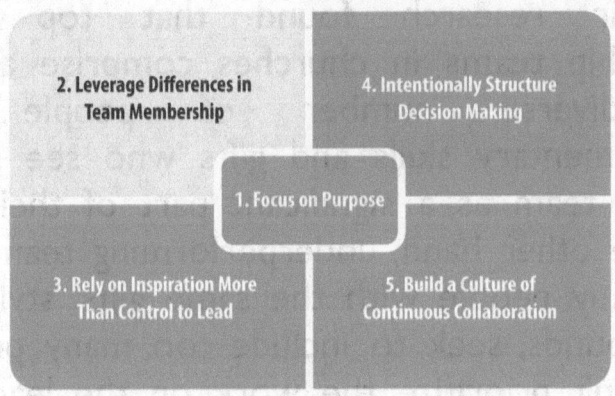

Figure 8.1. Teams that thrive leverage differences in team membership

To that end, this chapter tackles the issues associated with team membership head on as it
- explains the optimal size for leadership teams
- lists the characteristics of the right people to serve on a leadership team
- guides leaders on balancing team responsibilities with individual, departmental duties
- offers practical tips to implement those principles in regard to
    - finding the right people
    - gracefully narrowing a team's membership
    - creating space for the leadership team's work
    - managing compensation issues among the team
    - dealing with the loss (and replacement) of a team member

Our research found that top senior leadership teams in churches comprise a small, yet diverse number of people with complementary skills and gifts who see serving on the team as a significant part of their role. On the other hand, underperforming teams have too many people with the same gifts, styles and backgrounds, seek to include too many persons, and don't prioritize the work on the leadership team. Let's examine these components one by one.

THE RIGHT SIZE: FIVE OR FEWER

Smaller teams are better teams. As Larry Osborne noted in *Sticky Teams,* which narrates the story of North Coast Church in Vista, California, where he is long-term pastor: "When an ... executive team gets too big, it's hard to get anything done."[1] Indeed, our research found that teams composed of five or fewer members were more likely to be part of the top group of teams. Furthermore, the average size of the top teams was roughly two people fewer than mediocre teams. While that may seem to be a small difference, the addition of two voices, perspectives, needs and attitudes significantly multiplies the complexity of a leadership team.

> Smaller teams are better teams.

By simply looking at the number of communication channels that exist in a group of five versus a group of seven, it's obvious that the complexity of communication is doubled.

Teams with seven members must manage twice the communication channels as those with five members, as figure 8.2 illustrates.

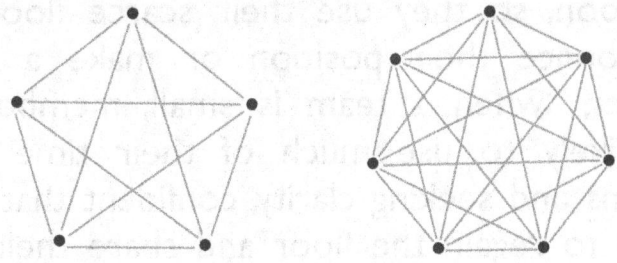

Figure 8.2. Communication channels of five-member versus seven-member teams

Yet, when considering that no human is one-dimensional, and that each person brings into the team attitudes, needs, perspectives, personalities, voices and connections, an even greater picture of complexity appears. A good rule of thumb to consider is to figure that every person on a team doubles the team's communicative and collaborative complexity. Doing so will encourage you to keep your team as small as possible to effectively accomplish your team's purpose.

> Every person on a team doubles the team's communicative and collaborative complexity.

Not only does complexity increase, but the way members communicate does as well. Patrick Lencioni explains: "When more than eight or nine people are on a team, members tend to advocate a lot more than they inquire. This makes sense because they aren't confident that they're going to get the opportunity to speak again soon, so they use their scarce floor time to announce their position or make a point." However, "when a team is small, members are more likely to use much of their time asking questions and seeking clarity, confident that they'll be able to regain the floor and share their ideas or opinions when necessary."[2] In essence, it is difficult to "be quick to hear [and] slow to speak" (Jas 1:19) on large teams. Consequently, subgroups inevitably form when a group gets bigger, which often causes rifts and disunity among the members of a team.

Two-Minute Tip:

Recall your team's most recent big decision. Rank each team member in two columns—advocacy and inquiry. Begin each list by listing persons who most advocated (discussed their opinions) or most inquired (asked others about their thoughts). Continue the ranking down to the ones who did so at the least at the bottom. What do you believe would happen if your team was smaller? What do these lists show you about how

> *you can, as a team, do a better job of advocating and inquiring?*

Furthermore, the larger a team gets, simple tasks like finding a time to meet grow more difficult. So do more challenging tasks, such as the team's core work of making key decisions and coordinating important leadership activities. More people means more voices competing for attention in conversations, hampering effective group discussion.

The bottom line: the best size for a top team is the smallest number of people who are able to sufficiently accomplish the group's purpose.

Before you decide, "Then let's make it really simple by limiting our 'team' to two of us," remember the best purpose of senior leadership teams: making key strategic decisions. As we showed in previous chapters, well-organized and carefully communicating teams typically outperform individuals due to the reality that multiple members offer additional perspective, provide necessary critique and advance creativity and innovation. If so, then three people's insights and perspectives are better than two, and often four is better than three. The dance, therefore, is to

1. Identify the important skills, experiences and perspectives that will enable the senior team to do its best work.

2. Invite a small group of people to the leadership team table who can best bring those attributes.
3. Relentlessly resist the urge to add any others to the leadership team mix.

THE RIGHT PEOPLE

Beyond a small number of people, teams that thrive comprise members with diverse yet complementary skills, experience and attributes. Certain characteristics tend to describe excellent team members, which we know from the best research on senior leadership teams over the last two decades filtered by biblical expectations for church leaders.[3]

1. Exemplary models of Christian character. The right leadership team members should be spiritually mature and possess the highest levels of Christian character, such as those traits that would qualify for eldership as described in 1 Timothy 3 and Titus 1. These passages suggest that the leaders of the church should be, among other qualifications,
- above reproach and respectable
- temperate, sober, patient, self-controlled, gentle and prudent
- able to advocate and refute false teaching (knowing the Word)
- not violent, pugnacious, contentious or quickly angered

- of good reputation with outsiders
- just, fair, holy and devout

Pastor Larry Osborne puts it well: "Finding leadership-oriented people is important. But it's even more important to find folks who meet the Bible's minimum requirements for spiritual leadership."[4]

2. *Diversely skilled and experienced.* The right people possess a diverse, complementary and balanced set of skills and abilities that are relevant to the team's objective. For a leadership team this likely means one or more members possess pastoral, financial, program development, strategic management and leadership skill sets and experiences. At Liquid Church, the senior team comprises a former corporate CFO, a church planter with excellent preaching abilities, a guru in church operations and strategy, and a ministry generalist with a huge pastor's heart. In essence, a great leadership team exemplifies the body of Christ, as various, diverse parts come together to make an incredibly influential whole.

Each one is very different from the others, and they all benefit greatly from it. These diverse abilities and skills offer the team a sharp skill set in several different areas that are crucial for providing outstanding leadership to a congregation. Numerous studies have shown the positive impact of member diversity in teams. They suggest that team member diversity promotes vigorous and constructive debate, increases creativity, prevents groupthink, normalizes the appreciation of difference as an undergirding team value, and produces better decision making.[5] On the other hand, teams with an overemphasis on the same skills or backgrounds risk lacking the various perspectives necessary to make quality decisions and ably lead the church.

3. Adept at solving problems. The right people are proven, mature problem identifiers and solvers. As we explain in chapters six and nine, the most important work that leadership teams do is make decisions in response to problems that typically defy simplistic analysis. Thus they must be populated with folks who can think conceptually and strategically about the church as a whole and process through issues in such a way to ably solve challenging, multifaceted problems. Further, they must have the internal fortitude to both push back on the most vigorous team members' assertions and ideas and to be pushed back by other members.

4. Motivated leaders. The right team members are action-oriented and possess a strong desire to contribute to the team's task. They take initiative, are fully "bought in" and are committed to the church beyond their particular area of ministry. In addition, they see themselves as leaders and they think beyond their current role. Because of their commitment to the mission of the church, they can be trusted to think about and make key decisions regarding the "big picture" of the church.

One caution is in order here. Motivated leaders are typically high-performers, people who have done good work and often expect to be given space to continue to do good work, who have been rewarded for independent achievement, who thrive on challenging, meaty tasks and who eschew micro-management. That means your team likely will regularly experience fireworks. Resist the urge to tame that energy too much; if you squelch it, you will likely lose your motivated leaders.

5. Committed to collaboration. The right team members "play nice" with others. In particular, they'll be able to work well with the other members of your leadership team. They are willing to surface problems, deal with issues and create an environment where others are free to express their ideas with confidence. In addition, they listen to and support the efforts of others, helping them to succeed. That means they do not see other team members as their competition. Finally, these people are optimistic, engaging, energetic and fun to work with.[6]

6. Aligned with the church's mission and philosophy of ministry. The right people "seek first the kingdom of God" (Mt 6:33) and therefore pursue the best for the church as a whole before their own personal preferences. At the most fundamental level, a team must agree on its direction and philosophy of ministry so that it is able to effectively weigh the issues and make important strategic decisions for the church. Thus members of a leadership team must be in general agreement with and alignment to the church's mission and vision, committed to fully supporting and actually implementing decisions agreed to by the team, and willing to fight to uphold the church's mission, values and ministry philosophy.

> **Two-Minute Tip:**
>
> *At your next team meeting, hand everyone a sheet of paper, asking each member to write out your church's philosophy of ministry (in their own words, not using formalized statements). Then compare them to see areas where your team is aligned or not.*

THE WRONG PEOPLE

If these six points describe what the right people are, it's probably helpful to also suggest what the right people are *not*.

1. Not merely the lead pastor's or executive pastor's direct reports. While it's common practice to identify the senior leadership team by drawing a circle around the top two or three layers of the organizational chart, doing so is neither necessary or advisable. Sitting at a particular place in the organizational hierarchy does not automatically qualify someone for senior team membership. For instance, the senior team at Irving Bible Church in Texas does not include the CFO, communications director or worship pastor, even though each of them report directly to the executive pastor. Though each of them brings outstanding individual skill and commitment to their roles, the leadership team was designed to be as small as possible, and so their positions on it were not guaranteed. As you determine your team's membership, you don't have to be a slave to your organizational chart.

2. Not a democratic representation of all church constituencies. Leadership teams are not mini-democracies. Every special interest group in your church does not need a seat—or direct representation—at the senior leadership team table. Representatives tend to lobby and protect their constituency rather than fight for what's best for the church as a whole. Also, because they are representatives, they tend to encourage even more representation, and therefore a larger number on the team.[7] Instead, it is important that the members of your leadership team—or at least one member of your leadership team—can think strategically and broadly enough to be able to generally understand the important interests of your church's various constituencies and consider them in the team's discussions. Special-interest pleading is a fatal practice of leadership teams.

> Special-interest pleading is a fatal practice of leadership teams.

3. Not people you include largely to make them feel special. A senior leadership team is no place to assuage a staff person who has been passed over for a promotion or whose role has been recently downsized. Nor even is it the group to offer an automatic seat solely because someone is a long-standing volunteer or senior staff member. While placing (or keeping) that person on the leadership team might soften someone's potential ego blow, you can be sure it will be a huge hit to your team's productivity and overall health. Don't fall to this temptation. At the same time, use extreme caution when using a seat on the leadership team as an enticement to lure a new staff member.

4. Not a coalition of "yes people." The primary benefits of a leadership team come directly *through* conflict. A team without robust, constructive debate over issues is not a team at all. Therefore, if you establish a team's membership based on a practice or desire of avoiding conflict, you will kill the team's potential before it even gets a shot at becoming effective.

Another form of "yes people" is the immature, unskilled, weak team member who really has no choice but to go along with the rest of the group. It takes great self-confidence for anyone to put people more gifted than themselves in positions of leadership, but those are the folks who comprise great teams. Andy Stanley underscored this principle: "One of the most important things you can do is surround yourself with smarter people."[8] Are the members of your team smarter than you? Are they both willing and encouraged to vehemently disagree (in a Christlike way) with all the members of your team, including the leader?

> A team without robust, constructive debate over issues is not a team at all.

Two-Minute Tip:
Engage an honest conversation by asking all team members to share a recent time and context when they were a "yes man" or "yes woman." What led to those circumstances? Affirm that in your senior team, you do not value that practice.

5. Not a constantly shifting group. If trust is built in the trenches, spending a significant amount of time together in the trenches is necessary. So when a group too often shifts its membership by adding or removing members, the team experiences a trust gap in how team members relate to each other. That's a recipe for disaster. Certainly, some change is good. It is also important to introduce fresh ideas and perspectives, and offer opportunities to develop leaders, or as Larry Osborne says, "let young eagles fly,"[9] resist the urge to play too constantly with your senior team's makeup. In cases other than massive growth, revisioning or restructuring, we suggest infusing your team with new blood in the way of new team members every few years. Additionally, simply bringing in other persons for single meetings to gain fresh perspective is another way to freshen your conversations without messing with the makeup of your team.

Another consequence of changing membership too frequently is that people don't even know who is on the team. When we asked members of the same team how many people were on their team, roughly two-thirds of the churches (63 percent) gave different numbers! We're puzzled by this statistic, but it provides evidence that too few churches are giving the attention to senior teams they deserve.

6. Not the "team" that was here when you got here. Just because you inherited a team doesn't mean you should keep that team. You may realize that the current members of the team don't possess the needed "stuff" to lead the church to new levels. Or perhaps history indicates a particular position has always sat on the team but doesn't contribute much. In these cases, make a move, and do it soon (and graciously). Too many leaders take too long deal with team members who sap the life out of the team; by doing so, they simply prolong the inevitable.

> The only reason a person should be on the leadership team is to bring a critical talent, perspective or skill to the group that enables the team to accomplish its unique purpose.

In essence, the only reason a person should be on the leadership team is to bring a critical talent, perspective or skill to the group that enables the team to accomplish its unique purpose. However, while the member characteristics of top teams are consistent, the particular makeup and tenure of top teams varies considerably. Table 8.1 illustrates the composition of several top teams.

THE RIGHT PRIORITIES

Beyond getting *only* the right people on the team, the next step to make your team's membership work is to prioritize the senior leadership team's work in members' job descriptions. If the team is committed to a $_5$C purpose, every member recognizes that his or her goals are shared among all the members of the team. Members contribute to the team's collective success: they win when the team wins, and they lose when the team loses. In our study, we found that members of top teams reported that they give more time to senior team tasks

(35 percent of their time) than do members of underperforming teams (27 percent of their time).

Table 8.1. Leadership Teams Come in All Shapes and Sizes

Church	Positions on top team and tenure
The Parks Church Attendance 400	Teaching Pastor—3 years (since founding)
	Executive Pastor—3 years (since founding)
	Worship Pastor—3 years (since founding)
The Church at Argyle Attendance 400	Lead Pastor—4 years
	Ministry Pastor and Administrator—7 years
	High School Pastor—5 years
	Middle School Pastor—1 year
	Children's Ministry Director—7 years
	Preschool Director and Financial Assistant—7 years
	Assistant Children's Director—2 years
Northstar Church Attendance 2,500	Lead Pastor—16 years
	Executive Pastor—2 years
	Executive Arts Pastor—12 years
	Spiritual Growth Pastor—6 years
	Financial/Admin Pastor—5 years
	Campus Operations Pastor—5 years

Faith Promise Church Attendance 5,000	Senior Pastor—17 years
	Executive Pastor—10 years
	Campus Pastor—3.5 years
	Pastor of Family Ministries—4 years
	Worship and Creative Arts Leader—14 years
The Ark Church Attendance 5,000	Senior Pastor—18 years
	Executive Pastor—11 years
	Worship Pastor—6 years
	Children's Pastor—8 years
	Adult Ministry Pastor—4 years
	Student Ministry Pastor—5 years

While that percentage difference might seem small, it's awfully significant. In a fifty-hour work week (for most pastors, that's a pretty conservative estimate), that's an extra four hours each week doing work as a member of the leadership team versus just doing work related to the individual ministry role.

Our data suggests that members of the best teams spend one-third of their time working as a member of a team and two-thirds performing their specialized ministry role. Spending one-third of the work time on senior leadership tasks should provide enough time—roughly fifteen to seventeen hours a week—to collaboratively establish and guide the church's strategic direction, and leave enough time for team members to ably perform their individual roles.

> ### Two-Minute Tip:
>
> *Go around the room. How much weekly time does each person spend doing leadership team work versus individual role work? How can you adjust your priorities to move closer to the one-third executive leadership, two-thirds job responsibility mix discussed in this chapter?*

On the other hand, work prioritization that puts too much emphasis on the team's work opens up a team to concerns from other staff that the members of the senior team don't do enough real work, or work for which they can be held individually accountable by other members of the organization. Years ago, team experts Jon Katzenbach and Doug Smith[10] argued that, on successful teams, every team member, including the team leader, does an equivalent amount of real work. In other words, they contribute in concrete ways to the team's work product rather than simply supervise the work of others doing real work. That principle applies to leaders at all organizational levels and all kinds of collectives. This principle explains why it's a bad idea for any person's entire job description to include only "supervision" tasks.

Applying this notion to the senior team, it is important that the team members do real work themselves beyond simply "leading" the church or "overseeing" the ministries. Indeed, it is the real work the team members do—preaching, directing building projects, implementing new systems, discipling and developing leaders, or running a particular ministry—that builds their credibility among the rest of the church staff and even into the congregation.

Indeed, Mike Erre, pastor of the EvFree Church of Fullerton, California, who is overseeing a massive church turnaround after several years of decline, understands this principle. In reference to the significant changes to the church's culture and direction he said, "The preaching and teaching I am doing week in and week out at EvFree affords me the favor to move ahead with change more rapidly than I would otherwise." He gets it: his real work, his performance of his individual role on staff—ably preaching the Word of God week in and week out—is the very thing that affords him the ability to move forward with sweeping changes to the church's direction and culture. So it is with members of leadership teams individually, as well as teams as collective entities.

MAKING MEMBERSHIP WORK

Finding the right people. Even when you know the kind of right people you need for your leadership team, where do you find them? When we talk to pastors, we consistently hear that one of their greatest needs is for more leaders, and especially the kind of leaders with robust skill sets and significant capacity to develop other leaders and disciple makers. To find the right people to populate your team, we urge you to address three questions:

1. Who is God raising up as leaders in our church? When we talked with the pastors at Cornerstone West LA (unrelated to Reality LA church introduced earlier), they emphasized that their eldership model of church leadership is fueled by God's movement in the lives of people in their congregation. Pastor Matt Kleinhans explains, "We don't appoint elders. We acknowledge the elders that God is raising up in our church." Thus, "we look for people whose character has been established over years and years and years, and [who] have been proven over years and years and years. So there's full confidence."

Confidence is full because past performance is the greatest indicator of future success. By looking at what they've done already and how they've served and led in the church and in the community, you'll know if they meet the criteria we listed above. You won't be surprised.

So prayerfully look around your church, keeping in mind the qualifications we mentioned in "The Right People" section above, and see who God is raising up, both on your staff as leaders of leaders or as volunteers with special gifting and discipline. Perhaps your next leadership team members are closer than you think.

2. *Who has great untapped potential?* While you look for people who are serving, consider who may be waiting for you to recognize and call out leadership potential and gifting. When you see something special in someone, seek them out, call out that gifting and invest in that person's development. Likely you (just like each of us) can think of a person who saw something in you that you never realized yourself, called it out or otherwise affirmed it, and, by doing so, was used by God to transform your life's direction.

Once you recognize those folks, don't stop there. Invest in them. Develop them. Quite frankly, some level of involvement with the senior leadership team—such as when the team is deliberating challenging decisions or charting out future plans—is a great way to expose young leaders full of potential to executive leadership tasks and to help them develop.

Two-Minute Tip:

> *As a team, discuss the following: Who is God raising up as leaders in our church? Who do we know who seems to have greater leadership potential? Of all those people listed, what can our team do to help cultivate the leadership capacity of those individuals?*

3. *What specific expertise does your team need?* Certainly there are times when, to accomplish your team's $_5$C purpose, you need additional horsepower from folks with specialized skill sets. When Liquid Church needed operational skill to champion their Past performance is the greatest indicator of future success. multisite expansion efforts, they brought in an experienced team member. Your church will likely need to do the same from time to time. The larger the church, the higher the percentage of staff that will come from the church's membership and other direct, proven connections. In those times you need to search beyond your immediate network, including seminary or denominational leads. Accordingly, it may be helpful to hire a placement organization that helps find available staff, such as our friends at the Vanderbloemen Search Group (www.vanderbloemen.com), which is one of the largest.

Repositioning the wrong people (to gracefully narrow your team's membership). To help your team thrive, you must be willing to take action to reshape it as necessary. If your team is too big, you will be wise to trim it. As pastor Larry Osborne notes, "Sooner or later the leadership table gets too crowded. Communication suffers, meetings run long, low-level conflict increases, and nothing much gets done anymore."[11] If your team is populated with a person who constantly shuts down your progress, we'd like to offer suggestions for the confrontation that needs to happen. If there are some folks who simply don't belong on your team because they don't bring the necessary skills and expertise, you need to remove or replace them.

The following are some general guidelines of how to gracefully downsize your team's membership.

1. *Pray until you have clarity and confidence from God.* He is the designer of the body of Christ and knows exactly where each member will thrive. Everything from timing to tone of voice needs to be guided by his promptings and orchestrations.

2. *Commit yourself (and your team) to doing what it takes, however uncomfortable that may be personally, to enable your team to provide the best leadership it can to your church.* Your commitment to improve your team (such as by going through this book as a team) powerfully demonstrates your willingness to put aside comfort and personal preference in favor of your church's mission.

3. *Clarify your team's purpose, according to the guidelines in chapter seven.* Your team's

membership should be derived from your team's purpose. Until you've established a $_5$C purpose, you are not ready to deal with team membership issues (unless you have a proven derailer on your team—in such a case, remember that the best day to plant a tree was twenty years ago; and the second best day is today). Once your purpose is clear, your team is ready to discuss who should be on the team and, by default, who should not be on the team.

4. *Determine who is most necessary on the team and who is not.* We acknowledge that these can sometimes be horribly difficult conversations. But they must be had. As you sort through your team's ideal membership, resist twin urges. First, don't simply draw a circle around the top of your organizational chart. Second, don't select or keep people on the team solely because of their particular technical skills. In fact, these urges account for many of the membership problems of leadership teams: defaulting to folks at the top of the hierarchy often robs the team of needed perspective, and selecting members solely based on technical expertise (or representation) often results in teams that keep growing and growing in size.

> Defaulting to folks at the top of the hierarchy often robs the team of needed perspective.

There is one conversation, however, that is often made harder than it needs to be. That is dealing with problem group members. Most know exactly who qualifies as an "extra grace required" member, to use an expression from Carl George's books on small groups.[12] These are folks who frequently complain about and criticize others in public, bring out the worst in people, attack people rather than issues, talk freely outside the room but not in it, constantly disagree with everything, display discrepancies between words and actions, and don't change even though they seem to understand their problematic behavior. If your team has this kind of person, we encourage you to confront that behavior right now. Don't wait another day. Here's why: "letting [this kind of behavior] slide teaches the derailer and other team members that such behavior is tolerable."13 There are lots of great resources out there to help you deal with the confrontation.14 If, after confrontation, the behavior continues, it's time to ask the person to move off the team. Do the hard thing; the cost will be worth it.

5. *Consider and develop layers of teams for different purposes.* Your senior leadership team certainly does not need to perform all of the leadership functions for your church. Lots of different tasks, including coordinating church activities like weekend services, discipleship programs and building plans; making sure everyone is on the same page by exchanging

information; and giving feedback to top-level church leaders, need to be accomplished. But they don't all have to be done by the leadership team. This is why it is so important to clearly establish your team's purpose. By limiting the leadership team's work, others can be invited into senior leadership activities.

One possibility is moving from a single top team to multiple top teams that each accomplish different leadership tasks. For instance, if you are in a larger elder-led church, you might establish three different leadership groups—the elders, the senior pastoral leadership team and all the director-level staff—as well as the leadership duties for each of them. In a smaller, pastor-led congregation, you might establish a senior leadership team that is responsible for key decision making, vision setting and establishing top-level strategy, and then formalize the entire staff, or a combination of staff and volunteer leaders, as a leadership team responsible for organizational alignment, program execution and coordination, and performance management.

One flexible model that we believe might be useful for many different types of churches involves three groups:
- Eldership or board: general oversight and policy-setting responsibilities according to church bylaws and governance
  - Senior leadership team (in some cases, this might also be the elders): a small team of four

to five persons devoted to key decision making, vision and top-level strategy

- Leadership council: a larger group of eight to ten senior staff members such as department heads (in larger churches) or key staff and volunteer leaders (in smaller churches) that focuses on organizational alignment, program execution and performance monitoring

Many churches already do something similar, as they establish separate service programming teams that own the weekend experience, teaching teams that steward all of the church's teaching content and delivery, and leadership councils that serve as brainstorming resources and own performance management. While some members of the leadership team might sit on these teams, they involve other key members of the staff and volunteer leaders in impactful work.

The point is this: the main senior leadership team doesn't have to do all the leading. If the senior leadership doesn't hog all the important work, moving someone off the decision-making leadership team and on to another team focused on churchwide alignment or ministry execution is much more palatable.

> The main senior leadership team doesn't have to do all the leading.

Of course, the particular way you might establish different layers and types of teams will vary by church size, denomination, polity, church age and more. We urge you to think through an approach that fits your church,[15] enabling more people to be involved in leadership while simultaneously ensuring that your leadership team is composed of only the people that must be on it.

7. *Follow through by actually giving the new leadership groups (such as the leadership council) important work to do.* Here it matters not only what the senior leadership team does (defining the work of the new council/group) but also what it does not do (nothing beyond its $_5$C purpose). In addition, wise leaders will be careful not to cut off general access to members of the senior team, especially initially. Many churches unnecessarily create angst among staff by cutting off access to, in many cases, the senior pastor, in association with staff reorganization. Taking an abrupt-change, heavy-handed approach ("you can no longer talk to me directly, but talk to the person you now report to") often does more harm than good. Instead, allow the work relationships to naturally change over time. Finally, support the work of the new team by celebrating their successes, highlighting their value to the board, staff and congregation (as appropriate), and continuing to hand out meaty assignments to the group.

Jesus did this with his disciples. Though Jesus invested his life and entrusted his church to the Twelve, he walked most closely with three of them: Peter, James and John. He needed those closest to him to provide the support necessary for him to fulfill his mission. That didn't mean that the other nine disciples were relegated to meaningless work. They were crucial members of the larger team that would establish Jesus' church. So can it be at your church.

Creating space for senior leadership team work. As mentioned above, our research suggests an optimal mix of one-third executive leadership, two-thirds specific job responsibility. We believe that in most cases this requires that team members spend more time (to achieve the full third) on senior leadership tasks. And that means adding responsibilities to an already full plate. Thus the solution must not only increase the depth and importance of senior leadership work but also create space in an already-full schedule to allow for it. Here are several strategies.

1. *Modify job descriptions to clarify responsibilities, removing some.* Each team member's job description should describe the specific responsibilities the team member carries, both as a member of the senior leadership team and as a staff leader, department head or similar. Putting these responsibilities on paper serves three purposes. First, it confirms for the team members their crucial executive leadership roles. Second, it reminds everyone involved that being a member of the senior leadership team constitutes real work, which helps prevent the unreasonable loading of additional expectations

into position descriptions. Third, it flags and draws attention to workloads that begin to contain an overwhelming number of responsibilities.

When a person's role is overloaded, ask: What can be taken off the plate? What is it that the team member must do and what is it that others could do, whether staff or volunteer? Even if that means that ministry area performance drops off a bit for a time, it is crucial to reduce the loads of staff members so they can offer their best to the leadership team.

2. *Train staff on how to lead with an entire-church mentality.* Once those expectations are clarified, train both new and existing team members to help them contribute their best to the team. Left alone, people often revert to what they know best—their own individual area such as youth ministry, finances, technology or worship. Thus they need to be prepared to use their differences to promote the good of the entire church and collaborate together.

In their seminal book on corporate senior leadership teams, Ruth Wageman and colleagues suggest that leaders do the equivalent of orientation sessions for new team members.[16] First, team leaders discuss outcome and behavioral expectations, both for the staff member's individual role and for his or her role on the senior leadership team. Second, leaders explore the new member's past performance to identify behaviors that could hurt the team as well as behaviors that could positively contribute to the team's work. Together, these conversation points enable new members to quickly identify how they can best contribute to the senior team's purpose and accountabilities while operating within the team's established norms.

3. Begin or continue leadership development efforts at your church. Ultimately, important tasks are able to be given away only when capable people are able to pick them up and run with them. Getting leadership team members to a mix of one-third executive leadership and two-thirds specific job responsibility might be one more reason why leadership development must remain or become a high priority for your church.

Dealing with team compensation issues. Churches that take teams seriously must seriously consider the implications of a team-approach on compensation.[17] Since the best teams are evaluated as a team on collective work products, not only as individuals, a portion of the paid staff 's compensation should be determined based upon the team's performance including each individual's contributions to the team. Our suggestion is to tie a percentage of individual compensation (such as annual merit increase or one-time bonus) to the percentage of one's role that is constituted as a member of the leadership team. If our suggested mix is used, that would mean that one-third of an individual's compensation is determined by the quality of the team's work (in relation to its purpose) and the individual's contributions toward that work.

> The best teams are evaluated as a team, not only as individuals.

This model offers flexibility to assess both the team's work and the individual's contributions toward it. First, it affords compensation based on both team and individual performance, which remedies problems with compensating everyone on a team equally when, almost certainly, not everyone contributed equally. Second, it recognizes multiple factors that comprise a person's performance rather than overemphasizing one role over another. Third, it can be customized for any role ratio, including those that make the team's work the primary part of the person's role, as well as those that minimize the importance of individuals' work on the team.

At the same time, some teams take equity in terms of team compensation incredibly seriously. One church staff we interviewed told the story of their three-person senior leadership team. The board had offered the senior pastor a raise, but he wouldn't accept it unless the other two on the team received equally generous raises.

Dealing with the loss (and replacement) of a team member. Sometimes membership transitions occur unexpectedly or abruptly. These can be hard to deal with, whether that member was a part of the team for five months or five years. They leave a hole, one that has to be filled somehow. When that happens, don't rush the decision about what to do next. Allow the team to feel the weight of the loss of the previous staff member. That will help you to appreciate and honor that team member's contributions, regardless of the reason that led to the departure. If the situation offers lessons for the entire team to learn, engage open discussion and process the challenges associated with the departure. Do all of that before you begin to figure out what to do next, though you will need to manage the departed person's day-today responsibilities in the short term.

Then and only then, consider what to do about moving forward. You may need to have someone take over the departed person's responsibilities temporarily, but avoid the trap of automatically putting this person on the leadership team. Instead, ensure that the new person is the right person not only for the specific job description tasks but also to join the leadership team.[18] Once you determine who will join the team, then walk through the process we explained above on training staff regarding how to lead with an entire-church mentality.

THE POWER OF YOUR TEAM

Those closest to us determine our success. The old adage "show me your friends, and I'll show you your future" can be applied to teams: show me your team members, and I'll show you your potential as a church. Leadership guru John Maxwell refers to this principle as the law of the inner circle.19 If you don't have the right folks on your team or the right folks contributing in the right ways, we urge you to discipline your efforts so that you can best leverage differences in your team membership. You won't regret leading in line with the law of the inner circle.

> Show me your team members, and I'll show you your potential as a church.

REFLECTION AND DISCUSSION QUESTIONS

1. Take stock of who sits on your team. Why is your team as big or small as it is?
2. If your team is three or less, what advantages might you experience by adding a member or two?
3. If your team is six or more, what advantages might you experience by narrowing your team's membership?

4. As you reflect on your member selection criteria in the past, which of the following has been most important to your selection?
    - Christian character
    - skill and experience
    - problem-solving ability
    - leadership motivation
    - collaborative competence
    - alignment with mission and philosophy
5. What important skills, experiences and perspectives are missing from your team? How could you go about adding those, either by adding people or developing existing members? Or, what skills and perspectives are overrepresented?
6. Think about your team's most recent discussions and decisions. When were your team members acting as representatives, and when were they acting as leaders?
7. What can your team do to minimize individual member advocacy and maximize taking a churchwide perspective?
8. Reflect on how I Corinthians 12 applies to your senior leadership team.
    - What diversity in gift, role and experience is your team missing?
    - How can you honor all members of your body as you work as a team?

EXPERT COMMENTARY: HOW ARTISTS AND NONARTISTS CAN LEAD WELL TOGETHER
Morgan McKenna

It's a common theme: church leaders and artists often don't play well together. They think with opposite sides of the brains. They are fluent in different languages. They value different kinds of responses and measure success in different ways.

Certainly, there's some truth in these generalizations. But consider this: to lead is an art, which is why we have so many leadership books—it's still as much mystery as mastery. And to create is an act of leadership. Art can shift a worldview in a nanosecond.

Without shoving our real differences under the rug, perhaps we might spend some time considering our common passions. After all, the interface of shared motivation between business and aesthetics has fostered the rise of many of the world's most innovative, game-changing companies, including Google, Netflix, Apple, Amazon and Tesla.

So, the following is a "what matters most" list: the top shared values and goals of some of the nation's most prominent church leaders and artists.

- God encounters
- changed lives (Is 6; Rom 12:1)

> - the well-told story (whatever that means in your context)
> - authenticity (real always trumps cool)
> - multisensory communication (most people are not auditory learners)
> - surrendered technology (technology serves the story and the experience, not the other way around)
> - co-creation (liturgy is the work of the people—find out where the gifts are in your congregation or community and release them)

- planning that breathes (start sooner, do less, take more time to noodle and create; communicate clearly, calmly and often)
- process (don't be fooled—how we treat each other in the process always speaks loudly in the "product")
- restraint (just because you can do something doesn't mean you should)
- presence (barring extreme circumstances, no one on the team attends by phone or video, pastors included)
- faithful innovation (creativity should serve all of the previous values)

The next time your team is tempted to divide and *not* conquer, take out this list and add some of your own team's essentials. You'll be amazed at how an open conversation about the core will free you up to scribble around the edges. You'll micromanage less, sabotage less—and you might actually enjoy working together.

***

Morgan McKenna is a veteran worship experience designer, worship coach, artist and published writer. Connect with her through mckennaimage.com and callahanstudios.com.

9

DISCIPLINE 3: Rely on Inspiration More Than Control to Lead

The first step that effective leaders need to take is not to ask "What can I do?" Rather they should ask "Am I needed at all? Will my actions, or even my presence, do more harm than good?" The best leaders know when and how to get out of the way.

Jeffrey Pfeffer and Robert I. Sutton, *Hard Facts, Dangerous Half-Truths, and Total Nonsense*

"I'll never forget my very first meeting as a senior pastor in this church," recalls Dan Steffen, who shifted from pastoral staff to lead pastor of Pure Heart Fellowship in Glendale, Arizona, one of the churches we visited for the book. "I brought all the pastors around a table and said, 'Everything's scrapped. We're starting over. What do we value as a church? What's our vision? What's our mission?' We then had a one-hour argument over the vision, the mission and what comes first. I thought I was going to lose my mind. I had walked in there going, 'This is going to be the greatest thing ever because we're joining arms, talking about our pain, praying for each other, ministering to each other. We're all in this now together.' But the reality was, our relationship was going to suck unless I could get the team on the same page."

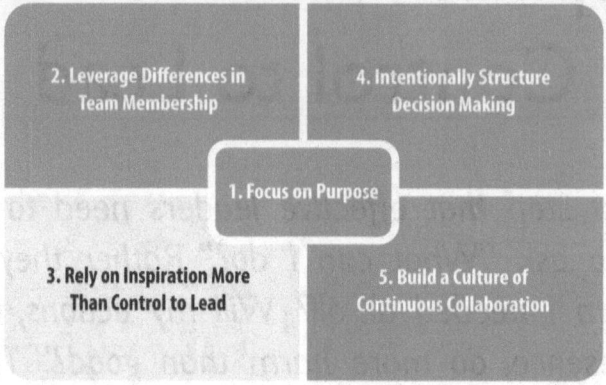

Figure 9.1. Teams that thrive rely on inspiration more than control to lead

Knowing everyone's previous experience helped Dan understand what happened that day. "Our former pastor had strong administrative gifts that enabled him to lead in more top-down fashion; he would give us lists of things and everybody had their job," Dan said. "He would plan the events and give us all our job assignments on color-coded charts. Then we'd knock out the assignments. I can see why some of the guys I used to work with before would do it this way: running top-down is faster, and often times easier. But I came to a personal conviction that this was not the healthiest way to lead. You don't keep good people long enough. They want to go somewhere they don't have to just march to somebody else's orders."

Dan decided to push against the previous culture and lead less by control and more by finding each staff member's best motivation (see fig. 9.1). "We just never gave up on it," he said. "Leading as a team is a really great way of doing ministry. Yes, it's messy. You're dealing with personalities, and everybody's hurt feelings, frustrations, bad days, struggles in their marriages, and struggles with their kids. It's not easy. But today we handle it better because we have more people who have more buy-in. I don't have to motivate those guys. I don't have to look over their shoulders to make sure they're getting these done. They have ownership on what they're doing. They flat-out love it. And I do better when I can come alongside and relationally encourage them and cheer them on. I get to be their relationship coach. I get to be that person that walks with people and thinks and dreams and plans the big picture stuff with them."

LEADERSHIP THAT MAKES A DIFFERENCE

If we've argued anything in this book, we've claimed that better leadership will be provided to a church when the leadership burden is shared by a diverse yet unified group of humble, competent leaders who function not simply as a work group but as a true team. Getting there usually takes some effort; but as Dan has experienced, it works better.

> Better leadership will be provided to a church when the leadership burden is shared by a diverse yet unified group of humble, competent leaders.

Like Dan, someone has to make the decision to do leadership by team. Most often, this is the lead pastor, or the lead pastor in collaboration with the executive pastor or another key player. Some person (or duo) then establishes the leadership team and determines what will be the parameters of its work. Then this person (or duo) "leads" the leadership team by calling its meetings, setting the team's agenda, determining who sits on the team and making other important decisions that shape the team's purpose, processes and players—or delegating such tasks to other team members.

These designated leaders of the leaders are the focus of this chapter. We want to help the persons entrusted to structure and lead the top team, whether that is the lead pastor, executive pastor or other person, do so with the greatest success.

Toward that end, this chapter
- explains the leadership behaviors of those who lead thriving teams

- highlights the kinds of relationships that team members report with team leaders
- discusses how leaders build trust within teams—and how that's different than often thought
- explores various approaches to "first among equals" on teams
- identifies ten essential team leadership practices
- shows leaders how they can cultivate greater shared leadership in their teams

For this chapter we'll address the team leader as the "lead pastor," but if that's a different person in your situation, please mentally switch the title as you read.

Our research indicates that lead pastors in teams that thrive act in a manner that inspires and frees the senior leadership team to perform with excellence while maintaining solid relationships. As table 9.1 illustrates, the best leaders exhibit transformational, inspirational and visionary leadership behaviors rather than directive, controlling and detail-oriented leadership actions. They also develop trust among their teams as they develop positive working relationships.

> The best leaders exhibit transformational, inspirational and visionary leadership behaviors.

Table 9.1. Thriving and Mediocre Team Leadership Differences

Thriving team leadership	Mediocre team leadership
Frees the team to do great work	Controls the team's work
Inspires the team	Directs the team
Builds trusting relationships	Neglects relationship development

BEHAVIORS OF THOSE WHO LEAD TEAMS THAT THRIVE

Our survey asked team members to identify the extent to which their lead pastors exhibited certain leadership characteristics. We then compared those ratings between the highest-rated and the lowest-rated teams in our study. We found statistically significant differences on the enactment of the following leadership behaviors.

1. *They are biblical.* Leaders of top teams remain fiercely committed to the authority of God's Word and allow it to guide every facet of their leadership efforts.
2. *They are transformational and motivational.* Classically defined by James MacGregor Burns, transformational leadership "occurs when one or more persons *engage* with others in such a way that leaders and followers raise one another to higher levels of motivation and morality."[1] In other

words, transformational leaders motivate followers to do more than they previously thought they could do.[2] That results in personal and organizational transformation. These leaders effectively motivate their teams to dream and accomplish big dreams.

3. *They cast vision and see and focus on the big picture.* Flying atop the trees, leaders of great teams keep their eyes on the horizon and focused on discerning the church's vision and accomplishing its mission. They avoid getting too involved in the details, at least to the extent that they distract from the most important matters.

4. *They are not laissez faire or hands-off.* While great leaders are focused on the big picture, they still remain involved in the team's work. Even if they have delegated operational leadership to another staff person (often the executive pastor), team leaders remain involved and hands-on in the team's work. Moreover, they do real work themselves, the kind of work for which other team members can hold them accountable. Even if that is work is primarily teaching, we saw many lead pastors submit their teaching to members of the leadership team for review and critique. As another example, at one point circumstances

necessitated that Chris Stephens, senior pastor of 5,000-attendance Faith Promise Church in Knoxville, Tennessee, step in to lead the small groups program for a time, even though that wasn't a typical aspect of his job description.

5. *They are not autocratic.* Leaders of top teams recognize the folly of "my way or the highway." Instead, they value the wisdom of the group, welcome dialogue and engage the team in making key decisions, even when that is messier than going it alone.
6. *They prioritize relationships.* Great leaders see team members less as tools to accomplish their purposes and more as persons made in the image of God. And they expend the effort needed to develop relationships with the members of their teams.

Two-Minute Tip:

At your next team meeting ask each member to share one characteristic of your lead pastor (such as those above) that they appreciate. Each should include an example of where that was recently demonstrated.

THE RELATIONAL CLIMATE OF TOP TEAMS

In addition to team leader behaviors, our data also pointed to two incredibly powerful findings regarding team relationships. First, we found that members of top teams reported they could disagree with the lead pastors and maintain relationship with them at a much greater rate than members of underperforming teams. These pastors had cultivated a climate that appreciates disagreement and cultivates debate while upholding positive relationships. We take up how to engage constructive conflict without destroying relationships in chapter eleven.

> ### Two-Minute Tip:
> *If you head a leadership team, how do you think everyone would rate your willingness to receive pushback about your ideas? If less than stellar, could you build time into your next meeting to brag on someone who gave you helpful feedback, to invite the group to give you pushback on some specific future plan and to genuinely thank everyone who offers it? If the group is largely silent, then reflect on whether they would say they're "punished" if they disagree with you, such as by you excluding them from future discussions, favors or decisions.*

Second, top team members stated that they experience less stress in their relationship with the lead pastor in both personal and work-related matters compared to underperforming teams. We suspect that by focusing on the big-picture vision and avoiding micromanagement, these lead pastors avoided causing greater stress to their staff members.

Cultivating relational trust and reducing stress. Sometimes when we talk with pastors and ministry leaders about their priorities in building a team, we hear an approach like the following:

> My team must be built on trust. The reason is simple: if we can't trust one another, we'll fail to achieve unity. Therefore we must focus first on being able to trust one another. To do that, we need to hang out together, build relationships and go on teambuilding retreats. Then, once the relationships are established and the trust is built, we'll start casting vision, clarifying our purpose and setting some goals for our work together.

This approach, we believe, stems from a misunderstanding of Patrick Lencioni's helpful triangle in the *Five Dysfunctions of a Team*, which argues that vulnerability-based trust is the foundation for effective teamwork.[3] Defining trust as "the confidence among team members that their peers' intentions are good, and that there is no reason to be protective or careful around the group," he argues that "teammates must get comfortable being vulnerable with one another."[4]

Did the previous quote make you mentally cue to awkward teambuilding activities as the primary pathway to get vulnerable with each other? Did you interpret Lencioni's words to mean it's time for new team members to vulnerably fall into the arms of their teammates (the classic trust fall) and to candidly share their most embarrassing moments, special childhood memories or greatest fears?

Unfortunately, these activities don't really build trust. In fact, trust isn't built by focusing on it.[5] Instead, initial trust is a byproduct of a team's focus and pursuit of a common purpose. It's easy to confuse the "chicken" and the "egg" here in terms of which causes the other. When people see two properties—in this case trust and performance—operating together, it's natural to seek to understand how they relate to each other. Often, though, we confuse the relationship, mistakenly thinking that trust *caused* performance to occur.[6]

> Trust is a byproduct of a team's focus and pursuit of a common purpose.

However, it's also a wrong interpretation to conclude that trust causes effective teamwork. An extensive body of literature7 indicates something else: that when team members focus on accomplishing a $_5$C purpose, they will begin to experience productive teamwork and trusting relationships. In other words, feelings of trust *follow* trust-building actions, those actions that focus on getting the work done. First comes the work, and then comes trust. As figure 9.2 shows, performance first begets trust, which then encourages greater performance, and greater trust development.

> First comes the work, and then comes trust.

1. Performance   2. Trust

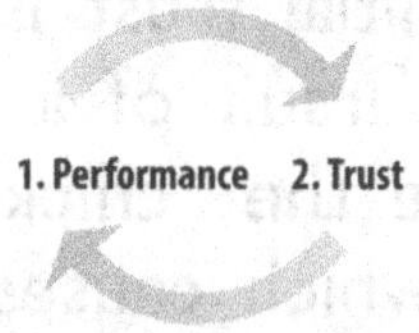

Figure 9.2. The performance-trust cycle

In our research, the top-performing teams—the same teams that focused on making the most important decisions for the church by using intentional decision-making processes—also reported greater relational satisfaction. Specifically, members of top teams reported the following, compared to underperforming teams:
- higher ratings of quality of relationships among team members

- feeling more confident that even if they disagreed vehemently with teammates, they would maintain positive relationships
- feeling more confident that even if they disagreed vehemently with the lead pastor, they would maintain a positive relationship
- feeling less stress about their relationships with other team members

The point is that teams build trusting relationships as they successfully complete difficult tasks. In fact, "the best way to develop a self-reinforcing cycle of trust is to help teams deal constructively with real conflicts,"[8] which are sure to emerge as a team focuses on accomplishing its purpose at an optimal level. Rarely do team-building activities like trust falls produce the results desired from them. Instead, they often spur greater dissatisfaction with the team as issues are surfaced but not sufficiently addressed. There are a few exceptions, and we take them up in chapter twelve when we discuss team retreats.

WHAT BUILDS TRUST?

Of all that has been said about the role of trust in teams, we find Onora O'Neill's exemplary TED talk most useful. She explains that the best way to build trust is to first be trustworthy. Based on her studies, she finds that people find someone to be trustworthy to the extent he or she is competent, honest and reliable.9

> The best way to build trust is to first be trustworthy.

First, team leaders initially build trust by *being competent* at their tasks, whether they be related to teaching, leading, visioning or whatever else. Pastors who build trust realize that more is caught than taught, and consequently they set an example for others in the excellence with which they approach their work. If you're responsible for leading your team, we commend you for seeking to grow more competent in your leadership by reading this book. If you have limited training in team leadership, you are in good company. As we mentioned earlier, less than 20 percent of leadership team leaders have received special training in how to lead teams.

Second, lead pastors build trust by *being honest and transparent.* That means they don't operate on a need-to-know basis. People don't like to be left in the dark. When a pastor constantly holds back plans and details, staff and lay leaders are forced to blindly trust or imagine about what is going on. These days very few people actually blindly trust anyone. Further, a culture that prompts leaders to try to figure out what's really going on in the church will foster rumors, back-door negotiations and a lack of trust. Secrecy typically breeds mistrust.

> Less than 20 percent of leadership team leaders have received special training in how to lead teams.

Just as lead pastors need to be careful not to keep team members in the dark, the same applies to entire leadership teams needing to communicate with others. At one church we observed, the staff felt the leadership team, as a whole, operated in secrecy and was constantly scheming, which developed a deep sense of mistrust among the staff.

> Secrecy typically breeds mistrust.

Honesty also requires vulnerability. We affirm Lencioni's call for team leaders to be vulnerable with leadership team members, setting an important role model. While forced vulnerability rarely yields positive results, real and natural vulnerability shows one's dependence upon God, invites community and models humble action. "At the heart of vulnerability lies the willingness of people to abandon their pride and their fear, to sacrifice their egos for the collective good of the team," he writes.10 As we mentioned in chapter seven, the team's purpose must drive the team's activities more than individual members' personal desires. To the extent that honest, vulnerable conversation helps the team to achieve its purpose, we urge you to engage in it.

Third, lead pastors generate trust by *being reliable,* by doing what they say they will do. In our research for this book, one pastor told us about a time when leaders at his church said one thing but then did another. The church recruited a strategic team, who was told they would focus on casting new vision, reaching millennials, researching new venues, developing a new website and strategizing new site locations. However, in reality, the team's first order of business was fixing the parking lot. As a result, many people felt lied to or tricked.

> ### Two-Minute Tip:
> *In your next meeting hold a quick but honest discussion about team member competence. Starting with the person who leads the team, each person discusses (1) one element of their position for which they are most competent, (2) one element for which they are least competent and (3) one action step they plan to take (or are taking) to grow in competence. This exercise will encourage you not only to appreciate one another's competencies but also to do it in a way that encourages some vulnerability.*

Lead pastors can develop trust with team members if they focus on becoming more trustworthy (competent, honest and reliable). Notice that none of those behaviors can be delegated; each one must be owned personally.

A FIRST AMONG EQUALS?

Give and take is part of the recipe for good teams. No healthy team effectively functions with everyone always enjoying equal say, power and input all of the time. Effective decision making requires at least one person to exert unequal influence and others to offer greater levels of submission than others from moment to moment.

Attempting to manage tensions among seemingly competing desires and needs for equality, authority and submission within leadership teams has prompted various ways to do eldership and church governance. One of the ways that some pastors have sought to address these tensions is through the notion of "first among equals." In many churches, the lead pastor is seen as the "first among equals," or the person who leads the leaders. Pastor and author Alexander Strauch explains this role among an eldership: "Although elders act jointly as a council and share equal authority and responsibility for the leadership of the church, all are not equal in their giftedness, biblical knowledge, leadership ability, experience, or dedication. Therefore, those among the elders who are particularly gifted leaders and/or teachers will naturally stand out among the other elders as leaders and teachers within the leadership body."[11]

Those particularly gifted leaders emerge as the "first" among equals in some churches, but in others, "first among equals" is a positional designation based on position, with lead pastors or preaching pastors often holding that position. No matter whether the first among equals leader emerges or is designated, Strauch suggests that understanding and implementing the first among equals principle "allows for functional, gift-based diversity within the eldership team without creating an official, superior office over fellow elders."[12]

Indeed, every healthy team understands the need for first among equals practices. We encourage you to determine the approach that fits best within your church's polity.

1. First among equals as the ultimate "leader." In some churches, first among equals is a permanent status conferred on the person who holds ultimate authority in the organization, most often the lead pastor. Believing one person must be established as having the final say, many teams are quick to explicitly define who is in charge. However, doing so is less important than many realize. In fact, numerous studies indicate that formal team leaders often account for only a small part (as little as 15 percent in one study) of total team performance.[13] The merging of all members' contributions and how the entire team works cooperatively accounts for much more variance. Too often, a leader's actions have very little to do with that. Harvard social psychologists Richard Hackman and Ruth Wageman termed the phenomenon of overemphasizing leadership as the *leadership attribution error*. Often, leaders are heralded for success or blamed for failure when, in reality, the team as a whole was the greater cause for the victory or defeat. As such, defining who is first among equals in an ongoing team is not as essential as many think. At the same time, however, most organizations, including churches, have identified a person at whom the buck stops. Our aim here is not to encourage you to change your leadership structure but to encourage you not to overemphasize the role of the leader at the expense of undervaluing other members of the team, and to consider alternative ways that the first among equals status can be negotiated.

2. First among equals as a rotating designation based on skill and expertise. For other churches, first among equals rotates among the members of the team, based on the topic at hand and the various skill sets and expertise among the team. At Reality LA, the leadership team members share responsibility of being first at different times. Executive Pastor Lorenzo Smith recounted a time when he was handling a rather complex matter. Because of the nature of the situation and his role at the church, he asked for affirmation from the leadership team, in essence, for him to be first. He said, "I didn't communicate as well as I would have liked in that moment, which gave the impression I was asking for total autonomy, but all I was asking for was some freedom." He asked the team for some leeway on handling the situation and for them to defer to and trust him. There are other situations, he noted, where the other pastors take the lead. Likewise, at Cornerstone LA, pastor Brian Colmery is first among equals when discussing and strategizing weekend service content and flow, but pastor Scott Mehl is first among equals when determining overall ministry strategy and administration.

"Plurality doesn't always mean democracy; it means deference," Lorenzo noted. Indeed, the best teams realize that some members are better educated, more passionate or more skilled in certain areas, and so they share leadership and regularly defer to one another. In more traditional arrangements, the lead pastor can let others lead from time to time, effectively rotating the first among equals status. Frankly, this notion of rotating first among equals is more consistent with a true team rather than a working group (see chap. 4).

> "Plurality doesn't always mean democracy; it means deference." Lorenzo Smith

3. First among equals based on hierarchy, age and respect. In some churches, especially those in traditional, hierarchical cultures, first among equals varies based more on custom. In some settings everyone assumes that the oldest, longest-tenured or highest-titled person must be the team leader. If so, we've seen many situations where that leader slowly, gradually but definitely over time empowers subleaders and invites true collaboration. "For this next section, I've asked Meifeng, who heads our young adult ministry, to bring us her recommendation and talk us through it." Or "For this next item, I really need your honest help. I fear I am so passionate about my idea that I can't see any potential downsides. Would each of you please name one potential unintended negative consequence if we do it?"

> ### Two-Minute Tip:
>
> *Engage a discussion about "first among equals." How does it work at your church? What are the various viewpoints that members of your team share? If you are the one that is always (or nearly always) first, how could you strategically share the first position with others? What are the leadership development implications of shared leadership?*

TEN PRACTICES OF GREAT TEAM LEADERS

Leaders are defined by what they do more than what they say or where they sit in the organizational chart. Thus our focus here is on what good leaders do. Of course, much advice is available for leading a team well. Here we've boiled down all of that advice into a top ten list to help you focus your efforts as a leader.

1. *Structure the team for success.* You cannot force a team to become great, but you can help put the pieces together and encourage greatness. Focus on structuring and facilitating productive team communication practices, as we've shown in this book.
2. *Establish with your team a $_5$ C purpose (clear, compelling, challenging, calling oriented and consequential).* Effective teams commonly aim toward a North Star. Good leaders facilitate processes to cast and clarify both vision and strategy (see chap. 7 for an easy process you can use).
3. *Get the right people on the team.* Great team leaders take team membership seriously, but not too seriously. Getting the right people on the bus won't solve all your problems, but it will help. Usually the right people possess essential skills and abilities

related to the team's purpose (in a balance with others), a strong desire to contribute to the vision and the capability to collaborate effectively. Leaders evaluate the strengths and skills of potential team members to find the right mix of skills the team needs (see chap. 8 for advice on getting the right people on and the wrong people off your team).

4. *Facilitate goal setting in pursuit of the team's vision.* Great leaders break down lofty vision into manageable chunks by setting specific, time-bound goals. Take some time to clarify, at minimum, monthly and annual goals.

5. *Set priorities and focus on achieving team goals.* Great leaders don't play politics within the team (that's not being trustworthy), don't focus on relationships at the expense of task accomplishment, don't make everything a priority and don't drown the team in a bunch of unimportant drivel. They laser-focus on accomplishing goals.

6. *Ensure a collaborative climate among the group.* Teams must work together effectively. Leaders help that happen. Leaders help set team ground rules (norms), encourage (and demand, at times) other team members to act cooperatively and work out their differences, recognize and reward

collaborative behaviors, and facilitate honest and respectful discussions (chap. 10 gives practical advice on how to develop this kind of climate among your team).

7. *Unleash talent by allowing others to do real work.* Great team leaders recognize that team members possess strengths they don't, so they step back and allow members to exercise those strengths. This isn't giving power away, or empowerment. It's self-control.

8. *Do real work themselves.* Great leaders don't just supervise, coordinate or delegate tasks. They do real work for which other team members can hold them accountable. Remember, much of what people learn is "caught, not taught." What are others "catching" from your leadership?

9. *Employ thoughtful, careful procedures for solving problems, making decisions and innovating.* Great leaders realize that unstructured, free-flowing discussion is problematic.[14] Thus they design intentional, structured conversations when making decisions or generating and vetting new ideas (which may, sometimes, be totally free-flowing by design). Chapter ten offers several strategies for doing so.

10. *Manage performance.* Great leaders hold team members accountable to team goals and norms. They *require results* by making performance expectations clear, *review results* by giving constructive feedback and resolving performance issues and *reward results* by recognizing superior performance.

Certainly one person doesn't have to do all of this. In our visits to churches, we saw these practices shared among two or several team members. These teams realize that everyone can lead, not just those at the very top of the organizational chart. Contrary to the elements of trustworthiness, these tasks can certainly be delegated, and we encourage you to create a team climate where every member of the team "leads" the team in various ways. Table 9.2 gives actual examples:

Table 9.2. Team Leadership Is Often Shared Among Team Members

Church	Team leadership functions of lead pastor	Team leadership functions of executive pastor	Team leadership functions of others
Cross Lanes Baptist Church Attendance 575	Casts vision and collaborates with the leadership team for implementation strategy; encourages and holds accountable team members	Provides administrative leadership and coordination, to encourage and focus other team members in carrying out the work	To practically and spiritually lead their areas of primary responsibility, consistent with the overall vision

Sunnybrook Community Church Attendance 2,000	Provides overall leadership, wisdom and direction	Schedules and drives team meetings	Provide spiritual and ministry perspective and insight
Lifepoint Church Attendance 2,000	Gives the leadership team the space to make key decisions, even occasionally stepping out of meetings to empower those leaders	Leads meetings; provides reports of key church health metrics	Develop plans of action for ministry areas; follow-up on key action items
Northstar Church Attendance 2,500	Casts vision and provides spiritual insight and direction for the team; helps set agenda for leadership team	Leads the team through execution; runs team meetings and project implementation	Provide spiritual leadership and financial oversight
Pure Heart Christian Fellowship Attendance 3,200	Clarifies vision and values	Leads meetings, focuses on execution, supervises other team members	Lead team in discussions that fall under their areas of responsibility
The Ark Church Attendance 5,000	Pastors the team, keeping the team aligned with God's Word and heart; clarifies macro-level direction	Leads the team through financial, personnel, facility and operational details involved with implementing the church's direction	Provide input and perspective for decision making for the overall church ministry

> **Two-Minute Tip:**
>
> *At your next meeting, go around the room. For each member of your team, state three or four ways that person "leads" your team. If it's difficult to identify the ways that each person leads, or if it becomes apparent one person does all (or the vast majority) of the leading, consider how you might more effectively share leadership among your team members.*

YOUR GREATEST LEADERSHIP DEVELOPMENT STRATEGY

If you, as a designated leader, lead the way we've encouraged you to in this chapter—casting vision, inspiring your team, allowing each member the space and freedom to do meaningful work, coaching the team and freeing them to collaboratively lead your church—you'll end up developing potent leaders. Leading well, quite frankly, is the best leadership development program you can offer. You role model doing what's most important and create space for others to contribute substantially to your church's mission and help accomplish your team's purpose. No matter where you find yourself today, take the next step to share the burdens, responsibility and actions of leadership with the members of your leadership team. The following are nine practical ways you can do this:

1. Establish a structure for success. Design meeting practices that offer space for people to empower themselves. For example, structure a meeting agenda such that each group member must contribute in a meaningful way at least once.
2. Shut your mouth. Allow silence to permeate the air in your meetings, showing you don't have all the answers, for "when leaders humbly admit that they don't have all the answers, they create space for others to step forward and offer solutions."[15] Humbly wait for your talented team members to speak up, offer ideas and move the conversation forward.
3. Don't be a "perfect" leader. Even if you can do it all, don't. Be "strategically incompetent."[16]
4. Take a humility pill. If you think you're better at most things than others, realize that's likely not true. There are other people who can do things far better than you. Allow them a shot. Plus, when you demonstrate humility, such as by learning from criticism and admitting mistakes, your team members are more likely to feel included, contribute innovative solutions,

suggest ways of working better together and go beyond the call of duty in their work with the team.[17]

5. Provide the education, funding and space necessary for others to proceed. Focus on gathering the kindling necessary for others to start and build a fire.

6. Collaboratively develop a compelling direction. Involve others in clarifying the direction of your team or organization, and let aspects of the strategy to get there remain murky. This kind of strategic ambiguity can reap huge rewards.[18]

7. Resist the urge to take over and control situations. Instead, step back, don't answer every question that comes your way and encourage others to make decisions, take risks and offer their best.

8. Step away from time to time. Especially when a team is doing creative (think creating, not artistry) work, research shows "the more that authority figures hang around, the more questions they ask, and especially the more feedback they give their people, the less creative the work will be. Why? Because doing creative work entails constant setbacks and failure, and people want to succeed when the boss is watching—which means doing proven, less

creative things that are sure to work."[19] Your presence (or lack thereof) casts a greater shadow than you might think; perhaps try to reduce the shadow from time to time to encourage your team to do its best work.

9. Do something that's not in your official job description. On select occasions when your team struggles to figure out who has bandwidth to take on a project or oversee a wayward ministry—one that's "below your pay grade"—take it on. In this role reversal leaders "not only facilitate employees' development, but they model the act of taking a different perspective, something that is so critical to working effectively in diverse teams."[20]

Often, the biggest obstacle to leadership development is *too much* leader activity, not too little. If you want to develop leaders, you have to create space where people empower themselves. Doing that requires not doing. Today, what's one thing you can do to *strategically not do*?

> If you want to develop leaders, you have to create space where people empower themselves.

WHAT TO DO IF YOUR TEAM LEADER DOESN'T MEASURE UP

Not every designated team leader leads as we've described in this chapter. If your team leader leaves lots to be desired, remember this: great leadership teams are great not so much because they have a great leader but because all the team members take responsibility to make the team great. Don't succumb to the temptation to evade responsibility for improving your team by simply deferring to the figurehead leader. Respectfully, gently engage the conversations, either one-on-one or as a team, that will help your team to realize it's not as effective as it could be, and start to cast some vision for what your team could look like.

Regardless of how well your feedback is accepted by other members of your leadership team, use what you've learned here to make the teams you lead as effective as possible. As you do, you'll not only earn the credibility to call for changes at other levels in your church but also provide a model for how a thriving team works. And when you do, you'll be providing outstanding leadership not only to your team but also to your whole church.

REFLECTION AND DISCUSSION QUESTIONS

1. What's the climate of your team? Are you able to disagree with one another and maintain healthy relationships? If the answer is no, this might be extremely difficult to discuss.
2. What does "first among equals" mean to your team?
3. How trustworthy are you? Where do/have you lacked competence, honesty and transparency, or reliability?
4. What's one thing you could do to increase your trustworthiness, especially among your leadership teammates, this week?
5. Which of the ten functions of effective team leaders could you do to enhance your positive influence on your team?
6. How might your team benefit from sharing leadership duties among all members of the group, rather than placing them on the one set leader?
7. If you're the designated team leader, what's one way you can strategically *not do* with your team?
8. Consider Jesus as team leader of the disciples. What did he *strategically not do*

that resulted in the leadership development of the disciples and the growth of the church? What insights do you glean about the way you lead your church teams?

> **EXPERT COMMENTARY: LEADING BY HUMILITY THROUGH RELATIONSHIP IS BEST—AND GETS YOU BETTER RESULTS**
> *Crawford Loritts*
> "The authority to lead is developed and cultivated not through a prominence and power but rather through acts of service from a sincere humble heart."[21] In this sense, others give us the "permission" to lead because they have experienced the authenticity of our acts of love and service on their behalf.
>
> I wrote these words in my book *Leadership as an Identity* to introduce a section that explores why it's better to lead with permission than with power. I based my conclusion on what I see in Scripture: that God's way of leading his people is through a profound humility. I see that as a model for how we should lead with humility—that intentional recognition that God is everything to you, and that you are nothing without him. Humility is the acknowledgment that life is not about you, and that the needs of others are more important than your own. Humility is an attitude, a way of thinking that touches your

approach to everything you do and especially the people you come in contact with. It reminds us of Jesus, our example who humbled himself in order to serve the purposes of God and to serve us.[22]

The translation for church leadership teams? People tend to follow who leaders are and what leaders do. We need to model not only desirable behavior but also desirable identity—a humble heart. As my friend Steve Douglass, president of Cru (formerly called Campus Crusade for Christ) says, "Serving is really the best posture from which to lead." It's the attitude and perspective that makes Christian leadership possible.

I also find humility in the popular phrase *servant leadership*. You may be the team leader, but you are also servant to all, just as Jesus was. Servant leadership is much more than a strategy. The key to embracing servant leadership is embracing a humble identity as a Christ-follower.

Servant leadership flows from humility. There cannot be genuine servant leadership apart from genuine humility. To the degree your team sees and believes that, they will want to follow you.

***

Crawford Loritts is pastor of Fellowship Bible Church in Roswell, Georgia, author of numerous books and host of the daily radio broadcast "Living a Legacy" on moodyradio.org/livingalegacy.

DISCIPLINE 4: Intentionally Structure Your Decision-Making Process

Part 1: Collaborating While Seeking God's Voice

Wise planning is not that I decide and then ask God to bless it, but I ask God what He desires of me, and then pursue it!

Ed Stetzer, executive director of LifeWay Research

Maybe one of the reasons our ministries are so ineffective is because we don't make room for God's power, since we are so enamored with our own.

Mike Erre, senior pastor of EvFree Church, Fullerton, California

When we observed a senior team meeting at Cross Point Church, a multisite congregation in Nashville, the five senior staff members were discussing the management structure for its Dream Center campus. Over the past several months, the staff had experienced some tension because of the existent leadership structure at the church. During the week, the campus provides outreach ministry services under the direction of the director of ministries (who was on the senior team). However, on the weekends, that campus, like the rest of the church's campuses across the Nashville area, holds regular services. In this way, the campus pastor, just as the other campus pastors, was responsible to the multisite director (also on the senior team). Feeling some tension caused by two people offering direction to the same campus leadership, the team set out to determine how to best move forward.

This conversation at Cross Point exemplifies the challenges faced by senior leadership teams. Not only do they deal with messy, difficult, strategic or precedent-setting matters, but they also face the typical challenges any group deals with as it tries to make decisions as a group.

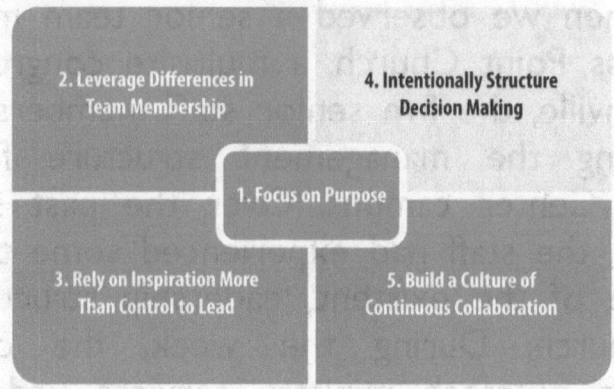

Figure 10.1. Teams that thrive intentionally structure decision making

Since decision making should be the primary role of the senior leadership team, thriving leadership teams must learn how to overcome these challenges to effectively make decisions. Our research suggests that when thriving teams make decisions, they employ careful, step-by-step problem solving or decision-making processes while seeking God for his perspective and leading. In other words, they intentionally collaborate while seeking God's voice (see fig. 10.1).

To help you explore the challenges of leadership team decision making and also to learn strategies to improve it, in this chapter, we
- discuss the particular problems senior leadership teams face when making decisions
- explore typical hang-ups and problems with group decision making

- offer a diagnostic to help you identify challenges with your team's decision-making processes
- present a solution to those problems: structured interaction that invites God to speak to the group

Then, in chapter eleven, we discuss the particular decision-making strategies of teams that thrive and provide a framework you can adapt and use with your team to make great decisions.

WHY LEADERSHIP TEAMS FACE "WICKED" PROBLEMS

Church senior leadership teams, by their very nature, face a tough challenge. *Spiritual* leadership chiefly involves "seeking to know and do the will of God."[1] And *senior* organizational leadership requires leaders to deal with thorny, complex problems and make consequential decisions, often in a room full of proven performers. These teams therefore confront several challenges.

First, leadership teams make extremely influential decisions that carry symbolic significance beyond even their material impact.[2] Leadership teams are forced to make the decisions that all others in the organization have either avoided making themselves, causing those problems to rise up the ranks to the senior leaders, or those that others at lower levels don't know need to be made, don't know how to make them or aren't authorized to make them. At Cross Point, a large, growing church with desires for additional campuses like the Dream Center, the campus leadership decision would not only dramatically influence the ministry direction of the existing Dream Center but also set precedent for other nontraditional campuses in the future. This situation illustrates how the decisions made by senior leadership teams are extraordinarily impactful for the direction and health of the church as a whole, both in the present and well into the future.

Second, leadership teams must make significant decisions in response to thorny problems. In fact, the issues that rise up the ranks often do so because they are so complex and reject typical decisional premises and principles. For instance, the confrontation pattern set forth in Matthew 18 escalates conflicts that could not be handled by an individual, or in the company of a few witnesses, to the church. Likewise, though Jethro advised Moses to establish bands of leaders to ease the leadership burden in Israel, he recognized the ultimate responsibility of senior leaders to manage the most difficult issues: "Every great matter they shall bring to you, but any small matter they shall decide themselves" (Ex 18:22).

Two-Minute Tip:

> *Look at your most recent meeting agenda. Is your team dealing mostly with thorny problems, the kind that are deeply complex and can't be answered easily or with decisions that likely could be made just as well by different people in the church? Depending on your answer, you may need to revisit the specific purpose of the senior leadership team.*

Third, leadership teams often have to manage tensions rather than simply solve problems.[3] In other words, leadership teams address "wicked problems,"[4] those issues that defy known algorithms for solutions and force teams to work outside the box and dialogue to actually define the problem, identify and invent possible solutions, and select the best course of action. The campus leadership arrangement, in which the campus pastors reported to the multisite director, worked just fine to guide the addition of other campuses in the past few years, but the Dream Center situation was different. The previously established structure didn't fit this unique situation, and the team had to reinvent their organizational structure to accommodate the complex problems arising from their leadership structure.

Fourth, leadership teams often comprise people who are considered to possess a "leadership" gift and who are accustomed to taking charge, making individual decisions and operating with a significant degree of autonomy.[5] These attributes, though perhaps the very ones that enabled great success in the past, can war against effectively contributing to a team decision-making process. In addition, the members of a senior leadership team, in most cases, direct a significant area of the church's ministry or operation. Though it'd be nice to think that church leaders never face these tensions, it is realistic to think that executives have to work at balancing an interest in doing what's best for the church as a whole with one in doing what's best for their particular ministry area. At Cross Point, delineating Dream Center reporting lines to either the multisite director or the director of ministries would likely impact those executives' staff, as well as give more organizational influence to one of them, while decreasing that of the other. For people who enjoy and excel at leadership, those realities play a prominent role in how those decisions are approached.

TEAM DECISION MAKING CAN BE HARD

Not only does your leadership team have to face unique challenges related to their role at the senior level of the church, but they also face the pesky issues teams of all stripes face. Use table 10.1 to rate your team on which (if any) of these problems you experience you try to make decisions:

Table 10.1. Rating the Level of Problems the Senior Leadership Team Addresses

Problem	Not at all	Happens sometimes	Occurs too often
The right people to offer input and perspective are often not at the table, or if they are they don't speak up.			
After the lead pastor offers input, the discussion centers far more on the pastor's words than ideas from anyone else.			
Some team members dominate the conversation while others offer virtually no input.			
You don't know if the team actually made a decision or merely had a discussion.			

Your team makes a clear decision, only to come back to it again two or three more times before actually taking action.			
The team deliberates for what seems to be hours, comes to consensus and then the lead pastor makes a completely different decision, either then or later.			
Team members self-censor their thoughts and ideas in order to keep the peace.			
The team often reverts to what's always been done, clearly wary of trying new, innovative ideas.			

Your team takes "forever" to make decisions.			
Tallies (points for each one)	_____ x 0 points	_____ x 1 point	_____ x 2 points
Your Score			

If your score is 10 or higher, frankly, your team is like most teams that face serious challenges in effectively solving problems, making decisions and developing and implementing innovative solutions. If you mostly checked "not at all," be encouraged, but also keep reading as you'll find many ideas in this chapter and the next for further improvement.

Interestingly, senior leadership team decision making is so hard that many folks shy away from giving senior teams decisions to make.[6] However, our research is clear that the senior teams that spent time making key decisions as a team outperformed those that did not. So, if you want a great senior team, your team needs to make important decisions. Thus if the answer to the question "should teams make decisions?" is yes, then we must explore how to actually do that well. Fortunately, many senior leadership teams have learned how to do it well, and we can learn from them.

> If you want a great senior team, your team needs to make important decisions.

THE ANSWER: STRUCTURING INTERACTION AND SEEKING GOD

We were not surprised when our statistical analysis told us that the more a team used a careful step-by-step process for solving problems and making decisions, the better the team performed. This parallels what group communication literature has suggested for many years: groups that conduct their business in a free-flowing, unstructured, haphazard manner tend to flounder, whereas those that intentionally structure and regulate their interaction generally perform at a much higher level.[7] Though sticking to a discussion plan or meeting agenda sometimes feels unnatural and awkward, it's clear that doing so supports team effectiveness.

However, we were delighted, but not too surprised, to see that the more a team sought God for his perspective, the better the team also performed. Apparently, seeking and hearing from God is an important contributor to team decision-making effectiveness for church senior leadership teams.

The most interesting insight, however, is the way that we believe these two practices—utilizing a careful step-by-step process and seeking God—interact with one another. On the surface, they appear contradictory. If teams are (vertically) seeking God for his direction, then they are not crunching numbers, employing critical analysis and vehemently discussing possible solutions. Instead, they are waiting on God to give the team his answers.

> Seeking and hearing from God is an important contributor to team decision-making effectiveness for church senior leadership teams.

On the other hand, if they're utilizing a robust, thoughtful (horizontal) group interaction process, they're not taking the time for vertical communication with God. But, after watching many of the top teams in action and talking to their members, we see a different relationship.

The best teams, in fact, do these things simultaneously. They vigorously pursue God and seek to hear his voice *and* they employ a rigorous, step-by-step approach to making decisions. In other words, they figuratively drive on a preferred road between two ditches (see fig. 10.2)—a ditch of adopting the best practices of business without any concern for how God might move, and another ditch of simply waiting for God to move while avoiding any real process that utilizes the collaborative potential of the team.

Figure 10.2. The preferred road between two ditches

Avoiding the ditches and staying on the road. Indeed, we've visited many churches that are stuck in one of the ditches. In churches that are stuck in the "best business practices" ditch, staff constantly refer to the church as "the organization," the lead pastor as the CEO and the congregants as clients, at best, and customers or wallet holders, at worst. While these teams do a great job availing themselves of the best thinking and practices for making great decisions, they fail to take advantage of the greatest gift to the church, the power of the Holy Spirit (Acts 1:8; Jas 1:5), and risk making bad decisions, like the Israelites did as recorded in Joshua 9, when they "did not ask counsel from the Lord" (Josh 9:14). In these environments, the church has adopted not only the language, metrics and practices of the corporate world, but unfortunately the values of it as well. When churches look only to butts, bucks and baptisms or the ABCs of attendance, buildings and cash[8] in ways that the Holy Spirit has no role, then it's time to recognize the unique nature of the church and her ministry—and perhaps to develop a new scorecard for measuring church and ministry health as well.[9]

> ### Two-Minute Tip:
>
> *Take a quick inventory of the most recent books you've read individually or as a team. Do those books indicate a greater reliance on best business practice or on the movement of the Holy Spirit for growing your church? As a team, what do you make of what you discovered in your reflection?*

Some churches are stuck in the other ditch. Listening to and following the Holy Spirit is the dominant agenda for their teams. In fact, in these meetings, it's incredibly obvious that you are in a church meeting, primarily because you know that if the church was any other kind of organization, it would not last for long! The team simply waits for a sense that God has moved and doesn't take any other proactive action to apply the wisdom God has put into the team members to collectively make key, strategic decisions. In so doing, these teams miss the model provided by Nehemiah, who not only prayed for God's wisdom but painstakingly inspected Jerusalem's ruined walls and strategically planned his approach for gathering the materials he would need.

Teams that thrive, however, avoid the ditches and stay on the road. They employ careful process and actively seek God's leading. Ruth Haley Barton, in her excellent book *Pursuing God's Will Together: A Discernment Practice for Leadership Groups*, offers a four-part framework for leaders to do just that—actively seek God together through a careful discernment process.[10] First, leaders prepare themselves for the discernment process by clarifying the question for discernment, gathering the team together, and affirming guiding values and principles. Second, those leaders situate themselves before God through prayers for wisdom and trust, acknowledging God is their source of wisdom and the One in whom they trust. Third, the team engages in the decision-making process by listening to one another, pertinent information and inner dynamics; creating moments of silence to continually listen to God; selecting and weighing options; and then agreeing together and seeking inner confirmation. Finally, leaders make plans to do God's will as they have understood it, communicating with those who need to know and moving forward together.[11]

Indeed, as table 10.2 illustrates, we found many leadership teams who employ myriad ways to seek God's direction and utilize their God-given wisdom, insight and analytical ability as they collaboratively make decisions.

Table 10.2. Thriving Teams Find Myriad Ways to Seek God and Collaborate Effectively

Northstar Church	Use Scripture as a benchmark; first seek God individually and then join together to make a collective decision; and seek wise counsel from board and spiritual advisors and mentors.
Freedom Church	Distribute discussion points a day or more before meetings so that prayer and forethought can take place; evaluate decisions based on life circumstances, influence of others, the leading of the Spirit, and the lens of God's Word; weigh the options as a team and then pull the trigger on the best decision.
Lifepoint Church	Cover major milestones, initiatives, and turning points in prayer; take advantage of the freedom to make decisions under the covering of James 1:5 ("If any of you lacks wisdom, let him ask God, who gives generously to all"); and ask God for wisdom at all times.
Sunnybrook Community Church	Prayerfully consider, honestly and colorfully discuss, and come to a consensus; take big decisions to the elders; and agree on time periods to pray (and sometimes fast) for particularly difficult or weighted decisions.
Country Bible Church	Ruthlessly ask and answer hard questions about each new plan or program and wait for a consensus to emerge that the new plan is the "right thing" to do.

In chapter eleven, we'll present several group problem-solving and decision-making practices that you can use with your team, demonstrating how you can integrate seeking God into each one. We hope those examples will provide inspiration and a model for how you might integrate more of seeking God or more of an intentional process into your team's decision-making practices, depending on where you fit in between the two ditches.

SEEKING GOD'S WILL TOGETHER

The distinctive finding in our study of church teams is the role of the Holy Spirit as teams seek his guidance, and we certainly don't want to underplay the importance of seeking and listening to God's voice. Thriving leadership teams take seriously James's instruction, "You ought to say, 'If the Lord wills, we will live and do this or that'" (Jas 4:15). As Haddon Robinson explains, "James is not against making plans, ... he is not taking a cheap shot at charts or making an argument against commitments.... What James warns us about is that our freedom to make plans is not a license to live free from God. To come to that conclusion would be arrogant. The phrase, 'If it is the Lord's will,' ought to infect our thinking. It ought to be a standard part of our vocabulary."[12]

The Ark Church in Conroe, Texas, recently tested their commitment to that truth. After experiencing great growth and needing more space, adding a third service seemed to be a no-brainer decision. All the facts and figures the team gathered pointed in that direction. So they set a date, communicated it to the church and set off to hit the target by launching a third service. However, as the date approached, they could not get clarity or peace from God about some of the specifics, even after they batted the issues around for hours as a team. They could never land the issues. Finally, Senior Pastor Alan Clayton pulled the team back, pointing out that if there was not clarity of direction from the Lord, it'd be better to serve the church by pressing the "pause button." So that's what they did. Using the reversal of decision as a great lesson of trust in and being led by God, Alan publicly recanted the third service launch. The Ark's leadership team, in essence, made their plans, just as James's audience did, saying, "Today or tomorrow we will go into such and such a town and spend a year there and trade and make a profit" (Jas 4:13). Depending on the Holy Spirit for guidance, they desperately clung to the phrase "If it is the Lord's will." Today, Alan says, "we are blessed to have a lot of quality, smart, high capacity leaders. Yet we fully realize that without being Spirit-led we could make decisions that are based simply on our thoughts, ideas, and facts, and miss what God is wanting to do in us, through us, and for us."

REFLECTION AND DISCUSSION QUESTIONS

1. Which decision-making problem in table 10.1 most resonated with you? Why?
2. Why do you find that making key decisions can be so hard at the leadership team level?
3. Thinking back to the image of the road and the two ditches (fig. 10.2), where does your team tend to mostly fall? If your team leans toward one of the ditches, what could you do to get back onto the road?
4. Which of the examples of how teams integrate seeking God and structuring their decision-making processes stuck out to you? How could you incorporate those practices in your team?
5. Read Acts 15:22-28 and Philippians 4:6. What do those passages teach you about making good and godly decisions?

EXPERT COMMENTARY: GOD'S SPIRIT, THE GREATEST ADVISOR
Ron Edmondson

"Without counsel plans fail, but with many advisers they succeed" (Prov 15:22). It has taken me a while to learn how true this biblical principle is in my leadership and to put it into practice.

As a doer, I am not good at waiting for an answer. Committee meetings wear me out and often seem a waste of my time. One of my strengths is the ability to make a decision. I have learned, however, that I stink at making decisions on my own. I almost always make a mistake when I don't include others.

Granted, we can have too many voices at the table and too many steps in our decision-making process, such that nothing ever gets accomplished. That is not good either, and I don't believe that is what this Proverb suggests that we do. When the decision is major, however, I know I need some help in making the right one. I need the help of people I trust and I need the help of The Helper, God's Spirit within me (see Jn 14:26).

One way we have attempted to do this in our structure has been to remove the word *vote* from our lead team. We believe that if God has assembled our team—and we think he has—then God will work within each of us to lead us to a unanimous decision. We are a large, intergenerational church and I don't expect everyone in our church to agree with every decision, but we certainly should have consensus among our leadership team.

Another thing we have done is to move slowly in making major decisions. Some decisions we can quickly make, but if it impacts the entire church then we want to make sure we are acting in obedience and not getting ahead of God. I am wired for progress, so the last thing I want to do is wait, but if we want to do things God's way, then we have to move forward on his timing and allow him to lead us to unity in our decisions.

Recently we were considering a capital campaign to pay off some existing debt and replace aging technology. We had reached what I believe was a unanimous decision among our lead staff team. Additionally, I had consulted with a dozen or more lay leaders in our church and everyone gave the green light to move forward. We hired a consultant and began making preparations.

As I continued to pray about the timing of this campaign I sensed an uneasiness in the decision to move forward. I called our lead team back together and ask them to pray with me again. This time the decision was unanimous the other direction. In our excitement, we had overreacted to our readiness, and none of us felt we were ready for this campaign. Had we not been sensitive to the Spirit's leading, we may have made a critical error.

Truly plans fail for the lack of counsel—and with many advisors they succeed—and the greatest advisor is God's Spirit within us as believers.

***

Ron Edmondson is pastor of Immanuel Baptist Church in Lexington, Kentucky, and a ministry consultant. He is a prolific blogger at ronedmondson.com and is active on Twitter (@ronedmondson).

11

DISCIPLINE 4: Intentionally Structure Your Decision-Making Process

Part 2: Collaborating in the Midst of Conflict

Find some happy people and get them to fight.

Robert I. Sutton, *Weird Ideas That Work*

"Pastor, you're killing our staff by something you do," said the executive pastor, after he pulled aside his boss for a private conversation.

"What am I doing?" the senior pastor asked.

"You come into our senior leadership team meetings and say, 'I want to know what you think,' but you've already made up your mind."

"I'm trying to be a better team player," the senior pastor responded. "What's wrong with that?"

"When you haven't decided yet, then ask for our help in making the decision. But if you have clearly gotten God's message already, just tell us—you're the leader—and we'll follow you."

The pastor got it, agreed, thanked his executive pastor, and their relationship continued forward without missing a beat. Honest talk, clear rules of engagement, and quick resolution. That's the rhythm often found in teams that thrive.

In one of the most representative studies ever conducted of US churches, involving over ten thousand congregations across every denomination and tradition, one factor rose to the top as the greatest predictor of whether a church is growing or non-growing. It is the presence or absence of lingering destructive conflict.[1] How a church deals with conflict—for this book, how its senior team models conflict resolution—has enormous consequences, not only for the growth of the church, but also for its health and effectiveness.

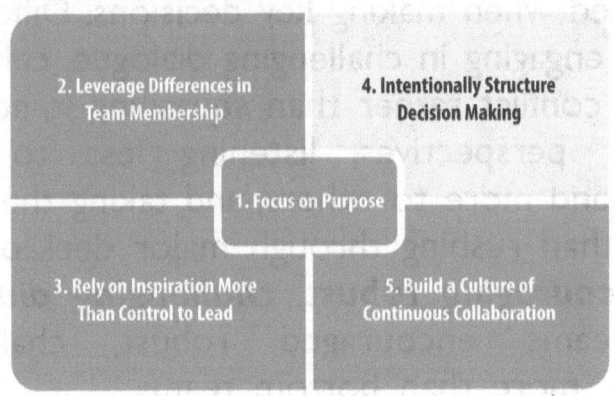

Figure 11.1. Teams that thrive intentionally structure decision making

Conflict in itself is not fundamentally bad. It's what we do with conflict that matters. In chapter ten we identified the need for teams to structure their interaction while diligently seeking God's voice. This chapter
- discusses the communication practices that make a difference for team decision-making performance, specifically dealing with conflict
- lays out a process you can use (and tweak) to help your team make better decisions

COMMUNICATION PRACTICES THAT MAKE A DIFFERENCE

We found that the top teams engaged in different decision-making practices than the underperforming teams (see fig. 11.1). Thriving teams differentiated themselves by the way they interacted when making key decisions. Differences include engaging in challenging dialogue, cultivating healthy conflict rather than squashing it, adopting broader perspectives, listening less to some people and more to others, and taking their time rather than rushing through major decisions.

Encouraging robust, challenging dialogue. Top teams encouraged robust, challenging dialogue more than bottom teams.

The genius of the leadership team is its collaborative potential. But to extract the full value out of a team, it must act collaboratively, which means its members must talk collaboratively as they go about their most important work of making decisions while eliciting and embracing conflict and debate. In fact, debate is the very thing that transforms a team's diversity into excellent performance.[2] Without vigorous debate, the team's diversity is a nuisance at best and a team destroyer at worst.

Members of excellent teams say what's on their mind; they offer their best to the team, even if it sparks conflict. They fear artificial agreement more than offending a teammate. The deleterious effects of groupthink—what happens when a group's desire for harmony overrides their commitment to critically examine issues—have been well-documented in the forty-plus years since Irving Janus famously coined the term, but many teams still regularly succumb to it.[3] Wary of offending another team members or overestimating the team's inherent goodness, team members fail to offer their best critical thinking or censor their novel ideas or hesitations about a pending plan. When that happens, groups make less-than-ideal decisions and suffer from groupthink.

> The genius of the leadership team is its collaborative potential. Debate is the very thing that transforms a team's diversity into excellent performance.

Great teams don't stand for such groupthink behavior. Instead, they engage in collaborative conversations,[4] during which they
- clarify the purpose of the conversation
- gather divergent views and perspectives
- build shared understanding of divergent views and perspectives
- create "new" options by connecting different views
- generate a conversation for action

These collaborative conversations require team members to not only advocate their own ideas, interests and positions with passion and resolve, but also to pursue a process of inquiry to explore others' interests and ideas. Adopting an inquiry approach tends to produce much better decisions for several reasons. First, a variety of options are considered rather than just the most persuasively argued ones. Second, colleagues are viewed as partners in discerning the optimal path forward rather than as opponents to conquer. Third, creative thinking is encouraged versus prematurely reducing all options down to just a few.[5] Fourth, all team members participate in the excavation, the unearthing of all relevant information that will enable the team to make a good decision.

However, inquiry is certainly not easy. In these conversations, authenticity and vulnerability reign supreme as the group seeks to create innovative solutions to their problems. In such discussions, conflict naturally arises, and the team embraces and utilizes it to make better decisions.

Cultivating and managing healthy conflict. "Conflict doesn't destroy strong teams because strong teams focus on results," argue Tom Rath and Barry Conchie, authors of *Strengths Based Leadership*.[6] Instead, strong teams welcome healthy conflict, for it is the catalyst of extraordinary performance, and manage it in such a way that it does not destroy the team. Certainly this is a tricky balance, and another stay-on-the-road-between-two-ditches situation. First, we'll discuss how to cultivate the kind of conflict that fuels great team performances. To spur healthy conflict, we suggest that members of senior leadership teams

> Healthy conflict is the catalyst of extraordinary performance.

1. Vigorously solicit critiques of plans, decisions and assumptions guiding decision making.
2. Model respectful, assertive, thoughtful and honest critiques of ministry ideas and plans, and invite others to do the same of your own ideas and plans.
3. Celebrate group members who say the hard thing even when it is uncomfortable to do so.

4. Cultivate a norm (expectation) of "If you see something, say it." Don't allow group members to keep their thoughts about a proposed direction to themselves, even if they are critical or contrary. They at least deserve to be heard and considered, even if dismissed later.
5. Hold group members accountable to that norm. If you find out later that someone was able to "see around the corner" on an issue but didn't voice that perspective, confront it, first privately and then perhaps with the rest of the team.
6. Assign one or more people to play the role of "devil's advocate" in every meeting. Make it that person's (or group's) job to search for problems, shortcomings and oversights with the group's decisions and plans. Rotating this role among team members reduces the likelihood of resentment toward a well-functioning devil's advocate.
7. On a regular basis, go around the table and ask each team member to identify one area in which the team, church or ministry could improve. Require every person to answer the question. Then, either talk about those issues immediately, or put them on a future agenda.

In any case, don't shut down this kind of conflict. Encourage it. It is the fuel your team needs to maximize its impact.

> ### Two-Minute Tip:
>
> *Do exercise 7 from the preceding list right now. Go around the table and ask each team member to identify one area in which the team, church or ministry could improve. Insist that every person answers the question, and then select one improvement you agree should happen. Discuss how you can implement it.*

A caution is in order here. Not all conflict is good. Studies overwhelmingly suggest that task conflict is good, whereas affective, or relationship, conflict is bad. In other words, team members should challenge each other's ideas, interrogate one another's beliefs and values, and willingly offer different perspectives while refraining from attacking others in the process, or making snide, sarcastic comments in the process. On many teams, sarcastic jokes can become a norm, and though they appear innocent, those sideways comments often have a greater effect than thought.

Thus engaging conflict over ideas without digressing into some sort of relationship conflict, especially when handling the kind of topics that senior leadership teams do, is quite the challenge. Just as we offered several tips for cultivating task-oriented conflict, we offer tips to manage relational conflict well when it arises.[7]

1. Don't freak out. When decision stakes are high, individuals' points of view are shaped by differing (usually taken-for-granted) values, belief systems or interests. When more about the problem is unknown than known—just as in nearly every decision made by a senior leadership team—relationship conflict is bound to surface.
2. Acknowledge the "elephant in the room" by addressing awkwardness or a conversation that has crossed the line. Pause the conversation to address the tension.
3. Pay attention to your emotions and to the emotions of others. If you experience a strong emotion or notice that someone else is, acknowledge it, and allow each person to express what they're feeling and why. Treat one another's feelings and perspectives as legitimate topics of concern and conversation.
4. If you are offended by what someone has said, consider alternative interpretations, and be willing to offer the benefit of the doubt. Seek to not be offended.

5. Engage in enough conversation so that your team can either resolve the conflict fully—if that can be done quickly—or get back to its work while leaving the conflict to more fully address it later. Get back to doing work together as soon as possible, without sweeping the conflict under the rug.
6. If the conflict is not resolved quickly, work it fully out in individual conversations between the persons with the conflict until they can come to a place of reconciliation.
7. Learn from it. Take some time in your next team meeting (or sooner, if necessary) to revisit the conflict. Ask all team members for their thoughts and feelings about the conflict. Discuss what your team learned from it—about one another's "touch points," about what it looks like to love and respect one another as brothers and sisters in Christ, and about how you can best work together in the future. When relevant, perhaps capture what you learned in your team ground rules (see later in this chapter).
8. Pat yourselves on the back. You're using conflict situations to learn how to work better together and how to love each other well in the process, which builds authentic trust and true community.

Welcoming, cultivating and effectively managing conflict is essential for a team to thrive in its decision-making work. When people have the opportunity to air their ideas and hesitations in an environment where their input is welcomed and truly considered, they are likely to unite around the decision that is made and walk out of the room unified in direction.

Listening to one another in equal amounts. Top teams reported listening less to what the lead pastor desires than did the underperforming teams. Great teams recognize that power can never be equally distributed on teams. They recognize that, in most churches, the voice of the lead pastor carries enormous weight and can easily sway the rest of the team. And so they listen less to what the lead pastor desires. They do so realizing that on great teams, everyone talks and listens in relatively similar amounts; no one dominates discussion. Now, of course, that doesn't mean that team members cover their ears when the lead pastor speaks. Instead, lead pastors speak less by holding back their opinions to create space for others to speak and resisting the urge to make a decision on every question that is posed to them.

Two-Minute Tip:

In your next team meeting, watch for who speaks first and last when important decisions are discussed and made. Then, before your next

> meeting, privately ask that person to wait until at least two other people have offered their perspective before entering the conversation.

These leaders, as Jim Collins has explained, are humble enough to aspire to be the dumbest person on the team.[8]

Additionally, these leaders encourage the input of other team members. "What do you think of this, Andrew? You haven't chimed in yet." Great teams don't take a chance that everyone will contribute. Instead, they find ways to ensure that everyone speaks at one point or another, and everyone listens.

At the same time, though, members of great teams don't feel like they always have to chime in. In fact, the members of Reality LA's senior team told us it's not uncommon for there to be abstainers in group decisions because they don't have strong convictions on the matter or because it might be an area that is outside of their expertise. They explained, "If someone is passionate about a matter and they are operating within their gift set, we tend to listen intently to those people; some of us, though, don't feel the need to chime in and bog down the decision-making process, and so we let those who feel passionately work it out. In such a case, there's no need to speak up at all."

Adopting a churchwide perspective. Members of top teams adopted a churchwide perspective rather than a position-based perspective (e.g., youth, business, technology, missions) more than members of bottom teams.

The primary value of a senior leadership team is *not* that it constitutes a representative democracy of all the church's department heads. Often, the team will be populated by the staff members at the top of the organization who oversee the church's various ministries (team membership is discussed in chap. 8). However, the team must focus more on its leadership of the church as a whole rather than advocating for their ministry area. In other words, members of great senior leadership teams, like the team members of the Ark Church in Conroe, Texas, hold fast to the idea that "the team you are on is more important than the team you lead." They are committed first to being members of the leadership team and secondarily to leading their respective ministry area (youth, kids, worship, etc.).

That's not to say, however, that team members should completely ignore their functional perspective.[9] Instead, it's advisable for team members to alternate between taking a holistic and functional perspective. A team member might say, "the concerns, as I see it from my role overseeing the budget, are..." and then say, "but if I take off my finance hat, I do see the value of this program for increasing the number of people involved in outreach ministries." Indeed, both perspectives are valuable, as they enable the team to look at each issue from several different vantage points, rather than just from a general leadership point of view.

That's a good thing, as it is hard to ask a team member who has spent an entire ministry career advocating for and ministering to students to not focus on what's best for students. Luckily, you don't have to do so, at least completely. You can encourage him or her to represent the students' interests but also to adopt a perspective of what's best for the church as a whole. One way to train team members to take a churchwide perspective is to ask them to think like another team member, such as the executive pastor or children's pastor, when viewing the decision.

Taking time when making decisions. Top teams took more time and didn't rush through decisions as much as bottom teams.

That's right. Great teams were less *efficient* than underperforming teams in the sense that they took longer to make decisions but benefited greatly from doing so. In fact, we learned that underperforming teams felt a great amount of stress due to not enough time to deliberate and make decisions.

The takeaway here is simple: *quantity time begets quality time.* For teams, it's often said that quick, standup meetings can not only substitute for longer ones but also actually increase the team's effectiveness because they help participants increase their focus.[10] But the rub is that quality time doesn't happen without quantity time.

Healthy, productive teams spend a good amount of time together. Andy Stanley adeptly recognizes the importance of time spent together: "Teams that meet only when they need to meet will never really function as a team; they act more a work group or a problem-solving task force. It's the regular meeting that creates the culture necessary to have healthy debate and effective problem solving."[11] Though distractions, fires and competing priorities vie for a leadership team's time, teams that thrive invest time to make their team great. They take time to negotiate vision, purpose and goals; establish team member roles; discuss how they will work together; plan out how they will solve problems and make decisions; work through conflicts; and get to know one another and each person's relevant strengths and talents. In fact, great teams tend to spend three and a half hours a week in team meetings, and another three talking informally with members of the team.

That's not to say, however, that meetings should drag on without a concern for efficiency. We take that discussion up in chapter twelve.

Putting these principles into practice will yield great results for your leadership team. To help you structure these principles into practice, we suggest that your team establishes some guidelines for decision making. Also called norms, plumb lines or ground rules, these principles articulate what your team values, what it seeks to accomplish and how it seeks to accomplish those

goals as it makes decisions together. The following is a sampling of the decision-making principles of several leadership teams that thrive.
- The best idea wins, no matter whose it is.
- We could do lots of *good* things but if not careful they will get in the way of the *best* things.
- We are principle driven and not pragmatically driven. We determine key objectives that we want to accomplish and then find the best ways to do so.
- Everything is always on the table. There are no sacred cows.
- We filter everything through the grid of our church's Nine Defining Values.
- We want honest and healthy conflict. We are always asking for the last 5 percent. We cannot make informed decisions without all ideas and opinions on the table.
- We don't let our organizational chart restrict us. If we feel we need other voices at the table, we'll invite those team members into team meetings. Meeting personnel can look quite different from time to time.
- We filter decision making through the following questions:
    - How does this further our church's vision?

- Where does this fit in our strategic recipe?
- How does this drive our core mission?
- Will it change lives?
- Does it keep costs low?
- Does it drive weekend attendance?
- Can it be done at a small campus in a small community (eventually anywhere in the world)?
- We apply tangible, measurable goals (clarify the "win") and then evaluate on the back side to see if the program was effective, if we will ever do it again and, if so, how it could be improved.

Whatever principles your team adopts, the important part is that your team uses principles and adheres to them.

A USEFUL TOOL TO FACILITATE ROBUST DIALOGUE IN MAKING DECISIONS: THE FUNCTIONAL APPROACH TO GROUP DECISION MAKING

Here is a decision-making process you can use to stimulate robust, challenging dialogue among all members of your team, cultivate healthy conflict and come to a unified decision, all so that you can make the most of your senior leadership team interaction.

There are no silver bullets to team decision making, but the functional approach to decision making, developed by scholars Randy Hirokawa and Dennis Gouran, lays out a simple and clear path for making great group decisions.[12] Over many years of research, scholars have repeatedly found that groups that fulfill the following five functions when making decisions make better decisions than those groups that use an unstructured, haphazard approach:

1. Analyze the problem.
2. Establish evaluation criteria and set goals.
3. Generate alternative solutions.
4. Evaluate positive and negative consequences of solutions.
5. Select course of action judged to most likely to satisfy goals.

Though studies have not shown that the order in which groups accomplish these functions matters more than simply ensuring they are all covered, approaching these five functions as steps is a wise way to create a habit of more comprehensively making decisions.

First, analyze the problem. Solid problem definition is often half the battle. Typically, decisions are made because problems exist. To solve problems, groups make decisions to mitigate the problem. Thus the first stage of this decision-making model is to develop an accurate, reasonable and realistic understanding of the nature of the issue at hand, based upon the necessary information available to the team. The team should investigate and dialogue about (1) the extent and seriousness of the problem, (2) the likely cause(s) of the problem and (3) the possible consequences of not dealing effectively with the problem. The team must answer the question, What's going on here, and why?

For instance, as Cross Point deliberated how to structure its Dream Center campus (see the beginning of chap. 10), problem analysis would entail the team clearly identifying what's problematic about the current structure, what problems will later develop if they don't decisively solve the issue, how many current or future campuses are affected by the confusion at the Dream Center campus and so on. In any case, fully understanding the causes and the consequences of the problem is essential for the team to make a good decision.

There are several simple discussion techniques, such as making a fishbone diagram, walking through a devil's advocacy or dialectical inquiry technique, or conducting a force field analysis, that could be used by teams in this problem analysis stage. See teamsthatthrivebook.com for a list of useful discussion tools and details on where you can find more information about them.

Regardless of the techniques a group uses to come to an in-depth understanding of the issue, it is essential that a group does this, for if a group doesn't recognize all of the possible reasons for the problem or extent of it, it's probable that the group's solution will not prove effective. Unfortunately, many groups skip this phase and move too quickly to simply generating possible solutions, *assuming* a common sense of the problem that actually doesn't exist. In this phase, teams might spend a meeting working through one of the above techniques but then take time before moving forward to pray, either individually or corporately, and ask God for his insight regarding what is really the problem, what the team might be missing and so forth. One practical way to invite God's direction during this stage is to create an intentional period—five, ten or fifteen minutes or more—to discern the Lord's leading, followed by a short time during which each person shares what he or she is sensing. These prayer times in the middle of a team's decision-making process underscore prayer as an essential element of the team's real work, not as bookends for the team's work of discussion and deliberation (as prayer at the beginning or end of meetings often does).[13]

During this process, it is important that teams have all the information they need to make important decisions. The Journey Church directional team understands the importance of quality information to support decision making.

That's why, at their quarterly directional team meetings, they go through nearly ten pages of metrics regarding baptisms, website hits, people serving in the church, small group involvement, worship service attendance, budgets, guest comment cards, leadership development and so on. They ensure they have the information they need at the time they need it to support important decisions.

At the same time, great teams don't allow themselves to become overwhelmed by the amount of information available to them. In today's world, gobs of information on every topic imaginable is available in a moment's notice, the use of which can cause decision paralysis. The group cannot sort through the information available to it and therefore fails to make sense of it in a way they can understand and move forward. To limit information overload but get only what they need, great teams designate certain members of the team to collect and provide important types of data the team needs. In particular, they designate persons who have a knack for not only collecting necessary information but also combing through it and presenting it in an accessible, understandable manner. Also, they routinely take breaks to ask, "What information do we not have in front of us that would help us to make this decision?" Then they wait to make the decision until they gather the necessary data. Doing so teaches the team what data it needs, and soon enough the team will gather the data proactively so that it does not have to suffer from waiting to make key decisions.

> ### Two-Minute Tip:
>
> *Ask your best data collector and presenter to become your team's data czar, responsible to ensure the team has the information it needs when approaching important decisions. Send the data czar your weekly agenda several days in advance so that he or she can gather the information you'll need for the meeting.*

Second, set goals that establish decision-evaluation criteria. In this phase, group members identify the characteristics of an ideal (or even acceptable) solution. Many groups assume that everyone understands and agrees on what the solution must accomplish, but this consensus is actually quite rare. The definition of "good" is contested in every facet of life, including decisions about programs, staff and vision. The characteristics developed here serve as criteria for judging the proposed solutions that are identified by the group.

Here the group identifies its interests in a decision. Doing so restricts the group from moving to positions (possible solutions) too quickly. Interests are desires and goals that people have in a situation, which can be accomplished in various ways. Positions, on the other hand, are ways to satisfy those interests. "I want to eat lunch at Chipotle across the street" is an example of a position statement, whereas the interests underlying that position might be concerns such as: "I want an inexpensive, delicious, nearby and organic lunch. Those interests could be satisfied in many different ways, including a meal at Chipotle."

In their bestselling book on negotiation, *Getting to Yes*, Roger Fisher and William Ury argue that by identifying underlying interests rather than positions, situations that seem to require compromise or only one winner are able to be solved in creative ways that satisfy all or as many of the criteria possible.[14] As such, focusing on interests enables the team to identify win-win solutions to problems that might not have been evident if the positions were identified too quickly.

This goal-setting phase is commonly the most overlooked element in team decision making. Often, the group does not take the time to agree on what a new plan needs to accomplish. Thus mediocre decisions are made that have to be revisited often to continually improve the programs so that they satisfy the needs (interests) of the church and its members. Or decisions are driven primarily by politics rather than careful reason. Most important, however, these criteria put constraints on the group, which research shows actually promotes creativity in groups.[15] Indeed, creativity research suggests that "innovation doesn't stem from wide-open spaces or from thinking outside the box. Instead, innovation happens when people work from inside the box, sometimes rethinking and reshaping the box entirely."[16] Evaluation criteria form the box that supports creative thinking.

The easiest way to develop a list of goals is to simply respond to the prompt:

An ideal _____ (meal, program, campus location, financial decision, etc.) will: _____ (listing as many ideas as possible for what it can achieve).

At Cross Point, this would look like developing a list of goals that completed this sentence: "An effective management structure for the Dream Center campus will: _____." We suspect they would identify goals such as: be sustainable as other campuses are added, increase clarity about authority and responsibility, streamline coordination with other campuses and ministry areas, and set the Dream Center up for continued success.

Once the group exhausts the list, the group can go through the list once more, determining whether each goal is a need or a want and then rank-ordering the importance of all of the wants (all of the needs are absolute, so no ranking is necessary).

As with the first phase, teams can seek God for his guidance through this process of identifying which desires are most important to pursue. In addition, teams might remind themselves of Scripture passages that refer to God's desires for the building of his church, soaking in the truth of these passages and ensuring their goals align with God's.

At that point, these criteria can be used to judge all of the proposed solutions.

Third, generate possible solutions. Once the group has a solid understanding of the problem and has established a set of criteria to judge possible solutions, it is then ready to generate possible solutions. Here, it is important that the group takes advantage of all its creative capacity.

Toward this end, the group will likely brainstorm ideas, which means more than throwing out some ideas. In particular, the traditional rules of brainstorming,[17] which do tend to produce better results than not following them, instruct groups to:

1. Generate as many ideas as possible. The more ideas the better.
2. Defer judgment on all ideas. That means avoiding criticism and praise.
3. Encourage wild, extreme, outlandish ideas. No idea is too ridiculous. Remember, no judgment.
4. Build upon one another's ideas. Piggybacking on and combining ideas is preferred, as doing so extends and synthesizes ideas.

Simply following these rules tends to promote much greater creativity, which increases the chances that an innovative solution can be developed that meets all of the evaluation criteria. However, just brainstorming won't necessarily be all you need. In fact, several elements of typical group discussion, including brainstorming, actually hinder creative output. Beyond what we've already mentioned, there are several things you can do to increase your team's creative output:[18]

1. *Alternate group interaction with individual reflection and ideation.* Because only one person can talk at a time, and because it takes time for a facilitator to write ideas on a whiteboard, individual production of creative ideas is often hindered. One way to address this issue is to try group brainstorming (as explained above) for three to five minutes. Then, offer the group members the chance to write down additional ideas for another three to five minutes. Repeat two or three times. This procedure takes advantage of piggybacking on one another's ideas, allows members to simultaneously create ideas and eliminates social inhibition caused by potential embarrassment, all in fifteen to twenty minutes total.

2. *Use a facilitator from outside the team (such as another staff member at the church) to record or collate ideas and manage the group's flow.* That allows all the members of the team to fully participate, without forcing one to record and facilitate discussion.
3. *Use a collaborative document projected on a screen.*[19] This simple technique eliminates any need to hold back ideas until another person is done talking yet takes advantage of the benefits of seeing each other's ideas, as each person can type into the document simultaneously while seeing what others are offering.
4. *Invite a diverse group of other staff or volunteers to participate in the ideation process.* Who says the leadership team has to be the only ones to generate possible ideas to challenging solutions? Bring a group—even with people who don't necessarily get along that well—into the room, explain the problem, tell them the criteria the solution needs to satisfy and then let them loose.[20] Just keep the group small; the more people in the room, the more that people's production will be blocked as they wait for someone else's idea to be articulated and recorded. Because they are not in the throes of the issue, they likely

will be able to generate ideas that are not constrained by traditional solutions or shaped by past practice.

5. *Practice creative thinking in every meeting of the leadership team and every other team.* Group genius must be practiced constantly and spread throughout the organization for it to be maximally effective.[21]

6. *Take some time away from the issue.* While away from the issue, creative sparks and connections may emerge as the mind has the ability to enter other conceptual spaces and ideas that were previously being incubated.[22] In addition, taking time away gives members time to deepen their knowledge of the problem domain through researching or talking to colleagues. Though a creative idea often comes in a spark, typically it takes time for that spark to grow into a fire that becomes a useful, innovative solution.

7. *Combine ideas in as many different ways as possible.* As you generate a list of ideas, push to say, "what if we put this together with that one?" Chances are these combinations will ultimately generate some useful ideas.

8. *Utilize various techniques to generate a large quantity of ideas.* Various techniques exist

that program in the principles discussed above.[23]

Fourth, evaluate the positive and negative characteristics of the possibilities. After a phase of generating ideas, the final step requires teams to evaluate the ideas developed against the goals established in the second phase. Typically, several ideas will stand out as the most feasible, and the list can be quickly narrowed. In the absence of that general agreement on a few key ideas to further explore, groups can score the ideas against the evaluation criteria. First, the ideas are simply scored against the needs: Does the proposed solution meet the needs identified? Only those that score "yes" across the board are kept for further analysis. Second, those that meet all of the needs can then be scored against the wants—those criteria that would be advantageous but not absolutely necessary. A simple way to do this is to rate each alternative on a scale of 1 to 10 (with 10 being the best) on each want. By weighting each of the wants on a scale of 1 to 10 in terms of importance (10 being the most important), a chart could be developed where each alternative is scored by multiplying its score against the weight and then adding up the totals for each possibility. The alternatives with the highest scores then are easily identified as the likely best candidates. Further discussion can identify the pros and cons of each alternative, including any adverse consequences of choosing that alternative until the group comes to a final decision.[24]

At Cross Point, functions three and four might look like throwing out several different possible solutions for managing the Dream Center campus, including wild, seemingly impossible solutions. Then, once those possibilities are listed, comparing and rating them against the criteria set during the second phase of goal setting. Pretty quickly, some consensus might emerge among the team about the best approach for the Dream Center's reporting structure.

Fifth, make a decision that best satisfies goals. After such a careful decision-making process, it's likely that a best solution will emerge, though the final decision may be made in various ways. Great teams use multiple decision rules to make decisions.

Achieving consensus all the time is unrealistic. There's no way the entire team is going to agree on every decision, nor does it need to. At the same time, it's a fallacy that the chief leader needs to make every decision, or even all the decisions that the team can't agree upon, or the leadership team has not learned how to effectively make decisions. However, there are certain times when it's best for one person—either the lead pastor or another pastor—to simply make the decision. Finally, though voting is a favorite American pastime, it's typically a worst-case option for making decisions, at least if you desire unity. The reason? Voting draws a line in the sand, causing some people be identified as losing.

So, what's the answer? It is different decision rules—consensus, majority and minority (one person decides)—for different situations. *Consensus* is best when everyone's commitment to the decision is essential and when adequate time exists to deliberate and come to consensus. *Majority* is best when the decision is less important, when time is of the issue and when those who are left in the minority opinion after the vote will not hold far-reaching anger or frustration. Finally, *minority* is good when one person is best prepared to make the final decision, taking into account the input from others. It's a misunderstanding of minority decision making to believe that the "team leader" always needs to be the one who makes the final decision. It's a better approach to vest decision-making authority with various members of the team for different situations because they are most prepared to make the final decision, again taking into account all of the input previously offered by the team. A team that vacillates among these approaches will do better than one that forces consensus 100 percent of the time, or resorts to the easiest, quickest method of majority voting.

Continuing to hold the decision up to the Holy Spirit is crucial. Acts 15 records an instance of decision making by the Jerusalem Council. Peter, Paul, Barnabas and James, among others, took their turns addressing the Council on the relation of salvation and circumcision. As they did, Luke records that the assembly listened to each speaker, referred back to the Scriptures, then made a decision that "seemed good to the Holy Spirit and to us" (Acts 15:28) and recorded it in a letter. In this way, it was a decision guided by the Holy Spirit (it "seemed good to the Holy Spirit") and made by the group (it "seemed good ... to us").[25]

Regardless of the way the decision is confirmed, following a careful, thoughtful process will often help members who didn't wish for that action initially to feel good about it and be able to support and present the decision in a unified front. And they'll feel like they're working as a team. As researchers Charles Kepner and Benjamin Tregoe conclude, "When people are provided with a common approach to decision-making, they find they can indeed work as a team. There is more sharing of relevant information. Differing positions are more successfully reconciled because the process of decision-making is less biased. Inevitably, the quality of decision-making improves."[26]

No matter how the final decision is determined, once the decision is made, teams would be wise to take Colin Powell's advice: "When we are debating an issue, loyalty means giving me your honest opinion, whether you think I'll like it or not. Disagreement, at this stage, stimulates me. But once a decision has been made, the debate ends. From that point on, loyalty means executing the decision as if it were your own."[27]

As mentioned above, as long as a group covers all five functions, the route taken is not the key issue. Nonetheless, groups that successfully resolve particularly tough problems often take a common decision-making path: problem analysis, goal setting, identifying alternatives and evaluating the positive and negative characteristics.

Following this process would be exhausting to do for every decision. However, discipline in learning to walk through this process several times until a team learns to do these things without having to go step-by-step through the stages will reap great rewards. The team will learn to fully think through its challenges, ideate creative solutions and make excellent decisions that propel the church's mission forward.

If the core work of the senior leadership team is making key decisions for the church, then it simply makes sense that the team should focus on doing so. Indeed, our research shows that the best teams use a structured, step-by-step approach to problem solving and seek God for his perspective as they make decisions. The functional approach to decision making offers a viable, flexible and practical way to do just that.

REFLECTION AND DISCUSSION QUESTIONS

1. What are the biggest challenges your team faces when making decisions?
2. On a scale from 1 to 5 (5 being the best), how consistently is your team:
   - Using a careful, step-by-step problem-solving or decision-making process?
   - Seeking God for his perspective?
   - Encouraging robust, challenging dialogue and task-related conflict?
   - Not listening only to what the lead pastor desires?
   - Taking on a churchwide perspective rather than a just a position-based perspective?
   - Taking plenty of time to deliberate, not rushing through decisions?
3. How can your team cultivate more healthy conflict?
4. In what ways is your team rushing the collaborative process? How can you ensure that your team has enough time to accomplish its objectives?
5. Why do tensions rise when discussing hot-button topics? What can you do to mitigate negative conflict stemming from those discussions?

6. Which of the five phases of the functional decision making does your team tend to do well? Not so well?
7. To better contribute individually as a team member, what are two action steps you will take based on what you learned in this chapter?
8. Read John 15:1-7. How could your team do a better job of abiding in Jesus as you go about your important work?

EXPERT COMMENTARY: SEVEN STRATEGIES TO LEVERAGE YOUR TEAM'S DECISION MAKING
Tony Morgan

As I wrote in the opening words of my book, *Take the Lid Off Your Church,* a solo leader "might draw a weekend crowd, but it takes a *team* to create healthy systems that foster sustained growth and opportunities for life change."

In short, the capacity of your team will determine the potential impact of your ministry. What you don't want is a team held back by conflict. What you do want is a team free to work at their peak. Here are seven strategies to leverage your team members' gifts and maximize the potential of your church.

1. Agree on the vision and values, and let your leaders make decisions. If the lead pastor

has to make all the decisions and come up with all the new ideas, that's an indication of micromanagement rather than empowerment. By clarifying vision and values and implementing systems that facilitate next steps, you can free your team to engage ministry without having to wait for permission.

2. Invite conflict privately and demand unity publicly. It's impossible to have unanimous agreement on every decision among your team. In some cases, leaders will have to make tough calls and the majority of the people in the room think it's the wrong decision. That's leadership. At the same time, though, you have to create an environment where pushback or alternatives are welcomed, but unity is expected.

3. Hold leaders responsible for outcomes rather than dictating the execution. As long as the execution fits within the framework of your vision, values and strategy, leaders should have freedom when it comes to the path from here to there. If you can't trust them with executing the tasks, you have the wrong leaders. On the other hand, the expectations need to be quite clear. What's the win? There should be no confusion over the expected outcomes. If you need help, see my most recent book, *Vital Signs: Meaningful Metrics That Keep a Pulse on Your Church's Health*.

4. Determine what the team needs to process together and what you need to monitor together. What you want to avoid is the situation where every decision has to rise to the leadership team. Your agenda should be action-oriented. There should be honest assessment of current numbers and trends. Your meetings should be relatively short and full of engaging conversation where everyone participates. If everyone isn't needed in the conversation, that's an indication you should be processing the decision in an email message or a sidebar conversation instead.

5. Give leaders ownership and accountability. Managers wait for orders and then go make it happen. Leaders grow frustrated over time taking orders. You need both managers and leaders in healthy organizations. Leaders, though, want a voice setting the goals and establishing the strategy. They want real responsibility for building the team and setting direction. At the same time, though, everyone needs clear expectations and accountability.

6. Invest time in the future rather than in what's urgent. What's the strategy for accomplishing your vision? Are you working as a team to move the ministry toward that vision? Analyze your meeting agendas or notes from recent months. Have you invested more time moving forward or putting out fires?

Leaders can get addicted to the urgent (I call that "killing cockroaches" and wrote an entire book on it[28]) because the challenge is right in front of us and there's immediate gratification when we fix it. It takes discipline to stay on the vision.

7. Welcome your team to look outside the organization for opportunities and threats. The culture around us is changing. People are changing. Families and communities are changing. Your "competition" is changing. The senior leadership team, in particular, has to look beyond the four walls of your organization to consider how your systems and strategies need to evolve over time.

Good leaders will leave your organization if they aren't empowered to make decisions or lead. That means you get to decide who stays and who leaves. Are you embracing an approach that empowers leaders to be who God created them to be or is your approach pushing them away?

***

Tony Morgan, a widely followed blogger, is the chief strategic officer and founder of The Unstuck Group and author of several books including *Take the Lid Off Your Church: Six Steps to Building a Healthy Senior Leadership Team*. Find him online at tonymorganlive.com.

12

DISCIPLINE 5: Build a Culture of Continuous Collaboration

Leaders of meetings can ... shape the conversation. Do your homework in advance and figure out who has something to say, and work hard to create interactions.
Either that or just send a memo and cancel the whole thing.

Seth Godin, "Let's Go Around the Room"

If you hang out in the hallways of a church named Cornerstone West LA, you'll watch three leadership meetings occur during the course of a typical week, each with a different configuration of people, goals, agendas and leaders. You'd also see a lot of informal collaboration between the pastors, especially because they share the same physical office. Most important, you'd affirm that the senior leadership team not only effectively leads the church but also shares an incredible sense of community.

Things weren't always that way. Cornerstone West LA is the result of a merger. One entity was a young church plant that was started by two young pastors with a strong conviction that shared leadership was God's design for the local church. The other was a long-standing church that struggled, in part, because it had three different boards that were constantly at odds with each other. When Cornerstone West LA was born, much was murky, but one thing was crystal clear: leadership by plurality of elders was nonnegotiable. They would make plurality leadership work by creating a culture of continuous collaboration.

Today, Cornerstone is led by eight men—five vocational pastor-elders and three lay pastor-elders. They work hard not only to value collaboration but to live it out, even when it requires more time, energy and occasional frustration. The pastor who oversees preaching, Brian Colmery, notes with a smile: "We're intentionally inefficient."

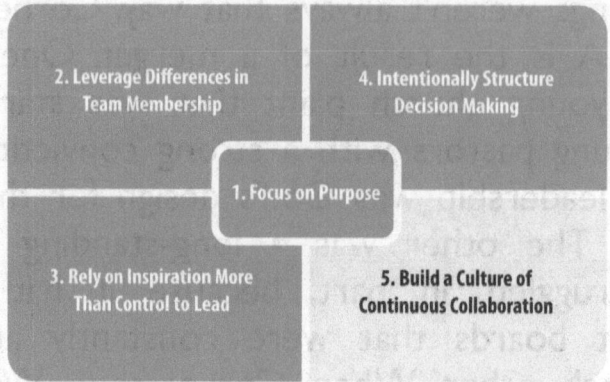

Figure 12.1. Teams that thrive build a culture of continuous collaboration

As part of their commitment to continuous collaboration, the vocational pastors share one office. In its previous life, the office they now inhabit was the senior pastor's waiting room and private office. Now by intention all five of them have a desk in one space, which spurs ongoing collaboration. When they need to work alone, the pastors retreat to one of two study rooms. In other churches team members typically office individually, and then come together for meetings. Cornerstone flipped the model—they office together and go away to work alone.

They also spend a good amount of time together regularly to pray, make key decisions for the church and coordinate ministries and pastoral care. Their meetings are highly structured yet remarkably relational. Pastor Scott Mehl convenes and facilitates two weekly meetings: a prayer meeting and an elders meeting, during which the team updates on a segment of the church's members, makes strategic ministry decisions and reviews key areas of ministry on a rotating basis. Pastor Brian Colmery leads a weekly "Sunday morning" meeting, which involves most of the elders along with the church's media director. Finally, the elders meet roughly once every other month for half-day planning meetings, during which they discuss their philosophy of ministry, review doctrinal matters, plan strategic activities such as setting the annual budget, and so on. These meetings are carefully planned and executed so that all of the team members contribute and provide leadership to the congregation. Most of the elders are in each of these meetings, which provides them with ample opportunity to not only speak into church matters but also spend time caring for one another and building community and trust.

Cornerstone LA's meetings are highly productive, even if a little inefficient. They're full of banter and true community, even though conflict is welcomed and desired. And they're nicely structured and well facilitated, even when most of the team is not organizationally gifted. If that doesn't sound like your meetings, this chapter will hopefully help you cultivate productivity and community inside and outside your team's meetings as you build a culture of continuous collaboration (see fig. 12.1). To that end, this chapter

- discusses the typical problems with meetings
- identifies best meeting practices that made a difference for thriving teams
- explores the relationship between getting work done and building community among team members
- offers simple strategies to effectively structure meetings with sample agendas and meeting practices
- provides advice for collaborating effectively and sharing information with people outside of the leadership team

THE PROBLEMS WITH MEETINGS

Meetings take a lot of blame for what's wrong in organizational life. In fact, Jason Fried and David Heinemeier Hansson, founders of a company named 37signals, claim that "meetings are toxic." They write:

The worst interruptions of all are meetings. Here's why:
- They're usually about words and abstract concepts, not real things.
- They usually convey an abysmally small amount of information per minute.
- They drift off-subject easier than a Chicago cab in heavy snow.

- They require thorough preparation that people rarely do anyway.
- They frequently have agendas so vague nobody is really sure of the goal.
- They often contain at least one moron who inevitably gets his turn to waste everyone's time with nonsense.
- Meetings procreate. One meeting leads to another meeting leads to another.[1]

Of course, some meetings are characterized by those things, but not all. Most important, meetings certainly don't have to be that way. The answer is not to throw out the baby with the bath water by getting rid of meetings. The answer is learning how to do better meetings. And that's what this chapter is all about: meeting in a way that allows your team to effectively and efficiently accomplish your $_5C$ purpose on a weekly, monthly and yearly basis, while growing more equipped as a team.

Simply put, meetings are the forum where leadership teams make the key decisions that define a church's vision, direction and strategy. As noted earlier, the best teams focus their team around making important decisions rather than advising the senior pastor on decision-making tasks or other tasks.

Though modern meeting advice, perhaps most notably *The Modern Meeting Standard* by Al Pittampalli, suggests that meetings should only be used to support already-made decisions, this is impractical for senior leadership teams. It is the decision-making capability of the team that offers some of the key value of doing leadership by team.

So, the key is not to have meetings or not, but how to meet.

THE MEETING PRACTICES OF TOP TEAMS

Meeting advice is ubiquitous; our goal is not to repeat that here. Instead, we just want to report the meeting practices that differentiated thriving teams from underperforming teams in our study. As you read what follows, notice what's missing: the number of meetings or the number of hours spent in meetings. Thus it appears that "too many meetings" or "too much time spent in meetings" aren't the scapegoats for poor team performance. Our data shows that there are many different ways to do effective meetings, but a few key practices make a great difference.

Teams do more than formally "meet" together. They collaborate continuously. On top teams, meeting times don't bound their teamwork. Instead, senior leadership teamwork is ongoing, not just occurring during meetings. In fact, we found that meeting informally for more than one hour per week was a contributing factor to differences between top and mediocre teams. Two key strategies best enable continuous teamwork. The first is to fight like crazy against overwork and busyness. As mentioned in chapter eight on membership, team members' job descriptions should be adjusted to allow for them to spend roughly one-third of their time on leadership team tasks. Doing so carves out schedule space to continue leadership team work outside of meetings. The second strategy is to develop office environments where it is easy for team members to bump into one another, just like Cornerstone West LA. Shared conference rooms and break rooms, stocked fridges, shared administrative support staff members and offices in close proximity to one another encourage team members to frequently bump into one another, creating additional opportunities to continue the team's important work outside of the boardroom. This active engagement carries over in the boardroom as well.

Two-Minute Tip:

Ask each member of your team to rate the strength of their communication with each other member of the team by comparing the strength of each relationship to a cell phone's signal strength. How many "bars" of strength in each relationship? Does low signal quality result in some dropped calls or fuzzy reception? Then, discuss how you can, as a team, increase your signal strength with one another.[2]

Meeting agendas are distributed to all team members, preferably at least one day in advance. Distributing meaningful agendas is so powerful for several reasons. First, it forces the meeting facilitator to spend time planning out the priorities and flow of the meeting beforehand, to an extent that it can be shared with others. Second, it informs all participants of the meeting's purpose and content, which enables each participant to come prepared. Third, it provides structure to the meeting that encourages the team to stay on task and focused throughout the meeting.

Meeting agendas are not solely developed by the lead pastor. Top teams get the whole team involved in setting the agenda. While most senior team meetings were convened and facilitated by either the senior pastor or executive pastor, top teams offered opportunities for other team members to shape the team's agenda. This input can be offered in a few different ways. First, meeting conveners can directly ask team members for items to include on the agenda several days prior to the meeting. Second, conveners can offer a standing invitation to send agenda items. Third, conveners can develop the agenda in such a way that a place to discuss the typical issues are slated on the agenda each week. For instance, each week an agenda may have a slot for "personnel issues," during which each team member is invited to broach discussions or to bring a decision to the group regarding personnel matters. To make this option work, however, conveners must create space for team members to bring up and discuss important issues, rather than overwhelm the meeting time with other agenda items.

Agendas clearly delineate the work for the meeting. For top teams, the agenda is thoughtfully developed enough to truly guide the team's discussion and progress through the meeting, rather than agendas that are so vague and routine that no one pays attention to them (see table 12.1). Such agendas include
- implicit or explicit time periods for each agenda item
- intentionally ordered items, often leaving the most important discussion items in the middle of the agenda
- consistent format so that participants know what you expect in each meeting and can find necessary information quickly
- enough detail to discourage participants from wondering what is coming later in the meeting

In line with our suggestions made in chapter seven, we advise minimizing information-sharing time and maximizing time spent on making key decisions. Agendas provide a forum to capture what has been decided during the meeting, individual expectations for followup and a framework to develop the agenda for the next team meeting.

> **Two-Minute Tip:**
>
> Consider your team's last meeting. Was the agenda distributed prior to the meeting, did it clearly guide the meeting, and who contributed to its development? Endeavor to answer "yes" to the first two questions, and "multiple persons" for the third question, for your next meeting.

Table 12.1. Principles That Guide Meetings of Top Teams

The team sends in recommended discussion points the day before to the meeting facilitator. If they do not apply to everyone, they don't make the cut. If they do, a goal of the conversation is established so it doesn't turn into a brainstorming session.
What we discuss in our team meetings stays in the team meetings, so we can work through things but walk out unified.
We practice vigorous honesty, always using an agenda and assigning who will implement decisions.
We maintain a very regular meeting schedule. However, if we feel bogged down with certain topics, we'll set up a separate offsite meeting to address larger issues. If we ever feel like we can't come to a good solution, we'll push the decision to later. Sometimes we'll push through the conversation or hump we are experiencing till we reach a decision we all are in agreement with. But we never force ourselves to make a decision. We are good at recognizing when fatigue or other issues are preventing us from thinking clearly about a subject.
Agenda items must be approved prior to meetings. We use open dialogue for pointing out ineffective methods. We try to make sure the right people are at the table and meet consistently at the same day/time. We read books and articles to stay on the same philosophical page, take quarterly extended retreats and run to difficult conversations rather than avoiding them.

> The best idea wins, no matter whose idea it is. We review data on a regular basis (if it's worth doing, it can be measured).

TAKING CARE OF COMMUNICATIONS—INFORMATION SHARING

Of course, information needs to be shared among team members—and beyond the team—to ensure the team members are on the same page and can effectively lead the church. Here are some tips to efficiently share information within your team without sacrificing your team's ability to do what's most important:

1. Establish expectations for reading updates and reports sent via email and other media before or after meetings, and then hold team members accountable. Don't take meeting time to remind staff of the deadline to submit reimbursement requests when you gave that same information in an email two days previously.
2. Resist the urge to overshare. Frankly, information overload impairs critical thinking, promotes indecisiveness, encourages binging and purging on information while never retaining or using it, and distracts from what's most important.

> **Two-Minute Tip:**
>
> *Take fifteen minutes in your next meeting to help separate the wheat from the chaff in terms of information shared. First, list all of the informational topics that typically come up in meetings. Second, make two columns on a whiteboard: "must share," and "maybe share" and "definitely don't share." Third, separate all of those informational topics into one of the three columns. Then, eliminate opportunities to discuss the topics in the "don't share" category, incorporate "must share" topics into the team's agenda, and continue to monitor the necessity of the "maybe share" items as they come up from time to time in future meetings.*

3. Establish informational dashboards that put key metrics and data at your team's fingertips. Often teams share so much because they're not sure what's important to share and what is not. Take the time to proactively establish the most important performance indicators, and then commission someone to develop a report that provides that data and eliminates the need to talk all of those topics through during meetings.
4. Allow specific, limited time in the agenda for sharing information members feel is

important. All the dashboards in the world cannot eliminate the need to share stories of life change that simply cannot be shared any other way. So, establish a framework where those stories can be told. The beginnings or ends of meetings are typically good times. However, if done at the beginning of the meeting, ensure those stories don't overtake the entire agenda. Set a time limit. If at the end of a meeting, ensure that time is still left for those stories to be shared and appreciated before people run out to their next commitment.

5. Extend information sharing to others outside of the team. Because leadership teams impact the work of the entire organization, they need to be keenly aware of how to effectively share information with staff and congregants outside of the team. We suggest a mix of routinized email communications and face-to-face meetings.

   a. First, a synopsis, brief or minutes should be sent to all staff, or the segment of staff who needs the information, right after the meeting. These briefs contain the most important decisions made, information shared and other basic need-to-know information. Too often, meeting minutes are so bland that no one reads them. One alternative is to begin the document with a series of action points: Jose is doing this, Fran and Maria that, and Felipe something else. This becomes a checklist that can be used when you meet next.

Here, the challenge is to make the minutes juicy enough that people actually read them right as they come out, and to hold staff accountable for the information in them. To ease this process, you might develop a template form that an administrative staff member fills out during the meeting and then sends out to staff within one hour of the meeting's conclusion. Your team can decide on what goes on the template and then out to staff after each meeting. In any case, we suggest that each point made includes the following information: what was decided, why, who it affects and when it goes into effect.

b. Second, even the juiciest printed information cannot replace face-to-face communication. Thus it is important for leadership teams to make themselves available not only to share with staff (and volunteers, maybe) what's on the horizon but also to receive feedback on what's working and what's not. Teams have developed several different ways to do this. One church hosts brown-bag lunch meetings every couple of weeks where the leadership team comes and just talks with the staff about new things on the horizon and asks for feedback. Another church hosts a once-a-month all pastors meeting (for smaller churches, this might be an all-leader meeting), during which all the pastors and leaders share information, connect relationally with one another and pray and worship together. Other churches do something similar, but add in staff recognition time, leadership development lesson or a vision snippet from the lead pastor or another staff member or outside speaker. Still, others ask leadership team members to individually share important information with their teams as part of their regular department or area meetings.

c. Third, and most important, we urge you to hold people accountable for knowing and acting on the information available to them. If you want people to read their email (or Facebook posts, or discussion board, or whatever), require them to do so; don't compensate for their irresponsibility by covering the information in another way and thereby reinforcing their bad behavior.

MAKING THE MOST OF YOUR MEETINGS?

The above tips certainly focus on getting the work done. What about relationships, you might ask? Our team can't solely be about the task all the time; we need to be able to relate to one another, cultivate relationships and build trust.

Our focus is very intentional. As we explained earlier in the book, trust is built by focusing on the task, not by focusing on building trust.

However, most teams engage some kind of team building, even if they don't benefit from it. If your experience is like many others, you find team-building exercises to detract from the team's real work. Thus they appear to be a waste of time. Often they are. But they don't have to be.

If you do team-building retreats or meetings, we offer a few suggestions to make the most of them. They should look different depending on the life stage and operating dynamics of your team.

When you launch a new team. Just because the senior team is composed of a great group of individuals, there's no guarantee they'll be able to work well as a team. Therefore, a thoughtful onboarding process and team launch can help a team to get off to a good start. To conduct a useful team launch, we suggest several steps (these steps also could guide a great re-launch of an ongoing team).

First, focus on determining or coming to a shared understanding of the team's purpose. Before you can do anything else, the team needs to know why it exists and how its work is differentiated from others at the church.

Second—and only once the team's purpose is clear—cultivate discussion about what each team member uniquely brings to the table to contribute to accomplishing the team's purpose. Here you might discuss previous experiences each member has had that relate to the team's purpose. Or, you might discuss each person's wiring—strengths, personality, spiritual gifts or talents—that might be useful for the team. Useful instruments to help shape these kinds of discussions include the Myers-Briggs Type Indicator (MBTI), the Strengths-Finder, the Strengthscope, a spiritual gifts assessment or even the Thomas-Kilmann Conflict Mode Instrument.

These instruments can help to see the positive dispositions and strengths each person brings to the task, as well as some areas the team needs to consider when working together.

One caveat: avoid the temptation to use these assessments to prescribe certain roles for each member. These assessments don't so much tell someone *what* to do. Instead, they should shape *how* one goes about their work. Just because someone has the gift of encouragement doesn't mean he or she needs to be the "official staff encourager." Nor does it mean that a person without the gift of encouragement should never encourage anyone. Moreover, a person with the strength of "woo" need not be deemed the presenter of all major change announcements.

Instead, these instruments are most useful (not to mention appropriately used) when they are used to help a team to recognize core strengths that each person tends to contribute or tendencies for how each person thinks and works. In addition, these instruments help people identify how to best accomplish their tasks. For all these reasons, conducting sessions with skilled facilitators can really help a team make sense of assessment results and draw out implications for how the team members can best work with each other.

There's nothing wrong with using fun activities to spur on these conversations; it's just vital that important conversations happen rather than fun activities.

Third, discuss what behaviors the team will require to do its best work. Thriving teams establish particular ways of interacting so that members will work together to fulfill the team's purpose and accomplish the performance goals. There's no right formula for success here; what matters most is that team members agree on a way to go about their work, both individually and collectively, as it pertains to their work on the team.

Group norms, or ground rules, establish acceptable and unacceptable behavior in the team. Great teams don't assume everyone's on the same page regarding what's appropriate and what's not; they take the time to discuss and develop a set of ground rules. For instance, the

Ark Church in Texas has developed a list of rules (see table 12.2) for dealing with conflict in leadership team meetings. These ground rules, by the way, have served as a model for other teams in the church.

Table 12.2. The Ark Church's Ground Rules for Conflict in Leadership Team Meetings

Acceptable	Unacceptable
Calling a time out if needed	Questioning/attacking personal character/integrity
Calling a "foul"	"Labeling"—generalizations/stereotyping
Completing the meeting (saying what needs to be said)	Piling on and tagging on
Responding, not reacting	Meeting after the meeting
Giving and receiving grace	Making private issues public
Fully listening	Hitting below the belt
Validating the person/issue (listening with your heart)	Cursing what you bless in the person
Believing the best in the person	Sugarcoating
Initiating items for feedback/discussion in your ministry area (inviting feedback)	Surprising someone publically with an item/questions/observation
Walking in sensitivity/awareness of each other	Wearing your heart on your sleeve
Speaking the truth	

Two-Minute Tip:

To quickly establish norms, ask your team: What excites you when you're working in a group

> setting, and what frustrates you? Next, come to consensus on the behaviors you agree to encourage and those you want to avoid. Then you'll have a list of ground rules for your team's work together.

Fourth, discuss each person's unique roles on the team. While norms dictate behavior for everyone in a group, roles establish expectations for individuals. It is important for each person to know what others are responsible for, so they can assist in holding one another accountable.

A caution is in order, though. Groups often make one of two common mistakes in dealing well with group roles. In the name of doing everything together, some groups resist establishing individual roles and do everything together. This mistake causes seemingly endless conversations about who is responsible for what, and precludes the group from capitalizing on the distinctive skills and expertise of members of the team. The other problem is overemphasizing roles, which leads to a problematic level of dividing-and-conquering the work. One person leads, one person provides spiritual counsel, another person does all the exegesis, only one person reviews the budget, and each person makes the final decision over his or her areas of individual responsibility.

When this is the case, there's no reason to even try to become a team. This creates a "goldilocks problem," as too little or too much clarity and distinction in roles is problematic. What is needed, instead, is just the right amount. Indeed, this common error is the reason many folks despise teams. Because they haven't approached their tasks in a way that benefits from teamwork, they find it would just be easier to do it apart from one another. In those cases, they're right.

Fifth, enjoy each other's company. If you focus this much on how you'll approach the team's work, your team will quickly realize that you might as well to get to know each other, because you're going to be doing a lot of significant work together. As that happens, allow relationships to form naturally. The key here is "to focus on the work and let the personal relationships in the team evolve as they will."[3] However, meeting in a place that affords fun opportunities, good food and comfortable accommodations creates a space for personal conversations to take place and relationships to begin to form.

Two-Minute Tip:

Over a meal or coffee, ask each member of your team to share a challenge they endured as a child or teenager. Here, you'll see unique facets of one another's backgrounds, as well as the inner strength and skill sets team members use to overcome adversity.[4]

A leadership team will inevitably struggle without the key building blocks of a team: a sense of purpose and direction, an understanding of the unique skill sets and roles of the team members and a constructive set of norms that guide the team's work. Thus focus the team launch on doing the team's core work, because "coaching the team as it does its work behind the closed doors of the conference room is far more likely to generate long-term improvements in teamwork than [team exercises like] climbing a mountain, crossing a desert, sailing boats, or driving race cars."[5]

At a natural breaking or refocusing time. Any team benefits from time away from the daily grind to look back on its work, recalibrate and prepare for the upcoming season. In essence, teams periodically need to take a "Sabbath" where they can rest, look back at what they've accomplished, look up to hear from God for a new sense of direction and then to look forward and plan out the coming time. Some teams do this monthly, others do it quarterly, others do it annually. Some may even do it at all of those intervals. Regardless the interval, four key tasks are essential for effective "Sabbath" team retreats:

1. Rest. The essential point of the Sabbath is to rest, to take a break from the daily, weekly grind. Effective retreats offer team members a time to rest, play and rejuvenate.

2. Look back. Great teams account for the work that has been accomplished in the previous season. They celebrate their wins and conduct autopsies on their failures. They investigate why they're wining or why they're losing. And they ask questions such as:
   - Where did we win?
   - Where did we lose?
   - Why did we win/lose?
   - What's working?
   - What's not working?
3. Look up. Great teams invest time in sitting before God, resting in his presence and asking for his direction. They carve out time for personal and corporate prayer and allow God to speak to them individually and as a team. Some teams read through books together.
4. Look forward. Great teams plan out the work ahead. They remind themselves of their team's core purpose and performance tasks, and then scope out key elements of the coming season. For many churches, that means establishing sermon series, identifying strategic ministry and operational priorities for the next year or taking an extended time to review and make crucial ministry decisions (such as pursuing a multisite

strategy or a building campaign or revamping a leadership development pipeline). In addition, they explore not only what they'll be doing but how they go about their work. They review their team norms and individual roles, holding members accountable for subpar performance and making adjustments to continually pursue outstanding teamwork. Some teams read books or bring in speakers or consultants to sharpen their focus or skills, while others take assessments that enable the team to learn to work better together.

Two-Minute Tip:

Imagine every member of your team has agreed to plant a church elsewhere. Your leadership team will be handing the baton to an entirely new team. With that in mind, ask each member of your team to write and share a short transition speech for the team. What would you hope others would say about your team and about the way you lead your church? After sharing your thoughts, discuss what it will take for your team to become the team envisioned in that speech.[6]

WE'VE TRIED ALL THIS, BUT IT DOESN'T WORK

Maybe you've tried until you're blue in the face to improve your team meetings, to build a culture of continuous collaboration, but your meetings still struggle. We feel your pain. In many cases, the missing ingredient is accountability. Indeed, team norms and roles will only be consistently followed if there is some sort of accountability. If your team has established ground rules but one team member consistently violates them without any repercussion, that person—and everyone else on the team—is learning that behavior is actually acceptable. And more of that violation, as well as other variations, will occur as those behaviors have been positively reinforced by silence.

Before you get too frustrated with your team's formal leader, recognize that, in true teams, all members of the team—not just the formal leader—hold the other members accountable. They say, "Hey, that's not how we do things here," rather than letting things go until the formal leader finally says something. What do you need to speak out against? How could you help your teammates recognize what's hindering your team from doing its best work? Now, go say something. You just might provide the critique and spark your team needs to develop the discipline it needs to thrive together.

REFLECTION AND DISCUSSION QUESTIONS

1. How often do the members of your team bump into one another during the week? What could you do to increase that likelihood?
2. Does your team's default position (think offices) privilege working alone or collaboratively?
3. Do your team's getaways focus more on relationship or work? How could you shift these meetings to a better balance?
4. What could you do to improve your team's weekly meetings?
5. Plan your team's next retreat. As a team, develop the agenda for it, based upon the guidelines offered in this chapter.
6. If "iron sharpens iron, and one man sharpens another" (Prov 27:17), how you could sharpen your teammates with regard to how you relate to one another in meetings?

EXPERT COMMENTARY: MAKING MALE-FEMALE DYNAMICS WORK AT THE SENIOR LEADERSHIP LEVEL
Jenni Catron

If collaboration is critical for successful leadership teams, how do you navigate coed work teams? How do men and women effectively work together especially with the level of engagement required for senior leadership teams to flourish?

Many churches wrestle with how to effectively engage men and women in ministry. Our fears of impropriety drive us to creating cultures where we avoid and alienate one another rather than seek to understand what healthy, God-honoring relationships can look like.

What are healthy practices that retain appropriate boundaries but allow for strong relationships to be established that support great team work? There are three things we need to be committed to as a leadership team.

1. Mutual respect. Respect is earned, and it's earned over time. As teams, we must be committed to one another and committed to allowing the strengths of one another to shine. There is no room for comparison or competition. We have to be dedicated to bringing out the best of each person and letting their gifts flourish on the team. Oftentimes men and women in the workplace misunderstand one another because they don't consider the other person's viewpoint or perspective. We can easily jump to conclusions rather than take the time to understand what the other person is thinking, feeling or perceiving. Respect is earned by bringing our best to the team every day, admitting our mistakes or misjudgments and celebrating each other's success.

2. *Mutual honor.* Men and women can be very apprehensive of working together. If you're a leader with even a smidge of a moral compass you (wisely) wrestle with the tension of appropriate interaction with the opposite sex. While healthy boundaries are essential, the problem with not addressing apprehension is that it often results in avoidance, which is dishonoring to the individual and ultimately to God. When we're apprehensive of one another we limit healthy, God-honoring community that is essential for great teams. If you find yourself apprehensive of the opposite sex, you may need to evaluate where those feelings are coming from. Are there healthy boundaries that you need to put in place to keep yourself accountable? What can you do to have a healthy view of the opposite sex? Romans 12:10: "Be devoted to one another in love. Honor one another above yourselves" (NIV).

3. *Mutual understanding.* Just as we seek to understand our personality types, our strengths and our spiritual gifts, we must seek to understand and value what each gender brings

to a team. God designed male and female with different strengths and sensitivities. When both genders are at the table and actively engaged in leadership, we most accurately reflect the staff and congregations that we lead. In reference to 1 Corinthians 12:14-31, John C. Maxwell writes this comment in the *Maxwell Leadership Bible:* "Leaders must build a team spirit that celebrates diversity. Teams must share a common goal, but not the same gifts. Teams mature when the leader insists on diversity and celebrates what everyone does together."

Because men and women typically think and feel from different perspectives, the chasm between our understandings of one another can feel very vast and insurmountable sometimes. But the truth is that it comes down to building relationships based upon mutual respect, honor and understanding.

***

Jenni Catron is shared resources leader and a member of the executive team at Menlo Park Presbyterian Church and author of *Clout: Discover and Unleash Your God-Given Influence.* Find her online at jennicatron.com.

PART FIVE

PART FIVE WHAT'S YOUR BEST NEXT STEP?

13

Six Ways to Avoid Sabotaging Your Team

We are what we repeatedly do. Excellence, then, is not an act, but a habit.

Aristotle

Folks often preach the value of teams and try to instill teams in their churches, all the while cheerleading and propagating organizational cultural dynamics that squelch any possibility for those teams to thrive. Though your strategy might desire to shift toward team leadership, you need to be aware of cultural values and practices that will support or destroy your efforts to lead by team. Indeed, consultant Sam Chand argues that "culture—not vision or strategy—is the most powerful factor in any organization."[1]

Just as planes in flight are eased by tailwinds and slowed by headwinds, so is your team unavoidably impacted by your church's culture. Some elements of your church's culture encourage your leadership team to thrive, while other facets threaten to sabotage your efforts to act more like a team and experience the benefits that come with a team approach.

In this chapter, we discuss six headwinds that can radically affect your ability to succeed as a leadership team. If you want to improve your leadership team, don't ignore these cultures that will kill your leadership team's ability to thrive.

> **Two-Minute Tip:**
>
> *Take fifteen minutes in your next team meeting to do a mini force field analysis.[2] In this exercise, first discuss a change you wish to make to thrive as a leadership team. Then, identify the cultural and practical driving forces (tailwinds) that encourage that change. Likewise, identify the restraining forces (headwinds) acting against that proposed change. Finally, develop strategies to increase the tailwinds and minimize the headwinds. Pick two or three of the most accessible strategies, and take action on them.*

1. A CULTURE THAT EMBRACES THE STATUS QUO

Change is scary. That's why we often prefer business as usual. Or we don't see any need to do anything different. So we say, "let's just keep doing things we've been doing." Of course, that does not require a team to do the hard work it takes to truly provide leadership.

One of the most intriguing findings of our study was that leadership teams that are facing organizational challenges related to growth tend to perform at higher levels. At first glance, that makes sense: better teams lead growing churches, and growing churches face growing pains. However, in the context of the remainder of our findings, we don't see it that way. Here's what we think it tells us: teams are propelled forward by performance challenges.[3] Those challenges—in particular, those that come from congregational growth—draw teams together and force them to learn how to perform at a higher level, and they provide quality leadership to their congregation as it bursts its seams. Just as stretching job assignments push people to grow to meet the demands of the position, so do challenges spur teams to become better. What's forcing your team to get better?

> Teams are propelled forward by performance challenges.

2. A CULTURE THAT ADOPTS THE LATEST FAD ADVICE THEN

GOES BACK TO NORMAL OPERATIONS

Acclaimed Harvard researcher Chris Argyris has famously noted the difference between people's espoused theories (what they preach) and their theories in use (what they actually do).[4] Insightfully, he recognized that what people say they do, or better what they say they *should* do, is often different than what they *actually* do. There is, however, an antidote to simply acting without intention or out of alignment with what you say you should do, especially during times of stress and pressure. Inviting and cultivating feedback about how your team works as a team helps narrow the gap between your espoused and enacted theories. This is good reason to make reviewing your team's work together a priority alongside your regular quarterly or annual evaluation and planning cycles.

Two-Minute Tip:

Set a calendar reminder twice a year to assess your team's performance against the "five disciplines of teams that thrive" model. (It's summarized in chapter fourteen.)

However you choose to do it, continually compare what you preach about teams with what you actually do in your team. Doing so will prevent the learnings from this book from simply residing in your espoused theories and instead enable them to sink deeply into your team's collective practices and culture.

3. A CULTURE OF SPONTANEITY THAT LIMITS PLANNING AND STRUCTURE

No matter how much we talk about wanting teams to thrive in our churches, they won't if teams don't have the organizational environment that offers fertile soil for teams to thrive in. In particular, teams thrive in organizational contexts that privilege thoughtful, deliberative action and provide structures that allow for planning. Fertile organizational soil typically exists when:

1. Leaders set crystal-clear mission, goals and priorities that guide team efforts and establish clear operating principles.
2. Organizational structures and systems foster effective group decision making.
3. Teams enjoy ample, planned time to stay connected and work jointly on problems.
4. Teams possess all the information they need to solve problems and make decisions.[5]

These structures offer the support a leadership team—and all teams in an organization—needs to be able to truly lead the church. Without them, teams spin their wheels and don't make progress. Before your team will be successful, you may need to engage some cultural change to enable the team to thrive.

At one less-than-exemplary church where we did interviews, the senior team's culture fought hard against any sort of planning. One pastor stated, we are more comfortable "fighting fires than building safe houses." As such, the team constantly deferred to the lead pastor rather than seek God together and work together to develop direction and strategy for the church.

Church cultures that prefer to fight fires rather than do the proactive work to avoid and protect against those fires are infertile ground for thriving teams. In such cases, addressing cultural challenges might be the first step in enabling a team to truly lead the church.

4. A CULTURE THAT REINFORCES THE ULTIMATE AUTHORITY OF THE LEAD PASTOR

In some churches, the senior leader's authority is spiritualized, making it seem uncontestable. When a church's culture emphasizes that no authority will be shared, a leadership team will never really lead the church. This dynamic plays out in three primary ways.

First, in some churches, church leaders assert that the lead pastor "hears from God" more often and more clearly than anybody else, giving de facto power to veto or otherwise trump any decision or direction. Second, some lead pastors populate their executive teams with persons much less talented, skilled and experienced, causing team members to frequently feel that their contributions could never be on par with the senior leader. Third, other lead pastors sideline their leadership teams by bringing only certain matters, but certainly not the most important matters, before their team, forcing discussion and decision making on the most important matters to side conversations with one or two selected staff, marginalizing the other members of the team and the influence of the team as a unit.

While spiritual authority certainly exists within the church, pastors, like any other organizational chief executive, often do have the ultimate say in determining direction. Not every decision can be made as a group, so senior or lead pastors seeking to employ leadership teams need to think seriously (and honestly) about the ways their church's positioning of pastoral authority affects their initiatives to build teams.

Chris Stephens at Faith Promise Church discussed how he balances his authority with the promotion of a team. He said, "The buck stops at my desk. I get it. We all also understand that at the end of the day, the best thing that I can do for Faith Promise is stay on my face [in prayer], communicate, motivate and cast vision, so I surround myself with people who do everything else. We are better than me. The more people that have input in the decision, the more buy in they have."

Though Chris, as the lead pastor, possesses the ultimate authority to direct the church, he realizes that the team leads better than he does, so he restricts himself so that the team truly leads the church.

5. A CULTURE THAT UNDERMINES THE LEADERSHIP TEAM'S IMPORTANT CONTRIBUTION

Even though many churches have a leadership team that leads the church on paper, it's not uncommon for many churches to truly be led by the benevolent dictator lead pastor, or the lead pastor's kitchen cabinet—a few confidants who run the show.

When this happens, the leadership team is not given the most important work to do, time is not allocated for the team to do its work, diversity is often squashed, and the team is reduced to mere information exchange. Talented leaders move on, because they want to be keenly involved in developing what's next for the church. And the church suffers from a lack of quality leadership.

6. A CULTURE THAT IGNORES BIBLICAL ACCOUNTABILITY

"Faithful are the wounds of a friend; profuse are the kisses of an enemy" (Prov 27:6). Feedback is the breakfast of champions, and *mutual accountability* is the not-so-secret success ingredient of exceptional teams. But too often, for a variety of reasons, team members avoid lovingly wounding a teammate, neglect offering feedback and refuse to hold one another accountable for their contributions to the team. That behavior is often learned in the larger church culture, where biblical accountability and confrontation is not pursued.

If your church avoids confrontation and biblical accountability, chances are that your team will never gel or perform at its peak. Your team as a whole needs feedback on its collective performance, and individual team members need feedback about what they contribute to the team. Your team needs faithful friends who will tell the truth, even when it stings. Without confronting the (sometimes painful) truth, your team doesn't have the insight to improve nor the fuel to do its job of effectively leading your church.

DON'T IGNORE CULTURE

Leadership teams, like all teams, can only grow and thrive in rich cultural soil. Before you take internal steps to grow your team, perhaps the best thing you could do is add some nutrients to your church's soil—its organizational culture. Embrace change, cement new ways of working deep in your team's practice, remain open to planning and structure, seek out the wisdom of the team, let the leadership team lead and cultivate biblical accountability. You'll give your team what it needs to thrive!

IF YOU NEED TO CHANGE YOUR TEAM'S COURSE

Sometimes teams need a significant reboot. Of course, change is hard, but John Kotter's eight steps to make organizational change offer great guidance.[6] Below we offer his tips, along with some commentary on how we helped one church leadership team address the resistance to change they experienced. Teams that change:

1. *Establish a sense of urgency.* When a feeling that "we're doing fine" permeates the team, someone, usually the lead pastor, has to be willing to say, "where we are is not where we are going to stay—we must press forward," and set performance standards at

a level that "business as usual" will no longer work.
2. *Create a guiding coalition for change.* Some team members, as well as other members of the staff or board, will resist change. In such a case, look around for other team members who share a sense of urgency to move forward and maximize the vision of the church. Rely on those who are willing to do whatever to takes to help the team get out of its rut and move forward. It might be time to limit the team's membership to that group for a time (you might reference the guidelines in chapter eight on reducing the team's membership).
3. *Develop a compelling vision and strategy.* Casting a vision for what the church could be like with a thriving team, as well as what it could be like to be a part of a thriving team, is vital. Many pastors love to live in the world of vision-casting; cast a vision for your church and for your team that only a thriving team can realize, and then work on developing a strategy (with the leadership team) that can bring that vision into reality.
4. *Communicate the changed vision over and over.* When vision is not kept in front of people, all sorts of other concerns become the

most important goals to accomplish, such as personal comfort, the number of meetings required and so on. But when the vision is compelling, people will do what it takes to accomplish it. Keep the vision fresh and out front. Mark Johnston of the Journey Church does this by reviewing the church's strategic statements (vision, strategy, targets and important metrics) at every quarterly team meeting. The Journey's team members not only can't forget the vision, but are so compelled by it they offer their best to accomplish it.

5. *Don't let obstacles block the new vision.* Too often the "can we?" gets in the way of the "we should." Tackle this head on. Discuss as a team (or as a guiding coalition) all the things that will get in the way of accomplishing the vision. Things like meeting structures, governance models, sacred cows, ways of "always" doing things and personnel shortages will likely come up. One by one, take action on those items, doing whatever it takes to declutter your team's efforts so it can pursue its vision of providing fantastic leadership to your church.

6. *Generate short-term wins.* Right away, define and pick some low-hanging fruit. Don't wait to identify all the issues before you start

taking action. Figure out one or two things you can do right away, and do them. Kill a meeting that's a waste of time (see chap. 12 on meetings). Knock off a routine report that no one does anything with. Cancel the program that's limping along. Then, when your team makes progress, celebrate it. Too many teams are so focused on what's ahead that they don't celebrate what's already been done. Don't succumb to that temptation.

7. *Consolidate gains and produce more change.* Use the energy gained from short-term wins to fan the flames of change. Avoid the tendency to bask in what's been done already and become complacent. Celebrate it, then introduce more and harder changes, bring in the horsepower needed to make the change stick, give stuff away to other individuals that the leadership team doesn't need to do, and clarify who's responsible for what. Keep up the momentum of change.

8. *Anchor new practices in your team's culture.* As your team makes changes and develops new principles for how it works together to lead your church, capture them and anchor them deep in your team's life. Develop new systems that make it easy for

your team to practice the disciplines that will make it great. Talk often about them with your team and with other. Share the new developments with other people, both inside and outside your church, so that they can hold you accountable to them.

Rebooting your team is hard work, but there is no better time to get started than today. As the old proverb goes, "the best time to plant a tree was twenty years ago. The second best time is now." Plant a tree of change for your team today.

REFLECTION AND DISCUSSION QUESTIONS

1. What elements of your church's culture most support your efforts for your team to provide true, effective leadership?
2. What elements of your church's culture most hinder your team from providing true, effective leadership?
3. How can you, today, add fertilizer to your church's cultural soil?
4. Who (inside or outside your team) needs you to be a faithful friend (Prov 27:6) today?

EXPERT COMMENTARY: CREATING AN INSPIRING TEAM CULTURE
Sam Chand

Some people have a "sixth sense" to pick up the unspoken and often invisible mood of a person or a group. That's a rare and valuable gift, but it doesn't take unusual perception to recognize a team has a culture problem. All you have to do is observe. The body language, facial expressions, tone and conversation are diagnostic tools. Too often, senior leaders don't recognize the health (or lack of health) of their teams because the problem has become "normal." For the leader and those who are struggling to fit into the twisted team dynamics, it's just one more day in paradise!

Team leaders have the privilege and responsibility to move their people toward inspiration, effectiveness and fulfillment. When they look around at the people on their teams, they may think it's impossible to make it work, but it is, indeed, possible. They need to implement the seven keys of CULTURE:

- *Control.* Team members function most effectively when the leader provides clear direction and then delegates control with responsibility. Clear control clarifies each person's role and eliminates turf wars.
- *Understanding.* The leader's primary job is to paint a picture of the future so that each person understands the big picture and his or

her part in seeing it take shape. In a healthy culture, no one is offended when someone asks why.

• *Leadership*. Healthy teams are pipelines of leadership development. Identifying, recruiting and training gifted leaders isn't an add-on activity; it's central to a healthy team.

• *Trust*. Trust is the glue of any relationship. On a team, trust grows in an environment that's HOT: honest, open and transparent.

• *Unafraid*. Many leaders are driven by hidden fears. Great leaders are secure enough to welcome dissenting opinions, as long as they are offered in good will with an eye toward a solution.

• *Responsive*. Great leaders have their eyes and ears open to notice what's going on in the team, the church and the community. When they notice opportunities and threats, they craft a plan to meet the needs.

• *Execution*. Great plans are worthless if the leader doesn't kick the team in gear to accomplish them. When plans aren't implemented, team members begin to believe what they do doesn't really matter.

To a large extent, teams are a reflection of their leaders. Poor leaders create stagnant, discouraging and toxic teams. Change is possible—and change is necessary—but change requires wisdom, vision, patience and compassion. Instead of sabotaging your team, create an inspiring culture.

***

Sam Chand, a leadership consultant, is author of several books, including *Cracking Your Church's Culture Code*. You can find Sam online at samchand.com.

14

Catalyze Your Team's Growth

I used to lead our church.... Now I lead our team and they lead our church. I'm loving it.

Mark Johnston, lead pastor of The Journey Church, Newark, Delaware

Mark Johnston Pastors one of the churches we visited for this book. He's convinced that his directional team's role is to figure out what's in the way of Jesus growing his church—and then get it out of the way. "God will never be saying, 'I really want my church to grow, but I'm not just quite sure how to do it,'" Mark said. "If anything is ever in the way of our church growing, it will always be us."

After eight years of leading his church as an entrepreneurial, driving pastor, Mark realized that his approach to leading the church had to get out of the way. He had to become more of a vision-caster and team-builder. Now he's leading a great team that's leading a "real church for real people" that's making a big difference across Delaware. Figuring out what was in the way of what God wants to do was a key step in that process.

WHAT'S IN THE WAY AT YOUR CHURCH?

As we wrap up this book, we want to encourage you to think through what's in the way, preventing your leadership team from thriving, and then to take a step, or a series of steps, to position your leadership team to truly and effectively lead your church. We believe you *can* be a team that thrives. This final chapter aims to help you determine what you can do to catalyze your team's growth.

Across this book, we've given reasons why leadership teams more than make sense for effective organizational leadership. We've affirmed how the team approach follows in line with key biblical principles. We've showed you what to do and how to do it to help your team thrive together.

All along we've said that it's up to you to actually shift leadership responsibility (or a large portion thereof) to your leadership team. Only you and the other members of your church's leadership team can take the needed steps for your team to go to the next level.

1. Make sure your team is really leading. Start by discussing the question we framed in chapter five: Does your team truly lead?

If you have a leadership team that doesn't lead, today is the day to begin allowing the team to lead.

If you are not yet utilizing a leadership team, we hope we've convinced you to do leadership as a team. To get started on a good footing, carefully think through who you might invite to be a part of the leadership team. Then, take the time to do an appropriate team kickoff by following our instructions under "When You Launch a New Team" in chapter twelve.

2. Ensure that your team is effective. If your team is truly leading, the next step is to ensure that your team is providing *effective* leadership. The metric we've recommended is the *disciplines of teams that thrive* framework of chapters seven through twelve (see fig. 14.1).

We encouraged you to develop five disciplines and showed you how. They are the practices, done over and over, that produce high-performance teamwork.

- *Discipline 1: Focus on purpose, the invisible leader of your team.* Great leadership teams realize that purpose drives every decision and every action of the team. Purpose is, in essence, the invisible leader of the team. As you clearly articulate your team's $_5$C purpose, remember that the best teams make critical, churchwide decisions regularly and continually.
- *Discipline 2: Leverage differences in team membership.* Thriving teams know that

differences make a difference. That is, they intentionally pursue diversity in personality, background and perspective as they strategically identify who should be on the team. Once together, those diverse members focus on what's best for the church while making their work on the leadership team a priority.

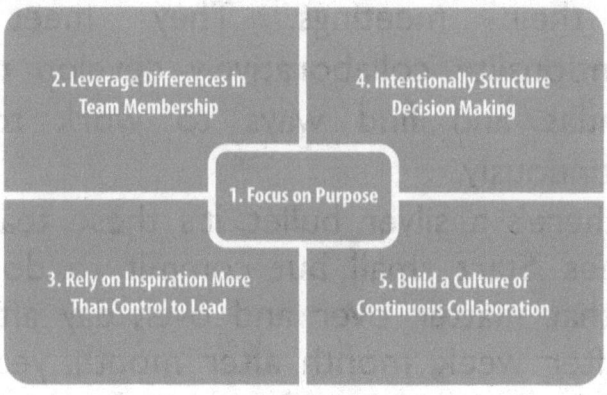

Figure 14.1. The five disciplines of teams that thrive

- *Discipline 3: Rely on inspiration more than control to lead.* Leaders of outstanding teams rely more on relationship-based inspirational leadership than role-based directive leadership. They build trust, cultivate positive working relationships and share leadership functions with others as they pursue the team's meaningful purpose.
- *Discipline 4: Intentionally structure your decision-making process.* When it comes to making decisions, thriving leadership teams

take advantage of divine inspiration and collaborative interaction. Specifically, they utilize a careful, step-by-step process that cultivates necessary conflict as they simultaneously seek God for his perspective and leading.
- *Discipline 5: Build a culture of continuous collaboration.* Effective leaders make the most of their meetings. They meet with intentionality, collaboratively develop meeting agendas and find ways to work together continuously.

If there's a silver bullet, it's these teamwork disciplines. Start small but commit to doing the things that matter, over and over, day after day, week after week, month after month, year after year. None of us can fix everything at once. Hopefully you've been discussing the questions at the end of each chapter with your team, doing some of the two-minute tips in your team meetings and putting into practice the many step-by-step processes we've laid out in this book. From here on out, each time you evaluate your team, identify two or three action steps and reference the appropriate chapter in the book that addresses how you might move forward to help your team thrive.

3. Keep evaluating. Continually monitor and cheer your team's progress. Regular evaluations will help you understand what's making a

difference for good or bad. The following are several ways to do that:
- Assess your team using a concise "Teams That Thrive Assessment" that synthesizes the numerous assessment elements throughout this book and is available online at teamsthatthrivebook.com. It's formatted so that you can easily print off a copy for each of your team members and perhaps for some staff, elders or volunteers who have a unique vantage point into the work of your team. Start by having each of your team members take the assessment and then come together and discuss each person's responses.
- Once every few months, ask one of your team members to step back from the action, take the perspective of an outside evaluator and simply observe a team meeting.
- Invite a trusted staff member, elder or outside pastor (hopefully one with a knack for building teams) to evaluate one of your team's meetings, noting strengths and areas for improvement.
- Send out an anonymous questionnaire to a group of staff or a group of volunteers (people who have a key stake in the leadership team's work) to comment on the quality of leadership being provided at the church. While you likely will not agree with

every sentiment, it might give you a good idea of how people perceive your team's effectiveness.
- Develop a regular rhythm for team self-assessment. Include in your annual or biannual retreat or offsite meeting an hour to talk about what's working or not on your team (feel free to use the "Teams That Thrive Assessment"). Also, review the suggested tips for a "Sabbath" team retreat in chapter twelve.

Whatever you do, find a way to step back from the action and ask, What is going on here? Harvard professor Ronald Heifetz refers to this skill as getting off the dance floor and onto the balcony, where you can see more broadly what is being accomplished by the team's work, the patterns of interactions among the team members, and the quality of the team's work together. Getting away from the action will enable you to pinpoint where your team needs the most immediate work.[1]

4. Invest in your team's development. Teams need coaching just like individuals do. The best pastors and the best leaders can point to mentors and coaches that have helped them to be the best they can be. So it is with teams. The best teams avail themselves of coaching and mentoring.

Interestingly, every top team we visited was genuinely surprised when we told them they were identified as a top team. When we asked them what has made them so successful, every one of them said something to the effect of, "I don't know, I just know that we're working hard to become a great team." It showed. The best teams are voracious learners. They don't rest on their laurels; they continue to push forward to become even better.

We urge you to follow their example. Keep learning and growing as a team. Avail yourselves of in-person or virtual team coaching. Maybe there's a person in your church who knows teams; give him or her a call for some help. Invest one or two hours during one of your retreats or off-sites in making your team better: identify a team weakness and bring in a qualified trainer, facilitator or consultant to develop your team's capacity. Utilize the many resources online to improve your team.

As a starting point, this book's accompanying website (teamsthatthrivebook.com) hosts numerous free articles and resources for yourteam to use, from sample meeting agendas to lists of team norms and ground rules to discussion procedures and more. You can also contact us through that website for additional consultation.

THE GREAT POTENTIAL OF YOUR TEAM

We're sure you're leading your church because you want to be a part of God's work of redeeming the world to himself (2 Cor 5). You want to change the world. Your team can be the group that actually does it, starting with your church. As Margaret Mead famously quipped, "Never doubt that a small group of thoughtful, committed citizens can change the world; indeed, it's the only thing that ever has."

Your leadership team is the primary determinant of the health, effectiveness and impact of your church. It affects every element of your church—your staff, your volunteers, your congregation, your weekend experience, your discipleship, your community, your financial position, your future, everything.

Ultimately, the call of the church is to, as Jesus said: "make disciples of all nations, baptizing them in the name of the Father and of the Son and of the Holy Spirit, teaching them to observe all that I have commanded you" (Mt 28:19-20). Your leadership team, to a large extent, gets to be a part of determining how your church goes about making disciples of all nations.

We close with three prayers for you.

First, we pray you'll take what you've learned here and apply it. As you do, we believe your team will develop the disciplines that will, as Paul wrote in Ephesians 4:12-13, "equip the saints for the work of ministry, for building up the body of Christ, until we all attain to the unity of the faith and of the knowledge of the Son of God, to mature manhood, to the measure of the stature of the fullness of Christ."

> I used to lead our church.... Now I lead our team and they lead our church.

Second, we pray that as you do, God will use your work and interaction as a leadership team member to mature you, as well, into "the measure of the stature of the fullness of Christ." Certainly, interaction with others in the church is the very thing God uses to shape and refine character. We pray God will develop your team into a group of faithful friends.

Third, we pray you'll get to echo what Mark Johnston recently exclaimed: "I used to lead our church.... Now I lead our team and they lead our church." And you'll get to say, "I'm loving it."

EXPERT COMMENTARY: HEALTHY TEAM LEADERSHIP IS A DISCIPLESHIP ISSUE

Mark DeYmaz

Years ago, as our college baseball team left my university campus for an out-of-state game, we raised quite a ruckus from the back of the bus. We had departed as scheduled, but the problem was our starting pitcher for that day was late. Consequently, he missed the bus.

"Coach," we complained, "Moon-man's not here. What are we going to do?"

After twenty minutes of listening to our noise and appeals, our coach calmly rose to address the situation.[2] "Fellas," he said, "I learned a long time ago: you play with who you got right now."

I've never forgotten his words, and they continue to serve us well in building a healthy church leadership team at Mosaic, a four-campus intentionally multiethnic church based in Little Rock, Arkansas. Yes, you'll continue to transition team members who don't fit and also to find new ones, but no matter who's on the team at any given moment, it's important to develop your current players by approaching team leadership as a discipleship issue. The following are key principles that have helped us:

• *We can't fulfill the Great Commission to make disciples of "all nations"* (Mt 28:19-20) apart from a team. Jesus gave the command to a group. All verbs in the command are plural.

• *In order to reach "all nations," we need a team that represents "all nations."* That world starts with the people our congregation can influence. The more diverse your congregation,

> the wider a range of the world you can reach. To influence an increasingly diverse and cynical society, church leadership—like the church itself—should reflect its community. By functioning in unity and diversity we model the love of God for all people, beyond mere words, on earth as it is in heaven. In so doing we present a credible gospel witness.

- *Our disciple making is a direct result of our personal discipleship.* Even as we pursue the Great Commission, we realize that we are following Jesus and growing up in him ourselves too. We're convinced that participating on a team with people who think and work differently challenges us to "put on the new self, created after the likeness of God in true righteousness and holiness" (Eph 4:24). Every team meeting we have gives each member of our team a chance to follow Jesus and emulate his character as we interact with each other. As Jesus transforms us, we get to participate in his transformation of others.
- *The teaching and practice of the early church was for Jews and Gentiles to walk, work and worship together.* The church at Antioch, described in Acts 13, had a leadership team from many nations, from central Africa to the Mediterranean islands. Paul taught the church in Ephesus that Jews and Gentiles are one in

Christ. The full-orbed perspective of God's love—the "breadth and length and height and depth" (Eph 3:18)—is best experienced with people different from you and me. Outreach through diversity doesn't come naturally; it requires intentional discipleship.

God's mission for the church is less about a program and more about who we are. Who we are is tested and tried in our relationships, including those on the teams we serve on. Certainly, we welcome the discipleship that occurs for our staff and volunteers as they serve on teams in our church. The Bible's teaching about discipleship through teams unavoidably informs and shapes the way we do church.

***

Mark DeYmaz is founding pastor of Mosaic Church in Little Rock, Arkansas, founder of Mosaix Global Network, author of several books, including *Building a Healthy Multi-Ethnic Church*, and blogger at markdeymaz.com.

Acknowledgments

This book is only possible because of the generosity and hard work of many.

To the more than one thousand leadership team members at over 250 churches who allowed us to peek into their teamwork—the good, bad and ugly—we're so grateful. We hope that we've captured what we learned from you in a way that benefits the cause we all hold so dear—Jesus building his church. To the dozens of churches that invited us into your meetings, took time to answer our long lists of questions and shared more than your insights and reflections about your team with us, thank you!

We're also grateful for all those who read, suggested improvements on early drafts of this book and helped improve it: David Anderson, Sam Chand, Stephen Coppenrath, David Fletcher, Jill Hartwig, Jeff Helton, Chris Lewis, Kep James, Marvin Nelson and Jim Tomberlin. Each of you certainly made this book better. Special shout outs go to Sid Buzzell for his expert contributions to the chapter on biblical foundations for leadership teams, to XPastor.org founder David Fletcher and his wife, Tami Fletcher, who opened many research and networking doors for us, and to the late J. Richard Hackman and also to Ruth Wageman, who allowed us to use the Team Diagnostic

Survey (team-diagnostics.com) for our research. Thank you.

Each of us enjoys a special system of support where we work. We acknowledge the research grant by the Faculty Research Council at Azusa Pacific University, which enabled the data gathering and analysis of this project, as well as many faculty and administrative colleagues that have made it possible for Ryan to pursue this research. Special thanks to Dr. Chong Ho (Alex) Yu and Dr. Rachel Castaneda, who assisted in data analysis and modeling, and three fantastic students—Lauren Villarreal, Bethany Weil and Gennavieve Carmazzi—who managed the research project, mined the data and provided editorial support throughout the project. Finally, our great thanks goes to Leadership Network who hosted and publicized the initial surveys we conducted and published our initial findings, "Searching for Strong Leadership Teams: What 145 Church Teams Told Us."

We couldn't do this without the support of the ones we love and who love us so well.

Ryan says: Jill, you've given me your best day in and day out for fourteen years. I love you more today than ever. Halle, Alia, Kate and Matt, there's nothing better in the world than being your dad. Thanks for loving me so well. I love you. To my family, friends and mentors who have paved the way for me, challenged me, put up with me, laughed with me, taught me, dreamed with me and sacrificed for me, I'm here today because of what you've invested in me. Thank you!

Warren says: Everything I have learned is because of the many mentors and friends who have shared from their lives, ministries and experiences. Heartfelt thanks to my wife, Michelle, to my supervisor, Leadership Network CEO Dave Travis, and to literally hundreds of pastors who have taken the time and trust to participate in surveys or who have let me sit in on their meetings and ask them questions.

Finally, we're most grateful to the triune God who modeled team ministry even in creation when he said, "*Let us* make man in our image" (Gen 1:26), whom we follow not just in how we worship and live, but also in how we work in community.

Appendix

Top Ten Tips to Help Your Team Thrive

Table A.1.

To help your team thrive:	For more information, see:
Biblical basis. Seriously consider the biblical admonitions for and practical benefits of shared leadership. You won't develop a true leadership team if you are not convinced of its value.	Chapters 3-4
Purpose. Clarify your team's $_5$C purpose. Make sure it's clear, compelling, challenging, calling-oriented and consistently held. Your team's purpose serves as its central organizing element.	Chapter 7
Assessment. Regularly review how well your team is doing. Thriving teams, like thriving gardens, require constant assessment and cultivation.	Chapters 6, 14
Big picture. Focus your team, taking a church-wide perspective as it considers decisions. Not only will your team make better decisions but you'll also develop leaders in the process.	Chapters 8, 11
Leadership. If you're the designated leader, determine what leadership is truly necessary. Remember, sometimes the best thing to do is to strategically not do.	Chapter 9
Conflict. Welcome healthy conflict into your team meetings. Diverse people, varied ideas and differing perspectives provide the fuel for great team performance.	Chapter 11

Collaboration. Make the most of your team's time together, and take steps to help your team work continuously together. Quality time requires quantity time.	Chapter 12
Decision making. Intentionally invite God to speak into your team's thoughtful decision-making processes. Discerning God's will for your church together will lead to the best decisions for your church.	Chapter 10
Holy discontent. Honestly take stock of who leads your church, and how that leadership is functioning. You might need to make some significant changes, but that will only happen if you are willing to be brutally honest with yourself.	Chapter 2
Next steps. Get moving! Don't wait another day to give your team the attention and resources it needs to thrive.	Chapter 14

More resources are available at teamsthatthrivebook.com

Notes

PREFACE

[1] J. Richard Hackman, *Leading Teams* (Boston: Harvard Business School Publishing, 2002), p.vii. The quiz wording is slightly edited.

[2] J. Richard Hackman and Diane Coutu, "Why Teams Don't Work," *Harvard Business Review*, May 2009, p.100.

[3] Dave Barry, "Dave Barry on Meetings," *Reader's Digest*, September 1986, http://dt.org/html/Meetings.html.

[4] Hackman and Contu, "Why Teams Don't Work," p.100.

[5] One recent study suggested that CEOs often perceive their senior team's performance as better than how other team members rate it. On a scale of 1 to 7, with 7 being the best score, the CEOs' average rating of their team's overall performance was 5.4, while other senior managers gave a score of 4.0. Misperception happens with identifying poor performance too: while 52 percent of non-CEOs said the CEO's team was performing poorly in crucial areas, only

28 percent of the CEOs agreed. Richard M. Rosen and Fred Adair, "CEOs Misperceive Top Teams' Performance," *Harvard Business Review*, September 2007, p.30.

[6] Andy Stanley, Twitter post, August 24, 2012, https://twitter.com/AndyStanley/status/239004423689474048.

[7] Alexander B. Bruce, *The Training of the Twelve* (Grand Rapids: Kregel, 1971); Robert E. Coleman, *The Master Plan of Evangelism* (Grand Rapids: Baker, 1963); George Barna, *The Power of Team Leadership* (Colorado Springs: Waterbrook, 2001); Kenneth O. Gangel, *Team Leadership in Christian Ministry* (Chicago: Moody, 1997).

[8] Hackman and Coutu, "Why Teams Don't Work," p.100.

CHAPTER 2: YOUR VANTAGE POINT

[1] Michael Schrage, *No More Teams! Mastering the Dynamics of Creative Collaboration* (New York: Bantam Doubleday Dell, 1989), p.5.

[2] We'll discuss more about the place of working groups and solo leadership in chapter four. The word *team* is often used

to designate any grouping of people. However, we believe the *team* label should be reserved for certain kinds of groups. We follow Jon Katzenbach and Doug Smith's classic definition of a team: "A small number of people with complementary skills who are committed to a common purpose, performance goals, and approach for which they hold themselves mutually accountable." On rare occasion when we use team in quotes ("team"), we are referring to team in the general sense, but when we do not use quotes (the vast majority of the time), we are referring to a team in the particular sense. Jon R. Katzenbach and Douglas K. Smith, *The Wisdom of Teams: Creating the High-Performance Organization* (New York: Harper Collins, 1999), p.45.

[3] Tony Morgan, *Take the Lid Off Your Church: 6 Steps to Building a Healthy Senior Leadership Team* (Seattle: Amazon Digital Services, 2012), pp.59-60.

[4] Bob Frisch, *Who's in the Room? How Great Leaders Structure and Manage the Teams Around Them* (San Francisco: Jossey-Bass, 2012), p.7.

[5] Ibid., p.2.

[6] You'll read many specific examples throughout the book. We use "we" for simplicity. Sometimes both of us were there at that moment, and sometimes just one of us was. Either way, each named church has vetted our accounts and given its okay (and edits) for us to use it.

[7] Peter Scazzero and Warren Bird, *The Emotionally Healthy Church* (Grand Rapids: Zondervan, 2010), p.20.

CHAPTER 3: THE BIBLE SPEAKS

[1] Charles Anderson, personal interview with the authors. Unless otherwise noted, all interviews for this book were conducted by Ryan Hartwig or Warren Bird (or both together) in person or via email from January 2013 to October 2014.

[2] Gratefully others have conducted rich analysis of biblical texts. Our favorites are Alexander Strauch, *Biblical Eldership: An Urgent Call to Restore Biblical Church Leadership* (Littleton, CO: Lewis and Roth, 1995); Joseph H. Hellerman, *Embracing Shared Ministry: Power and Status in the Early Church and Why It Matters Today* (Grand Rapids: Kregel, 2013); Bruce Stabbert, *The Team Concept: Paul's Church

Leadership Patterns or Ours? (Tacoma, WA: Hegg, 1982). We draw substantially on these texts throughout this chapter.

[3] Robert C. Crosby, *The Teaming Church: Ministry in the Age of Collaboration* (Nashville: Abingdon, 2012), p.131.

[4] E. Stanley Ott, *Transform Your Church with Ministry Teams* (Grand Rapids: Eerdmans, 2004), p.5.

[5] Sid Buzzell, who is professor of Bible exposition and leadership and dean of the school of theology at Colorado Christian University, generously provided much of the material we adapted for use in this chapter. Sid is also the general editor of the *NIV Leadership Bible: Leading by the Book.*

[6] Strauch, *Biblical Eldership*, p. 36.
[7] Stabbert, *The Team Concept*, p. 26.
[8] Strauch, *Biblical Eldership*, p. 39.

CHAPTER 4: PASSING FAD OR HERE TO STAY

[1] Alexander Strauch, *Biblical Eldership: An Urgent Call to Restore Biblical Church Leadership* (Littleton, CO: Lewis and Roth, 1995), p.45.

[2] Sherry Surratt and Wayne Smith, "Team Collaboration: Broadening the Church Leadership Platform," *Leadership Network* (2011): 2, http://leadnet.org/docs/11for11-2011-MAR-Team_Collaboration-Surratt_and_Smith.pdf.

[3] David A. Nadler and Janet L. Spencer, *Executive Teams* (San Francisco: Jossey-Bass, 1998), p.xi.

[4] For instance, see Tom Rath and Barry Conchie, *Strengths-Based Leadership: Great Leaders, Teams, and Why People Follow* (Irvine, CA: Gallup, 2009).

[5] David Burkus, *The Myths of Creativity: The Truth About How Innovative Companies and People Generate Great Ideas* (San Francisco: Jossey-Bass, 2014).

[6] Joseph H. Hellerman, *Embracing Shared Ministry: Power and Status in the Early Church and Why It Matters Today* (Grand Rapids: Kregel, 2013), p.18.

[7] Adam S. McHugh, *Introverts in the Church: Finding Our Place in an Extroverted Culture* (Downers Grove, IL: InterVarsity Press, 2009), p.161.

[8] Strauch, *Biblical Eldership*, p. 43.

[9] John Holm, "Here's Why Even Benevolent Dictators Need to Collaborate With Their Team," Churchleaders.com, June 25, 2014,

www.churchleaders.com/pastors/pastor-how-to/175113-john-holm-why-even-benevolent-dictators-need-to-collaborate-with-their-team.html.

[10] Jon R. Katzenbach and Douglas K. Smith, *The Wisdom of Teams* (New York: Harper Business, 1999).

[11] Patrick Lencioni, "Drucker Foundation's Leader to Leader, No. 29: The Trouble with Teamwork," *Table Group Blog*, June 2003, www.tablegroup.com/blog/drucker-foundations-leader-to-leader-no-29-the-trouble-with-teamwork.

[12] Ibid.

CHAPTER 5: REALITY CHECK

[1] Team performance or effectiveness is typically considered to be the composition of three interrelated elements: task accomplishment, member growth and ongoing teamwork capability. Effectiveness is measured based on the team's achievement of its task-related objectives in a manner acceptable to important stakeholders; the health, growth and development of team members, and the team's increasing capability as a unit. See Patrick Flood, Sarah MacCurtain and

Michael West, *Effective Top Management Teams: An International Perspective* (Dublin: Blackhall, 2001); Ruth Wageman, Debra A. Nunes, James A. Burress and J. Richard Hackman, *Senior Leadership Teams: What It Takes to Make Them Great* (Boston: Harvard Business School Publishing, 2008).

[2] Alexander Strauch, *Biblical Eldership: An Urgent Call to Restore Biblical Church Leadership* (Colorado Springs: Lewis and Roth, 1995), p.71.

[3] Tony Morgan, "The 'Culture of Honor' Is Hurting Churches," *Tony Morgan Live*, March 31, 2011, http://tonymorganlive.com/2011/03/31/honor.

[4] Annaloes M.L. Raes, *Top Management Teams: How to Be Effective Inside and Outside the Boardroom* (New York: Business Expert Press, 2012), p.68.

[5] Lawrence R. Frey, Carl H. Botan and Gary L. Kreps, *Investigating Communication: An Introduction to Research Methods* (Upper Saddle River, NJ: Pearson, 2000), p.28.

[6] Vernon E. Cronen, "Coordinated Management of Meaning: Practical Theory for the Complexities and Contradictions of Everyday Life," in *The Status of Common Sense in Psychology*, ed. J. Siegfried (Norwood, NJ: Ablex, 1994), pp.183–207.

[7] Quentin J. Shultze, *Communicating for Life: Christian Stewardship in Community and Media* (Grand Rapids: Baker Academic, 2000), p.19.

[8] Chris Grey, *A Very Short, Fairly Interesting and Reasonably Cheap Book About Studying Organizations* (Thousand Oaks, CA: Sage, 2013), p.16.

[9] Timothy Keller, *Every Good Endeavor: Connecting Your Work to God's Work* (New York: Penguin, 2012), p.13.

[10] Ed Catmull, *Creativity, Inc.: Overcoming the Unseen Forces That Stand in the Way of True Inspiration* (New York: Random House, 2014).

CHAPTER 6: OUR SURVEY SAYS

[1] See http://team-diagnostics.com.

[2] For a copy of the instrument, or for more details about the research project that grounds this book, please visit www.teamsthatthrivebook.com.

[3] Ruth Wageman, Debra A. Nunes, James A. Burress and J. Richard Hackman, *Senior Leadership Teams: What It Takes to Make Them Great* (Boston: Harvard Business School Publishing, 2008), p.163.

CHAPTER 7: DISCIPLINE 1: FOCUS ON PURPOSE, THE INVISIBLE LEADER OF YOUR TEAM

[1] Chris McChesney, Sean Covey and Jim Huling, *The 4 Disciplines of Execution: Achieving Your Wildly Important Goals* (New York: Free Press, 2012).

[2] Rick Warren, *The Purpose-Driven Life: What on Earth Am I Here For?* (Grand Rapids: Zondervan, 2012).

[3] Carl Larson and Frank LaFasto, *Teamwork: What Must Go Right/What Can Go Wrong* (Thousand Oaks, CA: Sage, 1989).

[4] J. Richard Hackman, *Leading Teams* (Boston: Harvard Business School Publishing, 2002), p.72.

[5] Will Mancini, *Church Unique: How Missional Leaders Cast Vision, Capture Culture, and Create Movement* (San Francisco: Jossey-Bass, 2008).

[6] Jon R. Katzenbach and Douglas K. Smith, *The Wisdom of Teams: Creating the High Performance Organization* (New York: Harper Business, 1999), p.49.

[7] Peter F. Drucker, *The Effective Executive* (New York: Harper & Row, 1967), p.44.

[8] Gill R. (Robinson) Hickman and Georgia J. Sorenson, *The Power of Invisible Leadership: How a Compelling Common Purpose Inspires Exceptional Leadership* (Thousand Oaks, CA: Sage, 2014), p.3.

[9] Adapted from Adrian Gostick and Chester Elton, *The Orange Revolution: How One Great Team Can Transform an Entire Organization* (New York: Free Press, 2010).

[10] Hickman and Sorenson, *Power of Invisible Leadership*, p. 3.

[11] For a great summary of group development as it relates to team performance, see Susan A. Wheelan, *Creating Effective Teams: A Guide for Members and Leaders* (Thousand Oaks, CA: Sage, 2010). In addition, Ruth Wageman, Debra A. Nunes, James A. Burress and J. Richard Hackman's *Senior Leadership Teams: What It Takes to Make Them Great* (Boston: Harvard Business School Publishing, 2008), among other resources, explains the importance of focusing on performance over trust in initial group development.

[12] Wageman et al., *Senior Leadership Teams*.

[13] Adapted from Jennifer Radin and Tiffany McDowell, "Making Decisions That Matter: How Improving Executive Decision-Making Can Lead to Better Business Outcomes," *Deloitte Consulting*, April 2012.

[14] John C. Maxwell, *How Successful People Think* (New York: Hachette Book Group, 2009).

[15] Vineet Nayar, "A Shared Purpose Drives Collaboration," *Harvard Business Review*, April 2014, http://blogs.hbr.org/2014/04/a-shared-purpose-drives-collaboration.

CHAPTER 8: DISCIPLINE 2: LEVERAGE DIFFERENCES IN TEAM MEMBERSHIP

[1] Larry Osborne, *Sticky Teams* (Grand Rapids: Zondervan, 2010), p.42.

[2] Patrick Lencioni, *The Advantage: Why Organizational Health Trumps Everything Else in Business* (San Francisco: Jossey-Bass, 2012), p.22.

[3] For solid research, see Carl E. Larson and Frank M.J. LaFasto, *Teamwork: What Must Go Right/What Can Go Wrong* (Thousand Oaks, CA: Sage, 1989); Jon R. Katzenbach

and Douglas K. Smith, *The Wisdom of Teams: Creating the High Performance Organization* (New York: Harper Business, 1999). For a great in-the-trenches view, see Larry Osborne, *Sticky Teams*.

[4] Osborne, *Sticky Teams*, p. 54.

[5] Ruth Wageman, Debra A. Nunes, James A. Burress and J. Richard Hackman, *Senior Leadership Teams: What It Takes to Make Them Great* (Boston: Harvard Business School Publishing, 2008), p.83.

[6] Frank LaFasto and Carl Larson, *When Teams Work Best* (Thousand Oaks, CA: Sage, 2001).

[7] Osborne, *Sticky Teams*.

[8] Andy Stanley quoted at Chick-fil-A-Leadercast, in Brian Dodd, "27 Leadership Lessons and Quotes from Andy Stanley—Live Notes from Chickfil-A-Leadercast," *Brian Dodd on Leadership* (blog), May 10, 2013, http://www.briandoddonleadership.com/2013/05/10/27-leadership-lessons-and-quotes-from-andy-stanley-live-notes-from-chick-fil-a-leadercast.

[9] Osborne, *Sticky Teams*, p. 114.

[10] Jon R. Katzenbach and Douglas K. Smith, "The Discipline of Teams," *Harvard Business Review*, March 1993.

[11] Larry Osborne, *Innovation's Dirty Little Secret: Why Serial Innovators Succeed Where Others Fail* (Grand Rapids: Zondervan, 2013), p.137.

[12] Carl George with Warren Bird, *Prepare Your Church for the Future* (Grand Rapids: Revell, 1991). See also Carl George with Warren Bird, *Nine Keys to Effective Small-Group Leadership: How Lay Leaders Can Establish Dynamic and Healthy Cells, Classes, or Teams* (Taylors, SC: CDLM, 2007).

[13] Wageman et al., *Senior Leadership Teams*, p. 101.

[14] See David Augsburger, *Caring Enough to Confront: How to Understand and Express Your Deepest Feelings Toward Others* (Ventura, CA: Regal, 2009); Kerry Patterson, Joseph Grenny, Ron McMillan and Al Switzler, *Crucial Conversations: Tools for Talking When Stakes Are High*, 2nd ed. (New York: McGraw-Hill, 2011); Kerry Patterson, Joseph Grenny, Ron McMillan and Al Switzler, *Crucial Confrontations: Tools for Resolving Broken Promises, Violated Expectations, and Bad Behavior* (New York: McGraw-Hill, 2005).

[15] Bob Frisch, *Who's in the Room?* (San Francisco: Jossey-Bass, 2012), is useful

for thinking through how to shift from one to multiple leadership groups. While we don't affirm the exact solution he champions, he offers great food for thought on what to consider in making a shift.

[16] Wageman et al., *Senior Leadership Teams*.

[17] Two excellent resources on church compensation, each updated every other year, are *2014-2015 Compensation Handbook for Church Staff* (store.churchlawtodaystore.com/20cohaforchs1.html), focused on churches of 50 to 1,000plusin attendance, and "Leadership Network/Vanderbloemen 2014 LargeChurch Salary Report" (leadnet.org/wp-content/uploads/2014/09/2014-Salary-Report_082914_reduced-print1.pdf), focused on churches of 1,000 and up in attendance. Leadership teams will need to consider how their team approach affects the way they think about salaries and benefits.

[18] William Vanderbloemen and Warren Bird, *Next: Pastoral Succession That Works* (Grand Rapids: Baker, 2014), emphasize the need to build a leadership culture where all players are regularly cultivating potential successors as part of

anticipating their own eventual and inevitable succession

[19] John C. Maxwell, *The 21 Irrefutable Laws of Leadership: Follow Them and People Will Follow You* (Nashville: Thomas Nelson, 2007).

CHAPTER 9: DISCIPLINE 3: RELY ON INSPIRATION MORE THAN CONTROL TO LEAD

[1] James MacGregor Burns, *Leadership* (New York: Harper Business, 1978), p.20.
[2] Bernard M. Bass, *Leadership and Performance Beyond Expectations* (New York: Free Press, 1985).
[3] Patrick M. Lencioni, *The Five Dysfunctions of a Team: A Leadership Fable* (San Francisco: Jossey-Bass, 2002), p.43.
[4] Ibid., p.195.
[5] For a more complete argument, see Ryan's ebook, *Burst: Bursting the Bubble of 5 Teamwork Myths* (Portland: BookBaby, 2012), www.amazon.com/Burst-Bursting-Bubbles-Teamwork-Myths-ebook/dp/B00AB3EZHA.
[6] See Seth Godin, "Getting Confused About Causation and Correlation," *Seth Godin*

(blog), March 21, 2012, http://sethgodin.typepad.com/seths_blog/2012/03/getting-confused-about-causation-and-correlation.html.

[7] For a great summary of group development as it relates to team performance see, Susan A. Wheelan, *Creating Effective Teams: A Guide for Members and Leaders* (Thousand Oaks, CA: Sage, 2010).

[8] A.C. Edmonson and D.M. Smith, "Too Hot to Handle? How to Manage Relationship Conflict," *California Management Review* 49, no. 1 (2006): 20.

[9] Onora O'Neill, "How to Trust Intelligently," *TED Blog*, September 25, 2013, http://blog.ted.com/2013/09/25/how-to-trust-intelligently.

[10] Patrick Lencioni, *The Advantage: Why Organizational Health Trumps Everything Else in Business* (San Francisco: Jossey-Bass, 2012), p.27.

[11] Alexander Strauch, *Biblical Eldership: An Urgent Call to Restore Biblical Church Leadership* (Littleton, CO: Lewis and Roth, 1995), p.45.

[12] Strauch, *Biblical Eldership*, p. 48.

[13] See Richard J. Hackman and Ruth Wageman, "When and How Team Leaders Matter," *Research in*

Organizational Behavior 26 (2005): 37-74, and James R. Meindl, Sanford B. Ehrlich and Janet M. Dukerich, "The Romance of Leadership," *Administrative Science Quarterly* 30 (1985): 78-102.

[14] For a summary of the problems with free group discussion, see Sunwolf and Lawrence R. Frey, "Facilitating Group Communication," in *The Handbook of Group Research and Practice* (Thousand Oaks, CA: Sage, 2005).

[15] Jeanine Prime and Elizabeth Salib, "The Best Leaders Are Humble Leaders," *Harvard Business Review Blog Network*, May 12, 2014, http://blogs.hbr.org/2014/05/the-best-leaders-are-humble-leaders.

[16] Sid Buzzell, PhD, professor of Bible exposition and leadership and dean of the school of theology at Colorado Christian University, teaches his students this concept as a way to generate greater involvement among team members.

[17] Prime and Salib, "Best Leaders."

[18] See Eric M. Eisenberg's *Strategic Ambiguities: Essays on Communication, Organization, and Identity* (Thousand Oaks, CA: Sage, 2007).

[19] Jeffrey Pfeffer and Robert Sutton, *Hard Facts, Dangerous Half-Truths, and Total Nonsense* (Boston: Harvard Business School Press, 2006), p.209.
[20] Prime and Salib, "Best Leaders."
[21] Crawford Loritts, *Leadership as an Identity* (Chicago: Moody Publishers, 2009), p.138.
[22] Ibid., pp.133-34.

CHAPTER 10: DISCIPLINE 4: INTENTIONALLY STRUCTURE YOUR DECISION-MAKING PROCESS, PART I

[1] Ruth Haley Barton, *Pursuing God's Will Together: A Discernment Practice for Leadership Groups* (Downers Grove, IL: InterVarsity Press, 2012), p.11.
[2] Patrick Flood, Sarah MacCurtain and Michael West, *Effective Top Management Teams: An International Perspective* (Dublin: Blackhall, 2001).
[3] Ibid.
[4] Though he did not originate the term "wicked problem," Michael Pacanowsky's description and exploration of wicked problems as different than tame problems offers a helpful resource for how to deal

with wicked problems. See Michael Pacanowsky, "Team Tools for Wicked Problems," *Organizational Dynamics* 23 (Winter 1995): 36-51.

[5] Flood, MacCurtain and West, *Effective Top Management Teams.*

[6] For instance, Bob Frisch, author of *Who's in the Room? How Great Leaders Structure and Manage the Teams Around Them* (San Francisco: Jossey-Bass, 2012), suggests that senior management teams are not suited for making major decisions and instead implores CEOs to employ a sort of "kitchen cabinet" for major decision-making tasks. In addition, Al Pittampalli, the author of *Read This Before Our Next Meeting* (Dobbs Ferry, NY: Do You Zoom, 2011), suggests that meetings are not places for groups to make decisions; instead, meetings simply support decisions that have been made by individuals.

[7] Lawrence R. Frey, "Introduction: Facilitating Group Communication in Context: Innovations and Applications with Natural Groups," in *Facilitating Group Communication in Context: Innovations and Applications with Natural Groups,* ed.

Lawrence R. Frey (New York: Hampton, 2006).

[8] Warren Bird and Meagan M. Taylor, "Pastors Who Are Shaping the Future," *Leadership Network Report,* 2011, http://ministryformation.com.au/attachments/338_RESEARCH-2011-DEC-PastorsWhoAreShapingtheFuture-Bird-Taylor.pdf.

[9] Dave Ferguson, *Keeping Score: How to Know if Your Church Is Winning* (Centreville, VA: Exponential, 2014), https://my.exponential.org/ebooks/keepingscore.

[10] Barton, *Pursuing God's Will Together.*

[11] A downloadable chart that summarizes this model is available at the Transforming Center website: www.transformingcenter.org/in/pgwt-book/Movements%20in%20Corporate%20Leadership%20Discernment.pdf.

[12] Haddon Robinson, *Decision Making by the Book* (Grand Rapids: Chariot Victor, 1991), pp.64-66.

CHAPTER 11: DISCIPLINE 4: INTENTIONALLY STRUCTURE

YOUR DECISION-MAKING PROCESS, PART 2

[1] Carl S. Dudley and Davis A. Roozen, "Faith Communities Today: A Report on Religion in the United States Today," Hartford Institute for Research, Hartford, CT, March 2001, p.62, available online at http://faithcommunities today.org/sites/all/themes/factzen4/files/Final%20FACTrpt.pdf.

[2] T. Simons, L.H. Pelled and K.A. Smith, "Making Use of Difference: Diversity, Debate, and Decision Comprehensiveness in Top Management Teams," *Academy of Management Journal* 42, no. 6 (1999): 662-73.

[3] Judith A. Kolb, *Small Group Facilitation: Improving Process and Performance in Groups and Teams* (Amherst, MA: HRD Press, 2011).

[4] Robert A. Hargrove, *Mastering the Art of Creative Collaboration* (New York: McGraw-Hill, 1997), p.185.

[5] David A. Garvin and Michael A. Roberto, "What You Don't Know About Making Decisions," *Harvard Business Review*, September 2001.

[6] Tom Rath and Barry Conchie, *Strengths Based Leadership: Great Leaders, Teams, and Why People Follow* (New York: Gallup, 2008), p.71.

[7] Some of these tips are adapted from A.C. Edmondson and D.M. Smith, "Too Hot to Handle? How to Manage Relationship Conflict," *California Management Review* 49, no. 1 (Fall 2006): 6-31.

[8] Jim Collins, *Good to Great: Why Some Companies Make the Leap and Others Don't* (New York: Harper Business, 2001).

[9] Bob Frisch, *Who's in the Room? How Great Leaders Structure and Manage the Teams Around Them* (San Francisco: Jossey-Bass, 2012).

[10] This kind of thinking is popularized in recent meeting management literature, such as Al Pittampalli, *Read This Before Our Next Meeting* (Dobbs Ferry, NY: Do You Zoom, 2011).

[11] Andy Stanley, "Leading a Team Meeting" (podcast), April 4, 2014, https://itunes.apple.com/us/podcast/andy-stanley-leadership-podcast/id290055666?mt=2.

[12] Dennis Gouran, Randy Hirokawa, Kelly Julian and Geoff Leatham, "The Evolution and Current Status of the Functional Perspective on Communication in

Decision-Making and Problem Solving Groups," in *Communication Yearbook* 16, ed. Stanley Deetz (Newbury Park, CA: Sage, 1993), pp.573-600.

[13] Paul Kaak, Gary LeMaster and Rob Muthiah, "Decision-Making for Christian Leaders Facing Adaptive Challenges," *Journal of Religious Leadership* 12, no 2 (fall 2013): 145-66.

[14] Roger Fisher and William L. Ury, *Getting to Yes: Negotiating Agreement Without Giving In* (New York: Penguin Group, 2011).

[15] For an excellent review of research on creativity, see Sunwolf, "Getting to 'GroupAha!': Provoking Creative Processes in Task Groups," in *New Directions in Group Communication*, ed. L.R. Frey (Thousand Oaks, CA: Sage, 2000).

[16] David Burkus, *The Myths of Creativity: The Truth About How Innovative Companies and People Generate Great Ideas* (San Francisco: Jossey-Bass, 2014), p.164.

[17] Kolb, *Small Group Facilitation*, p. 189.

[18] Ideas are drawn from Keith Sawyer, *Group Genius: The Creative Power of Collaboration* (New York: Perseus Books, 2007); Burkus, *Myths of Creativity;*

Sunwolf, "Getting to 'GroupAha!'; S. Jarboe, "Group Communication and Creativity Processes," in *The Handbook of Group Communication and Research*, eds L. Frey, D. Gouran and M. Poole (Thousand Oaks, CA: Sage, 1999), pp.335-68.

[19] Google Docs is one possible option for online collaborative documents.

[20] *Sawyer, Group Genius.*

[21] Ibid.

[22] Ibid.

[23] Our favorite techniques are the Lotus Blossom, the Delphi Method, Nominal Group Technique, Six Thinking Hats, Synectics, and Reverse Brainstorming. Instructions for using these and many other facilitation techniques can be found on www.mindtools.com or similar websites.

[24] Charles Higgins Kepner and Benjamin B. Tregoe, *The New Rational Manager* (Princeton, NJ: Princeton University Press, 1997). A simple adaptation of this process is also listed in Kolb, *Small Group Facilitation.*

[25] Kaak, Lemaster and Muthiah, "Decision-Making for Christian Leaders," p.157.

[26] Charles Kepner and Benjamin Tregoe, *The New Rational Manager: An Updated Edition for a New World* (Princeton, NJ: Princeton Research Press, 2006), p.77.

[27] Colin Powell and Joseph A. Persico, *My American Journey* (New York: Random House, 1995), p.309.

[28] Tony Morgan, *Killing Cockroaches: And Other Scattered Musings on Leadership* (Nashville: B&H, 2009).

CHAPTER 12: DISCIPLINE 5: BUILD A CULTURE OF CONTINUOUS COLLABORATION

[1] Jason Fried and David Heinemeier Hansson, *Rework* (New York: Crown Business, 2010), p.108.

[2] This tip is adapted from Auxano's *The VisionDeck*, available atwww.visiondeck.com

[3] Ruth Wageman, Debra A. Nunes, James A. Burress and J. Richard Hackman, *Senior Leadership Teams: What It Takes to Make Them Great* (Boston: Harvard Business School Publishing, 2008), p.163.

[4] This tip is adapted from Patrick Lencioni, *The Advantage: Why Organizational Health Trumps Everything Else in Business* (San Francisco: Jossey-Bass, 2012), p.28.

[5] Wageman et al., *Senior Leadership Teams*, p. 163.

[6] This tip is adapted from Auxano's *The VisionDeck,* available at www.zvisiondeckcom.

CHAPTER 13: SIX WAYS TO AVOID SABOTAGING YOUR TEAM

[1] Samuel R. Chand, *Cracking Your Church's Culture Code* (San Francisco: Jossey-Bass, 2011), p.9.

[2] Kurt Lewin, *Field Theory in Social Science* (New York: Harper & Row, 1951).

[3] Jon R. Katzenbach and Douglas K. Smith, *The Wisdom of Teams: Creating the High Performance Organization* (New York: Harper Business, 1999).

[4] Chris Argyris, *Knowledge for Action* (San Francisco: Jossey-Bass, 1993). An interview with Chris Argyris in which he dives deeper into the theories presented in his book can be found at Joe Kurtzman, "An

Interview with Chris Argyris," *Strategy&,* January 1, 1998, www.strategy-business.com/article/9887?gko=c19c5.

[5] Frank LaFasto and Carl Larson, *When Teams Work Best* (Thousand Oaks, CA: Sage, 2001), pp.157-95.

[6] John P. Kotter, *Leading Change* (Boston: Harvard Business Review Press, 1996); John P. Kotter, "Leading Change: Why Transformation Efforts Fail," *Harvard Business Review,* March-April 1995.

CHAPTER 14: CATALYZE YOUR TEAM'S GROWTH

[1] Ronald A. Heifetz and Marty Linsky, *Leadership on the Line* (Boston: Harvard Business School Publishing, 2002).

[2] Coach Al Worthington is a former pitcher who played fourteen seasons in Major League Baseball. He was the first and founding coach of Liberty University's Division I baseball team.

Additional Resources

Visit teamsthatthrivebook.com for additional resources to help yourteam thrive. There you'll find:
- suggested resources, including videos, books, articles and assessments
- additional discussion tools to help your group collaboratively make decisions
- more information about our research study
- sample meeting agendas and annual meeting schedules
- information about opportunities for additional training, coaching and consulting, and more

About the Authors

Ryan T. Hartwig, PhD, is associate dean of the college of liberal arts and sciences and associate professor of communication at Azusa Pacific University, an evangelical Christian university in Greater Los Angeles. As a practical academic, he helps leaders develop thriving leadership and ministry teams, and design and cultivate collaborative organizations.

Ryan earned a PhD in communication from the University of Colorado Boulder. His scholarship has been published in the *Journal of Applied Communication Research* and *Group Facilitation*, and recognized with several awards from the National Communication Association. Blending his teaching, research and leadership practice, Ryan has consulted with and trained leaders at numerous universities, churches, seminaries and nonprofit organizations.

Ryan has taught classes in group, organizational and leadership communication for more than ten years, and he has led, trained and developed teams focusing on community development, discipleship, missions, leadership development, academic excellence, fundraising and marketing for more fifteen years in universities and churches. He's active as a lay leader in his church, where he spearheads leadership development initiatives, facilitates a growth group and frequently teaches in various venues.

Ryan journeys through life with his wife, Jill, and their four children. Connect with Ryan at ryanhartwig.com, or follow on Twitter(@rthartwig).

Warren Bird, PhD, is director of research and intellectual capital development for Leadership Network (leadnet.org), a nonprofit that helps North America's leading innovative church leaders leverage their ideas for greater influence and impact. An ordained minister, he has served as staff pastor for fifteen years, for most of which he also served as a teaching faculty member at Alliance Theological Seminary in Nyack, New York.

Warren has authored or coauthored twenty-six books, over two hundred magazine articles and more than two dozen in-depth research reports. He is an award-winning writer and has been quoted by a wide variety of national media. He is among the nation's leading experts on megachurches, multisite churches and current trends in greater church effectiveness.

Warren and his wife, Michelle, live in New York City.

Follow Warren on Twitter (@warrenbird).

> **"...TO EQUIP HIS PEOPLE FOR WORKS OF SERVICE, SO THAT THE BODY OF CHRIST MAY BE BUILT UP."**
> **EPHESIANS 4:12**

God has called us to ministry. But it's not enough to have a vision for ministry if you don't have the practical skills for it. Nor is it enough to do the work of ministry if what you do is headed in the wrong direction. We need both vision *and* expertise for effective ministry. We need *praxis*.

Praxis puts theory into practice. It brings cutting-edge ministry expertise from visionary practitioners. You'll find sound biblical and theological foundations for ministry in the real world, with concrete examples for effective action and pastoral ministry. Praxis books are more than the "how to"—they're also the "why to." And because *being* is every bit as important as *doing*, Praxis attends to the inner life of the leader as well as the outer work of ministry. Feed your soul, and feed your ministry.

If you are called to ministry, you know you can't do it on your own. Let Praxis provide the companions you need to equip God's people for life in the kingdom.

www.ivpress.com/praxis

www.ingramcontent.com/pod-product-compliance
Lightning Source LLC
Chambersburg PA
CBHW011718220426
43663CB00018B/2916